TRANSNATIONAL ACTORS IN WAR AND PEACE

TRANSNATIONAL ACTORS IN WAR AND PEACE

Militants, Activists, and Corporations in World Politics

DAVID MALET
and
MIRIAM J. ANDERSON
Editors

Georgetown University Press
Washington, DC

The publisher is not responsible for third-party websites or their content. URL links were active at time of publication.

Library of Congress Cataloging-in-Publication Data

Names: Malet, David, 1976- editor, author. | Anderson, Miriam J., editor, author.
Title: Transnational Actors in War and Peace : Militants, Activists, and Corporations in World Politics / David Malet and Miriam J. Anderson, editors.
Description: Washington, DC : Georgetown University Press, 2017. | Includes bibliographical references and index.
Identifiers: LCCN 2016035821 (print) | LCCN 2016058220 (ebook) | ISBN 9781626164420 (hc : alk. paper) | ISBN 9781626164437 (pb : alk. paper) | ISBN 9781626164444 (eb) |
Subjects: LCSH: Transnationalism—Political aspects. | International relations.
Classification: LCC JZ1320 .T717 2017 (print) | LCC JZ1320 (ebook) | DDC 327.1—dc23
LC record available at https://lccn.loc.gov/2016035821

18 17   9 8 7 6 5 4 3 2 First printing

Printed in the United States of America

Cover by Rebecca Lown Design.
Cover images from left to right, top to bottom: NATO Mercenary (INTERFOTO / Alamy Stock Photo); employee of the German Red Cross (dpa picture alliance / Alamy Stock Photo); United States Social Forum (Jim West / Alamy Stock Photo); No More War Demonstration, ca. 1920 (Swarthmore College Peace Collection #B8); masked militants holding the ISIS black banner of Muhammad (Handout / Alamy Stock Photo); African Union Commission for Somalia and AMISOM Senior Political Officer at a meeting with Somali Diaspora Community (Africa Collection / Alamy Stock Photo); demonstration in Myanmar (REUTERS / Alamy Stock Photo).

To my family across three countries,
who have given me love, support, and continuity

D.M.

For Sarah Marie Anderson and Amanda Kathleen Anderson,
my strong, vibrant, and supportive sisters

M.J.A.

CONTENTS

ACKNOWLEDGMENTS

This book is the result of an ambitious project to bring together the work of scholars in numerous subfields of international relations studying transnational actors in war and peace. Achieving a common framework and an overview of a multitude of international relations literatures required multiple meetings and the input of many scholars over a number of years.

The publication of this book owes to the support and perseverance of our editor, Donald Jacobs. Gratitude is also due to the staff of Georgetown University Press and the two anonymous reviewers who provided useful suggestions and critiques.

This project began when we initially met at the 2006 International Studies Association (ISA) annual conference while we were both PhD students working on our dissertations. Our discussions about networks and mobilization led us to quickly recognize interesting similarities between how two starkly different types of entities operated in transnational politics—women's peace groups and foreign fighters—that would never be noticed without conversations across subfields. We were able to further this discussion at a panel at the 2008 ISA conference with participation from Charli Carpenter, Betcy Jose, Thomas Olsen, and Christine Sylvester.

In 2012, we received a Catalytic Grant from ISA to hold a conference workshop, "Transnational Actors and Conflict Outcomes," which included the participation of Jennifer Brinkerhoff, Mohammed Hafez, Cerwyn Moore, and Sparsha Saha. A reporting panel on transnational violent actors at the following year's conference benefited from the additional participation of Max Abrahms, Jonathan Agensky, and Daniela Pisiou. In 2014, we received a Venture Grant from ISA for a workshop to plan this volume, with new participants including Virginia Haufler, Phil Orchard, and Michael Schroeder. We were assisted in this workshop by two graduate students, Ryan Webb and Mark Winward.

The School of Social and Political Sciences at the University of Melbourne supported this project with funding for the symposium "The Influence of Non-State Actors in War and Peace" in November 2013, which included the participation of Phil Orchard and Sarah Percy. Andrew Walter was also very helpful in providing suggestions about and resources on transnational corporations.

In July 2014, we held the conference "Transnational Actors in War and Peace" at Memorial University in St. John's, Newfoundland, which included the following participants from institutions in four countries (Australia, Canada, the United Kingdom, and the United States): Luke Ashworth, Derick Brinker-hoff, Jennifer Brinkerhoff, Terry Bishop-Stirling, Catia Confortini, Thomas Davies, Luke Flanagan, Ann Florini, Virginia Haufler, Matthew LeRiche, Adrian Little, Jeremy Littlewood, Kate Macdonald, and Lorraine MacMillan. Three graduate students who assisted in the organization of the conference and prepa-ration of the book manuscript were Lucy MacDonald, Karalena McLean, and Kathryn Wesley.

The 2014 conference and the production of this edited volume were spon-sored by the Social Sciences and Humanities Research Council Connection grant program and the Canadian Department of Public Safety. We also received support from various sources at Memorial University, including the Scholarship in the Arts grant, the School of Graduate Studies, the Conference Fund, the Living Memorial Commemoration Fund, the Office of the Dean of Arts, and the Arts on Violence fund.

And last but not least, we especially owe a debt of gratitude to each of the book's contributors, many of whom we have now worked with for years. We look forward to continued collaboration and exchange to better understand the transnational dynamics and actors key to comprehending contemporary armed conflict and peace.

Introduction

The Transnational Century

DAVID MALET and MIRIAM J. ANDERSON

In late June 2014, exactly one century after the assassination of Franz Ferdinand by a terrorist cell with nationalist aspirations triggered World War I, a transnational terrorist network known as the Islamic State of Iraq and Syria (ISIS) proclaimed a caliphate intended to erase post–World War I national borders. Although it immediately embarked on a state-building exercise to provide social services and infrastructure, ISIS maintained its fundamentalist religious interpretation of political order, rejecting the legitimacy of the Westphalian international system of states and the possibility of membership in any state-based international organization (IO).

ISIS financed its activities through black-market sales of oil and looted goods via transnational criminal channels. Prevented from using traditional banks by both international law enforcement and sharia law, it funded its activities through the traditional hawala system of financial transactions across a transnational network of private lenders. It rapidly built a force of foreign fighters from dozens of countries and featured Western, English-speaking militants in videos distributed via the platforms of social media companies that found it impossible to shut down pro-ISIS accounts quickly enough. These videos regularly featured the brutal executions of humanitarian aid workers from transnational civil society

1

(TCS) groups and journalists working for transnational corporations (TNCs). A female cadre also used social media to successfully recruit young women from Western Europe, Southeast Asia, and elsewhere to serve as brides of fighters and to perform gendered social-services roles. Transnational violent actors (TVAs) aside from the jihadis were drawn in as well.

While Western states that had withdrawn from occupying Iraq only within the preceding couple of years launched airstrikes, their leaders immediately claimed that their armies would not put "boots on the ground" to fight ISIS. Instead, they first turned to multinational private security companies to engage in logistical and public-outreach operations to counter further ISIS advances. Meanwhile, ISIS was engaged in combat first with other transnational jihadi groups and then with Kurdish fighters, who were joined by Western Christian and Kurdish diaspora volunteers. At the same time, ISIS's social media operation came under assault by the transnational hacker collective Anonymous, which pirated its Twitter account and engaged in other cyberattacks as a form of protest. While the ISIS declaration of the end of the state system in the Levant may have been premature, clearly it did establish a milieu for a complex transnationalism featuring a variety of nonstate actors interacting directly.

Transnational Actors in the Twenty-First Century

This book compares the structures, effects, and interactions of an array of transnational actors on warfare and contentious politics. It does not attempt to provide an encyclopedia of transnationalism but rather to analyze the characteristics of the most prominent transnational actors participating in both armed conflict and in building conditions for peace. It stems from our observation that diverse transnational actors operate in strikingly similar ways in how they seek to influence conflicts as well as peacemaking and that they are in turn influenced directly by each other rather than just operating as separate entities outside of the formal international system.

Initially we were surprised to discover that the transnational actors we studied, jihadi foreign fighters and women's advocacy networks, shared a number of commonalities in organization, communications, and operational strategies and methods. We soon learned from colleagues who studied a range of violent and nonviolent nonstate transnational actors that these similarities are evident across the spectrum. Yet these patterns normally go unnoticed because we were all "stovepiped" into subfields of literature on transnationalism that typically do not reference each other. Works concerned with transnational activists and those examining transnational militants turn out to have almost no overlap in their bibliographies. In searching for a unifying paradigm for transnational actors, we also discovered that 2016 marked the centenary of the introduction of the term "transnational," in the context of examining citizenship-versus-ethnic ties during World War I, making it a particularly appropriate moment for reevaluation.

Ever since 1916, scholars have been claiming that globalized nonstate actors are becoming more prominent, powerful, or effective and that the nature of world politics is changing as a result. Developments in international relations, such as trade expansion and petro-conflicts in the 1970s and major terrorist attacks in the 2000s, have led to waves of interest in new facets of transnationalism that had not previously been significant concerns within the discipline. So, to an extent, transnational actors in war and peace, including most described in the ISIS example, are nothing new.

At the same time, technological developments and cultural liberalization have lowered the cost of participation in formal and contentious politics by nonstate actors, increased the velocity with which they communicate with various audiences and with each other, and democratized the locus of political discourse away from control by traditional elites to mass, increasingly online participation. Instead of expending resources to organize mass meetings when permitted to do so by the state, transnational groups can organize and procure funds online. And while private individuals and community groups were raising money to fund revolutions in other countries during the eighteenth century, in the twenty-first century every blog or tweet has a greater reach than any printing press of the Enlightenment era, and their authors can connect with the like-minded instantly and nearly cost-free to marshal their efforts.

States have clearly created some of the opportunity structures for modern transnational actors to thrive, such as the absence of major wars, the end of colonialism, and the supply of arms on the global market that contributed to a surge in civil conflicts. Shifting norms of human rights, often promoted by state entrepreneurs, have increased the number of armed interventions. States have delegated authority to nongovernmental organizations (NGOs) with presumed issue expertise and with transnational private-donor bases whose primary concerns are not necessarily state interests. Outsourcing and political imperatives have led to military services performed by private firms. Regulatory changes in trade and the continuing development of transportation and communications infrastructure have increased contact between employees of TNCs and local populations and cosmopolitanism that impacts public policy via the so-called CNN effect, in which the immediacy of global real-time news and communications builds empathy with peoples who are geographically remote and stokes public pressure for humanitarian interventions.

Along with the increased prominence of transnational actors, there appears to be a greater legitimation afforded to them by both actors in world politics and scholars of international relations.[1] States may see value in transnational actors such as diasporas that provide them with political and financial support, and national, even patriotic chapters of TCS organizations reify the state and international system, retaining voice and loyalty despite their exit from purely domestic regulatory constraints.

Cooperation between NGOs in different sectors and with TNCs that have overlapping interests indicates a growing self-consciousness of transnationalism and perhaps even solidarity. Women's rights NGOs are now common participants at negotiations for civil war peace settlements, and private corporations are invited by IOs to develop global governance guidelines for regulating trade of conflict resources or reconstruction and development. Likewise, among TVAs, illicit collaboration builds networks and global supply chains between different entities with political and profit motivations. After becoming ubiquitous in the first decade of the twenty-first century, foreign fighters, pirates, and mercenary armies now seem familiar elements in international security rather than aberrant challenges to the Westphalian sovereign order.

Individual participants' conceptions of affiliation, political space, and global order have been transformed by their roles within transnational actors, and they in turn forge partnerships and shape discourse that intensifies the acceleration of these trends.[2] We therefore argue that, at the end of the first century since the concept of transnational actors was identified, the growing and interconnected web of interaction between these actors and states has produced a complex transnationalism in international security.

Defining Transnationalism

The term "trans-national" was introduced by Randolph S. Bourne in an article titled "Trans-national America" published in the *Atlantic Monthly* in 1916. The article was written to address the mistrust of Americans of Anglo-Saxon descent toward other immigrants living in the United States and argued that a unique advantage of ethnic diversity was that it prevented the country from easily joining either side in the Great War.

Bourne's "trans-nationality, a weaving back and forth, with the other lands, of many threads of all sizes and colors," transcended nationalism and created a uniquely strong cosmopolitan state. But whereas Bourne coined the term to mean "cosmopolitanism," the subsequent study of transnationalism in international relations has tended to focus on border-crossing actors or networks. Initially the interdependence literature of the 1970s was concerned with the web of relationships traversing borders termed "complex interdependence." Joseph S. Nye and Robert O. Keohane defined "transnational relations" in 1971 to mean "contacts, coalitions, and interactions across state boundaries that are not controlled by the central foreign policy organs of governments."[3] In other words, their definition refers to the crossing of state borders by nonstate actors. It is the physical boundary itself that is traversed according to this definition.

Nye and Keohane delimit what types of issues are relevant to their study of transnationalism. These include the degree to which the state's power is eroded, the degree to which the relative power of states among themselves is changed, and the degree to which transnational relations impact IOs.[4] They conclude that the presence and influence of transnational actors does merit a shift from a state-centric paradigm to a world politics paradigm but note that states "remain the most important actors in world affairs, acting both directly and through intergovernmental organizations to which states, and only states, belong. States virtually monopolize large-scale, organized force which remains the ultimate weapon and a potent bargaining resource."[5] Not being able to wield or compete with the resources of the state, nonstate actors must use other means to carry out their objectives.

In defining transnationalism, we wish to distinguish it from Keohane and Nye's useful explanations of "interdependence," "globalization," and "globalism." These are related to transnationalism in that interdependence and globalization refer to "an increased sense of vulnerability to distant causes."[6] Globalism may be understood as "a state of the world involving networks of interdependence at multicontinental distances."[7] Interdependence, on the other hand, relates to bilateral relationships between states, while "globalism is a type of interdependence, but with two special characteristics," which are "networks of connections (multiple relationships), not to single linkages" that "must include multicontinental distances, not simply regional networks."[8] And "complex interdependence" relates to there being multiple channels between societies; multiple actors, not just states; multiple issues, not arranged in any clear hierarchy; and the irrelevance of the threat or use of force among states linked by complex interdependence.[9]

We posit that complex transnationalism is *the increasing number, scope, interactions, and influence of transnational actors on diplomatic and governance processes where states have invited as participants, been forced to respond to, or have become reliant upon the expertise of transnational actors and where transnational actors increasingly interact directly with each other.* In developing a framework for examining transnational actors, we treat them as a category distinct from state actors involved in transnational processes or descriptions of transnational flows of material or ideas. We propose that transnational actors in international politics are (1) entities that work through nonstate mobilizing structures, (2) entities that are perceived to be beyond the state, and (3) those who self-identify as transnational.

The Increasing Importance of Transnational Actors in Global Politics

Numerous entities throughout history have operated in conflicts across borders under the conditions created by the opportunity structures of the day. The Crusades produced multinational armed companies motivated by religious convictions and greed to fight and plunder. The quest for resources driven by industrialization led to corporations such as the East India Company employing private armies to support the extraction of resources from colonized territory. During waves of globalization in the nineteenth century, newly formed TCS groups worked to end slavery, and transnational societies of peace formed during the Napoleonic Wars.

However, two major developments during the late twentieth and early twenty-first centuries have intensified the transnational dynamics of international security. The first is the significant reduction of transaction costs associated with acting transnationally. For example, by communicating online, individuals can more easily locate and join peace advocacy groups and they need not leave home to participate in transnational entities. Due to the availability of air travel, humanitarian aid workers and foreign fighters can easily traverse continents.

The second is the increased attention, both positive and negative, afforded to transnational actors in both public discourse and by states. Now governments funnel money through NGOs to engage in peacebuilding, and the United Nations (UN) Security Council has passed a resolution condemning foreign fighters and others calling for women's participation in peace processes. TCS often plays an active formal role in peace negotiations and in postconflict reconstruction. And since 2001, states have spent billions of dollars in the name of combating terrorism.

The Evolution of Transnationalism in International Relations

There is an extensive well of resources within the international relations discipline from which to draw in developing a framework for examining transnational actors, one fed by several separate streams from various subfields. While scholars have worked in each of these areas throughout the existence of the discipline, particular developments in world politics triggered waves of increased interest in particular types of transnational actors. In this section, we present an overview of the study of transnational actors in war and peace that is both thematic and chronological.

Transnationalism became a significant concern of the international relations literature in the 1970s with the emerging study of interdependence and TNCs beyond the sovereign juridical authority of the state. It expanded in the post–Cold War period with the integration of critical studies that brought feminist analytics into the discipline and then adapted in the 1990s as globalization and a spike in civil wars made other identity politics particularly salient and with them concerns of diaspora and religious identity. By the late 1990s, the constructivist turn had foregrounded TCS nonstate actors who influenced states through norms and the politics of protest. In the wake of the 9/11 attacks, terrorist networks were the main security preoccupation of the first decades of the twenty-first century, with other TVAs seemingly reemerging from pre-Westphalian history or materializing out of cyberspace.

Globalization scholars across the transnational century consistently articulated an expansion and acceleration of the global market in commerce, communications, and affiliations, with the more static sovereign states lagging in regulatory power and centripetal authority.[10] Nye and Keohane claimed in 1971 that "transnational organizations are immensely more powerful and significant now than before 1914 or 1945," and the contemporary reader would no doubt imagine transnational actors to be more consequential in global affairs than they were at the beginning of the 1970s when their edited volume appeared as the touchstone of literature on globalization.[11]

Transnational Corporations

Both liberal and critical theories of market transactions predating the literature on TNCs were predicated on the activities of private transnational actors engaged in commercial activities that shape the fortunes of states and on the formulation of transnational classes of labor and ownership.[12] These divisions of labor resulted in colonialism, anti- and postcolonial revolutions, and continuing patterns of political and economic inequality in international relations. They also shape both the alliances and domestic policies of states, which seek to attract private capital investment.[13]

Some of the first private firms to exploit global markets afforded by colonization and industrialization were arms manufacturers seeking new markets, who began to sell directly to other regimes outside of states in transactions that went unregulated by their home governments.[14] In the twentieth century, the rise of American-originated multinational corporations (MNCs) impacted political and development conditions in host countries, in some cases reducing state capacity in exchange for capital investment. They were clearly beyond the full reach of national laws, and they became symbolic of both concerns about United States dominance within the Western economic order and the need for global governance (what Phillip C. Jessup called "transnational law" in the 1950s) to maintain international order in an increasingly interdependent world.[15]

By the 1990s, although the global political order shifted into post–Cold War unipolarity, the truly globalized economy that emerged was increasingly diversified, with MNCs from a range of countries, including the global South, operating ubiquitously. Thus, the nature of the concern changed to one of TNCs operating globally, buying favorable regulations from compliant regimes at the expense of workers and customers, or shifting operations as required, ultimately with no sovereign state truly holding them in sway.[16]

Additionally, the networked globalized economy now meant that finance could be transferred nearly instantaneously, with consequences evident in the 1997 Asian financial contagion that resulted in both democratization and ethnic violence in Indonesia. The 2008 global economic crisis subsequently demonstrated the influence of bond-rating agencies, TNCs that could destabilize or reinforce national economies based on credit reports.[17]

However, such concerns had featured throughout the transnational century. Fears that the wealth of private transnational financial actors would undermine the security of the nation state had existed at least since J. P. Morgan helped finance interwar reconstruction in Europe.[18] According to Edward L. Morse, "The international monetary crises of the 1960s have demonstrated the emergence of financial markets that seem to operate beyond the jurisdiction of even the most advanced industrial states of the West and outside of their individual or collective control."[19] The emergence of TNCs with the power to influence the laws of host states had also long signaled the possibility that firms were now in a position to engage in diplomacy and conflict negotiation, often with other corporations directly.[20]

Complex Transnationalism in the Global Market

TNC control of critical communications, transportation, and energy infrastructure also challenges state sovereignty. While states reserve ultimate control over telecommunications media, they are regulating operations that, in the cases of the radio spectrum and the Internet, were usually developed and maintained by private actors that are increasingly subsidiaries of TNCs.[21] Service providers such as Google have influenced the civil liberties policies of powerful states such as China and tacitly sided with dissidents by threatening to withdraw operations.[22] Both TCS and TVA groups use telecommunications TNCs to their advantage by using them to reach global audiences.[23] The CNN effect has acted as a constraint on states and potentially saved lives in armed conflict, but the omnipresence of media TNCs has fueled resentment against the West and contributed to antihegemonic militant activity.[24]

TNCs that contribute to globalization through transportation service can also destabilize international order, from the French firm that built the Suez Canal in 1858, which "emptied the South Atlantic of shipping,"[25] to the global aviation industry, which has been blamed for accelerating the spread of pandemics.[26] Competition within the global energy sector that is required to fuel transnational commerce has also been a source of war between states.[27] Other studies find that the shift from nationally based corporations to TNCs produces instability in developing countries.[28]

Yet TNCs must also contend with other transnational actors that constrain them. Ulrich Beck notes the argument that the flow of transnational capital has limited the autonomy of the sovereign state because TNCs are able to dictate favorable state labor policies by threatening to relocate to more compliant jurisdictions.[29] But consumers are also a transnational class, and, by organizing boycotts and other "naming and shaming" campaigns, TCS can use the market to regulate TNCs in a way that states cannot.

Keohane and Nye offer the example of environmental NGOs imposing costs on energy companies by calling for regulation of their extractive processes, but the environmental, development, and energy price impacts also have human security implications.[30] Elsewhere they note that TNCs actively influence state foreign policy but may be thwarted by TCS groups. For example the petroleum sector's preferred policy for the United States on Israel has been mitigated by the efforts of Jewish diaspora groups.[31]

Transnational Feminism

An increased focus on the study of nonstate actors came with the end of the Cold War and a reduced preoccupation with great power politics in international relations, opening up space for more diverse perspectives and approaches.[32] Feminists forged a place for themselves in the discipline, throwing light on the prior invisibility of women there,[33] which meant the expansion of the terrain of the discipline to include the contributions and experiences of women—who were often excluded from prominent leadership roles, such as head of state, general, politician, and diplomat.

Feminist scholars have produced work on various transnational aspects of war and peace, as well as expanded the definition of both to pay attention to women who are often members of nonstate groups. Transnational feminist praxis involves "shifting the unit of analysis from local, regional, and national culture to relations and processes across cultures."[34] Scholars involved in this endeavor have charted the development of feminist peace advocacy and how it took on an increasingly transnational character near the end of the Cold War, marked by the UN's Third World Conference on Women, held in Nairobi in 1985.[35] The increased interconnectedness of feminist advocates worldwide has meant that women lobbying for particular policies within their own state may often call upon nodes of the feminist transnational advocacy network, which includes other women's groups, various politicians, and allies in IOs worldwide.[36]

The Women's International League for Peace and Freedom (WILPF) is the oldest women's peace international NGO. It seeks "to end and prevent war, ensure that women are represented at all levels in the peace-building process, defend the human rights of women, and promote social, economic and political justice," has developed chapters worldwide, and plays a prominent role in promoting the women, peace, and security agenda at the UN.[37] Numerous women's advocacy groups, such as the Women in Black, which originated in Israel and Palestine, have developed linkages and partnerships with other organizations worldwide and have seen new chapters created in the former Yugoslavia and the United Kingdom.[38] The NGO Development Alternatives with Women for a

New Era, founded in India in 1984 as a network for women of the global South to affect international development policy, has influenced international policy through organizing Third World women's participation at UN conferences on women, producing publications on development from the perspectives of third world women, and serving as consultants for international bodies such as the UN Development Fund for Women, the UN Population Fund, the UN Development Programme, the International Labour Organization, and the UN Educational, Scientific, and Cultural Organization.[39]

Feminists have long claimed a close relationship between the private and public spheres, and accordingly women's advocacy groups have not strictly differentiated between violence that occurs during armed conflict and that which is experienced during peacetime. Margaret Keck and Kathryn Sikkink detail how transnational women's networks successfully framed violence against women as a human rights issue, expanding the strength of their network and gaining traction in states worldwide, while Brooke Ackerly has examined transnational networks of human rights activists.[40]

Now, due to the efforts of feminist activists worldwide, the issue of women, peace, and security has been placed on the international agenda. From 2000 onward, at least seven UN security resolutions have been passed calling for the right of women to participate in all stages of peacebuilding and for women's rights and needs to be taken into consideration in any policy decisions related to women, peace, and security broadly. These resolutions were the first of their kind to address women's experiences during peace and conflict,[41] and they occurred due to the efforts of transnational feminist networks over decades.[42] Feminist international relations theory has served to make the lives of women and their transnational alliances relevant in the discipline.

Identity Politics

The end of the Cold War heralded not only the emergence of feminist international relations theory but a new period in which security studies was compelled to examine the import of a variety of other sociopolitical identities competing with the assumed primacy of the nation-state. Early attention shifted to subnational schisms as genocidal ethnic conflicts erupted in the Balkans and the African Great Lakes region. However, the impact of ties between local belligerents and their transnational kin communities, and of the global networks that enabled militant groups to buy arms, soon made it evident that few civil wars were purely local matters. Thereafter, the 9/11 attacks and the subsequent war on terrorism made transnational religious affiliations the most salient divide in the first decade of the twenty-first century.

Samuel Huntington's article "The Clash of Civilizations?" predicted in 1993 an era of conflict between largely sectarian transnational primordial blocs with divergent cultural values and political philosophies.[43] It enjoyed renewed interest after 9/11, with Osama bin Laden even citing it in one video to explain his framing of a war by the West against Islam. Daniel Philpott described the post-9/11 era as being characterized by the resacralization of international relations after 350 years of a Westphalian secular basis for world high politics.[44] As early as 1977, Hedley Bull had questioned why nonstate groups could not have armies of their own, and the trend appeared to be moving in that transnational direction.[45]

Transnational Insurgencies

Jeffrey T. Checkel contends that civil wars are rarely purely local affairs but are inevitably both causes and effects of "the dark side of global politics."[46] In particular, the economic dimensions of modern civil wars "do not observe sovereign borders," according to Karen Ballentine and Jake Sherman.[47] Lootable resources such as "blood diamonds," even when sold through licit transnational market channels, finance armed groups, exacerbating civil wars, and permit them to remain active as bandits and warlords long after their political causes have fallen away.[48] At the same time, insurgencies are increasingly being directly targeted by TCS actors with their own interests as well, such as Invisible Children's *Kony 2012* viral campaign urging international intervention against a Ugandan insurgency.[49]

Imperial and colonial boundaries are responsible for many kin groups being divided across state borders,[50] and both local villagers and state regimes frequently provide aid and shelter to their ethnic or sectarian compatriots in conflicts that spill over from neighboring territories.[51] More than half of insurgencies since World War II have had external linkages to neighboring states,[52] with rebels strong enough to fight but not to win unaided reaching out to kin.[53]

However, many of those insurgencies have also attracted transnational volunteers from dozens of countries around the world. It is common practice for state military forces to offer positions to noncitizens to augment their forces, such as in the case of the French Foreign Legion. This has also been true for insurgent groups, from George Washington's Continental Army to the International Brigades in Spain to the Islamic State in Iraq and Syria. Because rebels are typically resource-poor, they attract volunteers with pleas for defenders of their shared transnational identity community, which they portray as facing existential threat as a result of the conflict, rather than offering them material incentives.[54] The practice has become ubiquitous among Islamist groups in the twenty-first century, in part because they have successfully established the master frame of a global siege against the *ummah* (transnational community of the Islamic faithful), and it is expected that militant fighters will travel to new conflict zones as part of their role.[55]

Refugees, who are treated as victims in the literature on TCS, human rights, and norms—but are often not themselves considered part of TCS—are viewed as sources of instability in the security literature.[56] They may aid insurgencies by expanding rebel social networks and introduce conflict to the states around them by facilitating the spread of arms and ideologies and by changing the ethnic composition of host societies.[57] They also become conduits for transnational criminal activity.[58] Dislocated refugees resettle in other states along with economic migrants from their same groups, with "nesting pigeons" attempting to assimilate in new home societies while "birds of passage" plot triumphal returns and lend their financial and political support to parties and armed groups who oppose settlement efforts they view as accommodationist.[59]

Diasporas

Diasporas come in various forms and influence politics in their homelands as well as in their adopted states.[60] For example, through communications from abroad, they can support or oppose integration in postconflict divided societies.[61] They may organize politically in their adopted state and lobby it to take on particular foreign policies.[62] Their new state, then, becomes an instrument to wield in the service of the political objectives in the state of origin. Transmigrants therefore hold a unique place in international politics by virtue of simultaneously occupying several social locations and holding multiple identities.[63]

Some birds of passage use their new home societies only as secure bases of operation, much like cross-border rebels.[64] Such actively transnational diasporans often employ rejectionist rhetoric and collected funds to prompt their kinsmen to accept only victory rather than compromise,[65] although their influence is dependent on conditions in the homeland,[66] and they can be effective advocates for peacemaking as well.[67] Transnational migration flows can present challenges to states that do not have the capacity to accommodate new groups, particularly those who also import their contentious politics.[68]

Transnational Civil Society

International relations scholars since the Cold War have increasingly focused on transnational actors as conveyers of issues and norms. Recent scholarship has demonstrated that transnational, usually religious NGOs were actively promoting humanitarian relief during the major wars of the nineteenth century and have since branched out in numerous other forms.[69] During the 1990s, constructivist scholars also examined cases from the early twentieth century that indicated the influence of TCS to create normative constraints on states.[70] These studies provided context for contemporary events, as various networked activists campaigned to eliminate categories of weapons,[71] advocated on behalf of indigenous rebel groups,[72] and eventually became belligerents themselves in massive antiglobalization protests targeting meetings of intergovernmental organizations.[73]

This body of work has sought to show the relevance of transnational advocacy networks (TANs)—"sets of actors linked across country boundaries, bound together by shared values, dense exchanges of information and services, and common discourses"—in affecting the behavior of powerful actors through various strategies. Keck and Sikkink explored human rights advocacy networks in Latin America, environmental advocacy networks, and transnational networks focused on violence against women in their seminal 1998 work *Activists beyond Borders*, a text commonly referenced across different subfields of transnational studies.[74] A key phenomenon they proposed is the "boomerang model," in which activists, facing obstacles in their own state, appeal to allies outside of their country who then apply pressure on the recalcitrant government "from above." To achieve their objectives, TANs "generate politically usable information and move it to where it will have the most impact" and use "symbolic politics" or "framing" to make issues relatable to global audiences. In this way activist groups, which rely on "soft power," are able to exert influence on their states, often in order to pressure them to moderate their use of "hard power"—that is violence—targeted against their own citizens.

TANs have been instrumental in the creation of multilateral treaties regulating the conduct of warfare, such as an international convention banning the use of land mines.[75] They were also key in the adoption of the Rome Statute, which created the International Criminal Court.[76]

NGOs are effective in producing these changes because they are situated within networks of TCS-connected actors and regimes.[77] They succeed when they are able to produce cosmopolitan senses of shared affectedness, as with emerging environmental consciousness,[78] or with transnational indigenous solidarity movements.[79] They must also expand networks to incorporate local actors who might resist or subvert external norm diffusion into their polities.[80]

Transnational Violent Actors

Alongside the TNC and the TCS actors that have existed throughout the modern era but flowered in the waves of twentieth-century globalization was another category of private nonstate entities that used violent coercion to attain their political or financial goals. The TVA group encompasses illicit transnational criminal enterprises, including organized criminal networks, gangs, pirates, nonstate cyberhackers, terrorist organizations and networks, and foreign fighters who join insurgencies in other states. Mercenaries are often included in this category, but the prominent private military companies of the twenty-first century have generally acted as government contractors (or at least with state sanction), rather than used violence against authority and operated as registered TNCs. There has not until now been a widely used acronym denoting this category of transnational actor, but we propose TVA for comparability to the more familiar TNC and TCS.[81]

The Westphalian system gave sovereign states a monopoly on the legitimate use of violence, and they therefore attempt to delegitimize private actors who use violence or coercion by using terms such as "mercenary" that have over time acquired negative normative connotations.[82] Regular military forces are instruments of states and thus do not challenge international order, but mercenaries are not necessarily constrained by national interests or allegiance to citizenship in their use of violence. Both TCS groups and TNCs have hired private military companies to rein in other TVAs (examples include environmentalists using them against criminal poachers in the Democratic Republic of the Congo and oil companies against separatist rebels in Angola).

Despite any public relations problems, private military security companies (PMSCs) potentially make it easier for regimes to go to war and to avoid regulation because their publics do not care about the fate of mercenaries—particularly noncitizens—as they would for their own children in uniform.[83] By offering themselves as an instrument through outsourcing, PMSCs, and particularly those with transnational employee rosters, can actually empower state interventions by displacing costs.

By contrast, transnational criminal organizations and networks pursue profits through completely illicit means. They do not have political agendas, but transnational organized crime, including the activities of Mafias and large gangs such as MS-13, influences regional and global security governance by trafficking through "dark networks," co-opting governance through extortion, and degrading the capacity of states to exercise internal sovereignty. Smugglers were vital to efforts to bring jihadi foreign fighters into Iraq in the 2000s, and there is evidence of gang members serving as mercenaries in transnational terrorist groups.[84] Maritime pirates, transnational in operations and sometimes membership, require the littorals of weak states. In their resurgence in the 2000s, they prompted both increased international cooperation to curtail them and an increase in private security operations in areas far beyond home territorial waters.[85] Failed states and conflict zones provide havens and attract a variety of TVAs who build networks and supply chains.[86] The increased prominence and connectedness of globalized nonstate actors in armed conflicts is a feature of the "new wars" of the post–Cold War globalized order.[87]

While criminal activity drives some cyberspace security concerns, other online transnational actors are more challenging to characterize. For example, Russia and China routinely claim that cyberattacks originating from their territories against foreign government and financial websites are the effort of private "patriotic hackers."[88] Individual, locally rooted hackers are not a part of global transaction chains like online shoppers and do not fit neatly into existing models of transnationalism, but their activities impact across countries. Others employed by transnational terrorist organizations such as Hezbollah and Hamas occupy a more readily familiar position in the international security ecology.

Another transnational cyber threat has been posed by Anonymous, which, since its emergence in 2003, has been described as a leaderless "hacktivist collective" with splinter factions. Multinational teams of Anonymous members have engaged in online protest activities and cyberattacks against state targets but also against other transnational actors, including the Church of Scientology, Wall Street, the Zetas drug cartel, and ISIS.

The architecture of global telecommunications has permitted other TVAs to operate transnationally as well. Shortly after the advent of global satellite broadcasting in 1967, major terrorist groups moved from being essentially domestic organizations to international actors playing to a global audience, notably with the attack by the Palestinian Black September Organization at the 1972 Olympics. Unlike primarily profit-seeking criminal actors whose success is aided by secrecy, the immediate objective of terrorists is publicity. Unable to influence governance through available means, they seek to coerce states into granting their policy goals and expect that an informed public will ultimately rally behind them.[89] The advent of the Internet means that radicals have less cause to moderate their activities out of concern for editorial presentation to the public by mainstream media. Instead, they are free to go over the top of content providers and program directly to the demographics and communicated preferences of their likeliest audience.[90]

The rise of global Islamist terrorism by regional al-Qaeda affiliates and self-starters inspired by the familiar brand provided international relations scholars a new impetus to examine networks, both transnational networks of coordination in international plots like 9/11 and local social networks that self-organize into cells with limited or no contact with a major terrorist organization.[91] Al-Qaeda never had more than a couple hundred members in its formal organization; its success came from establishing a narrative of the transnational (Sunni) Islamic community under attack by Western hegemony, facilitated by complicit regimes in Muslim states and the imperative for individuals to fight a global war of resistance and liberation. By providing a template for action and a moniker associated with effectiveness, the group could encourage alienated individuals or small groups to initiate action without direct transnational coordination.[92] Therefore, jihadi TVAs, like humanist TCS groups, pursue a strategy of mobilization based on the perception of values-based, shared transnational affiliation beyond the formulation of national interests.

Transnational Actors in Comparison

In many ways, diverse transnational actors appear to behave similarly, whether through deliberate emulation or because of parallel operational requirements. Most also appear to have increased visibility and authority in conflicts and peacebuilding because the costs of disseminating their messages and organizing support have diminished with advances in technology. But beyond these generalizations, it is necessary to examine the actors in depth and using the same measures to determine the significance of these similarities and also how they interact with states and with each other.

We therefore present for comparison case studies of transnational actors spanning the past century and across different areas of involvement in contentious politics. For comparability, each chapter examining a different transnational actor is structured around five components: how the actor is organized; how it interacts with other actors, including other transnational actors and states; how it communicates both internally and externally; how it influences conflict or peace; and how it reflects developments in transnationalism.

Luke Flanagan introduces the Knights of Columbus, a Catholic service organization, and its humanitarian work during World War I, the period during which transnationalism was proposed as an alternative to belligerent nationalism. Indeed, the case evidences tension between the Knights' desire to be cosmopolitan while at the same time being constrained by their respective national war efforts to appear patriotic in order to retain access to state resources.

Catia Cecilia Confortini examines WILPF in the decade following World War II. In contrast to the preceding case, with the emergence of a Western liberal regime changing opportunity structures, WILPF selected a cosmopolitan strategy with an explicit tie to universal human rights norms.

Virginia Haufler moves forward to the post–Cold War period, analyzing the leadership of transnational corporations in the Kimberley Process to restrict conflict minerals. TNCs coordinated their efforts with a host of other actors, including IOs and civil society NGOs. This coordination with other nonstate actors pointed the way for the complex transnationalism evident in the governance of twenty-first-century conflicts.

Jennifer M. Brinkerhoff considers the role of diasporas and the impact of transnational individuals in public policymaking in developing states. Using African postconflict cases, she juxtaposes the authority enjoyed by a civil servant who returned with Western training with the influence of mobilized expatriates on electoral politics. Her data demonstrate that transnational actors often have "hybrid identities" across more than one state that can either facilitate or hinder postwar peacebuilding.

Ariel I. Ahram and John Gledhill offer an alternative view of transnational individuals by examining political exiles who orchestrate contentious politics from abroad. They contrast the experiences of two exiles, Ayatollah Ruhollah Khomeini of Iran and bin Laden of Saudi Arabia. They argue that Khomeini's transnational experiences, counterintuitively, served to sharpen his focus on a strictly *national* popular uprising. By contrast, the political opportunity structures and organizational resources that bin Laden encountered while in exile reinforced his inclination toward a *global* revolt.

David Malet surveys the major groups that brought foreign fighters to the Syrian Civil War, culminating in the declaration of a transnationally oriented

Islamic State (the ISIS caliphate) governed by foreign fighters. Unlike the transnational exiles who mustered resources to fight domestic battles in their home states, the jihadi movement created a global convergence of militants with no prior local ties to a local conflict, using framing strategies similar to those of TCS groups to broaden involvement and likewise exploiting new communication technologies.

Matthew LeRiche presents insights into private military security companies operating in conflict zones such as Syria and the contractors who work for them, describing how their services to states have grown well beyond soldiers for hire. These firms are now responsible for the broad logistics upon which states rely to implement their foreign policies, including humanitarian assistance. They are also being emulated across developing states, in a sense acting as entrepreneurs for new modes of contemporary warfare led by transnational actors.

Phil Orchard examines how humanitarian relief NGOs are constrained by the emergence of the international humanitarian regimes that support their activities. He applies regime theory to transnational actors to develop a unique model of interaction effects. In the case of the Syrian conflict, states and IOs clearly retain structural advantages in determining the implementation of human rights, even in the context that gives TCS groups their legitimacy in expertise.

Miriam J. Anderson examines how local women's advocacy groups, embedded in transnational feminist networks, shape peace negotiations. These groups perceive peace processes as opportunities to advance gender equality and due to their transnational ties reproduce international women's rights norms in the process. Because of the efforts of transnational feminist advocacy, the right of women to participate in all aspects of peacebuilding has been recognized in a series of UN Security Council resolutions making their presence at peace negotiations a global norm.

Kate Macdonald presents the merging of international and transnational authority in nonjudicial grievance bodies created by multilateral state agreements but that draw their legitimacy from the perspective of appellants by representing impartiality beyond state interests. In the human security–charged area of conflict between TNCs and traditional local authority over land ownership rights, maintaining peace requires the political acumen to mollify a variety of types of transnational actors.

We conclude by assessing conditions of complex transnationalism and anticipating potential developments in transnational politics and scholarship for the second transnational century.

Notes

1. There have been works in other disciplines cataloging the transnational broadly, although without presenting cases of actors in international relations or a means of comparing

them. These include sociologists Peggy Leavitt and Sanjeev Khagram's cross-disciplinary reader excerpting major works on transnationalism, *The Transnational Studies Reader: Intersections and Innovations* (New York: Routledge, 2007), and historians Akira Iriye and Pierre-Yves Saunier's dictionary of the transnational that included major events and technological developments, *The Palgrave Dictionary of Transnational History* (New York: Palgrave Macmillan, 2009).

2. This phenomenon has been evident throughout the transnational century. See Donald P. Warwick, "Transnational Participation in Peace and International Peace" in *Transnational Relations and World Politics*, eds. Joseph Nye and Robert Keohane (Cambridge, MA: Harvard University Press, 1972), 305–21.

3. Joseph S. Nye and Robert O. Keohane, "Transnational Relations and World Politics: An Introduction," *International Organization* 25, no. 3 (1971).

4. Ibid., 331.

5. Ibid., 344.

6. Robert O. Keohane and Joseph S. Nye Jr., "Globalization: What's New? What's Not? (and So What?)," *Foreign Policy*, no. 118 (2000): 104.

7. Ibid., 105.

8. Ibid., 104–5.

9. Ibid., 115.

10. Randolph Silliman Bourne, *Towards an Enduring Peace: A Symposium of Peace Proposals and Programs, 1914–1916* (New York: Association for International Conciliation, 1916); Charles Kindleberger, *American Business Abroad: Six Lectures on Direct Investment* (New Haven, CT: Yale University Press, 1969); Raymond Vernon, *Sovereignty at Bay: The Transnational Spread of U.S. Enterprises* (London: Longman, 1971); Richard W. Mansbach, *Web of World Politics: Non-state Actors in the Global System* (Englewood Cliffs, NJ: Prentice Hall, 1976); Anthony Giddens, *The Consequences of Modernity* (Cambridge, UK: Polity Press, 1990); Jean-Marie Guehenno, *End of the Nation-State* (Minneapolis: University of Minnesota Press, 1995); Gary Gereffi, "Global Commodity Chains: New Forms of Coordination and Control among Nations and Firms in International Industries," *Competition and Change* 1, no. 4 (May 1996): 427–39; John Ruggie, *Winning the Peace: American and World Order in the New Era* (New York: Columbia University Press, 1996); James Rosenau, *Along the Domestic-Foreign Frontier: Exploring Governance in a Turbulent World* (Cambridge, UK: Cambridge University Press, 1997); David Held et al., *Global Transformations: Politics, Economics, and Culture* (Cambridge, UK: Polity Press, 1999). By contrast, a minority have claimed either that the long-standing ubiquity of such claims is evidence that nothing is new and that states do not face meaningful challenges to their sovereignty (Michael Veseth, *Globaloney: Unraveling the Myths of Globalization* [Lanham, MD: Rowman & Littlefield, 2005]; Paul Hirst and Grahame Thompson, "Globalization and the Future of the Nation State," *Economy and Society* 24, no. 3 [1995]).

11. Nye and Keohane, *Transnational Relations and World Politics*, 342.

12. Adam Smith, *The Wealth of Nations* (1776); Karl Marx, *Das Kapital* (1867).

13. Raúl Prebisch, *Power, Principle and the Ethics of Development* (1949) ; H. W. Singer, "The Distribution of Gains between Investing and Borrowing Countries," *American Economic Review* no. 2 (May 1950): 473–85; Immanuel Wallerstein, "The Rise and Future Demise of the World Capitalist System," *Comparative Studies in History and Society* 16, no. 4 (September 1974): 387–415.

14. Held et al., *Global Transformations*; Daniel W. Drezner, "The Global Governance of the Internet: Bringing the State Back In," *Political Science Quarterly* 119, no. 3 (Fall 2004): 477–98.

15. Phillip C. Jessup, *Transnational Law* (New Haven, CT: Yale University Press, 1956); Vernon, *Sovereignty at Bay*; Cynthia Enloe, *Bananas, Beaches and Bases: Making Feminist Sense of International Politics* (Berkeley: University of California Press, 1989); Martha Harris, "Energy and Security," in *Grave New World: Security Challenges in the 21st Century*, ed. Michael E. Brown (Washington, DC: Georgetown University Press, 2003); Derick W. Brinkerhoff and Jennifer Brinkerhoff, "Public-Private Partnerships: Perspectives on Purposes, Publicness, and Good Governance," *Public Administration and Development* 31, no. 1 (February 2011): 2–14.

16. Andrew Walter, "Do They Really Rule the World?," *New Political Economy* 3, no. 2 (1998): 288–92.

17. Tim Sinclair, *The New Masters of Capital: American Bond Rating Agencies and the Politics of Creditworthiness* (Ithaca, NY: Cornell University Press, 2008).

18. Herbert Feis, *The Diplomacy of the Dollar: First Era, 1919–1932* (Hamden, CT: Archon Books, 1965).

19. Edward L. Morse, "Transnational Economic Processes," in Nye and Keohane, *Transnational Relations and World Politics*, 23.

20. Arnold Wolfers, *Alliance Policy in the Cold War* (Baltimore: Johns Hopkins University Press, 1959); John M. Stopford, Susan Strange, and John S. Henley, *Rival States, Rival Firms: Competition for World Market Shares* (Cambridge, UK: Cambridge University Press, 1991).

21. Stephen D. Krasner, "Global Communications and National Power," *World Politics* 43, no. 3 (April 1991): 336–66; Craig Murphy, *International Organization and Industrial Change: Global Governance since 1850* (New York: Oxford University Press, 1994); Drezner, "Global Governance of the Internet."

22. Bingchun Meng, "Moving Beyond Democratization: A Thought Piece on the China Internet Research Agenda," *International Journal of Communication* 4 (2010): 501–8.

23. Held et al., *Global Transformations*, 59.

24. Diana Owen, "Transnational Mass Media Organizations and Security" in Brown, *Grave New World*, 237–42, 250.

25. James A. Field, "Transnationalism and the New Tribe," in Nye and Keohane, *Transnational Relations and World Politics*, 6.

26. Robert O. Keohane and Joseph S. Nye, *Power and Interdependence* (Boston: Longman, 2001), 229.

27. Jeff D. Colgan, *Petro-Aggression: When Oil Causes War* (Cambridge, UK: Cambridge University Press, 2013).

28. Stephen G. Brooks, *Producing Security: Multinational Corporations, Globalization, and the Changing Calculus of Conflict* (Princeton, NJ: Princeton University Press, 2005).

29. Ulrich Beck, "Counter-Power in the Global Age: Strategies of Civil Society Movements" in *Power and Transnational Activism*, ed. Thomas Olesen (New York: Routledge, 2011), 25.

30. Keohane and Nye, *Power and Interdependence*, 225.

31. Keohane and Nye, *Transnational Relations and World Politics*, 342.

32. Lucian M. Ashworth, *A History of International Thought: From the Origins of the Modern State to Academic International Relations* (New York: Routledge, 2013), 269.

33. See, for examples, Jean Bethke Elshtain, *Women and War* (New York: Basic Books, 1987), and Enloe, *Bananas, Beaches and Bases*.

34. M. Jacqui Alexander and Chandra Talpade Mohanty, "Introduction: Genealogies, Capitalist State Practice, and Feminist Movements," in *Feminist Genealogies, Colonial Legacies, Democratic Futures*, ed. M. Jacqui Alexander and Chandra Talpade Mohanty (New York: Routledge, 1997), xix, as cited by Catia Cecilia Confortini in chapter 2 of this volume.

35. Valentine M. Moghadam, *Globalizing Women: Transnational Feminist Networks* (London: Johns Hopkins University Press, 2005).

36. Ibid.

37. Catia Cecilia Confortini, *Intelligent Compassion: Feminist Critical Methodology in the Women's International League for Peace and Freedom* (New York: Oxford University Press, 2012).

38. Linda Etchart, "Demilitarizing the Global: Women's Peace Movements and Transnational Networks," in *The Oxford Handbook of Transnational Feminist Movements*, ed. Rawwida Baksh and Wendy Harcourt (New York: Oxford University Press, 2015), 702–22.

39. Moghadam, *Globalizing Women*.

40. Brooke A. Ackerly, *Universal Human Rights in a World of Difference* (Cambridge, UK: Cambridge University Press, 2008).

41. Nicola Pratt and Sophie Richter-Devroe, "Critically Examining UNSCR 1325 on Women, Peace and Security," *International Feminist Journal of Politics* 13, no. 4 (2011).

42. Carol Cohn, Helen Kinsella, and Sheri Gibbings, "Women, Peace and Security: Resolution 1325," *International Feminist Journal of Politics* 6, no.1 (2001); Cynthia Cockburn, *From Where We Stand: War, Women's Activism and Feminist Analysis* (London: Zed Books, 2007); Pratt and Richter-Devroe, "Critically Examining UNSCR 1325."

43. Samuel Huntington, "The Clash of Civilizations?," *Foreign Affairs* 72, no. 3 (1993).

44. See also Magnus Ranstorp, "Terrorism in the Name of Religion," *Journal of International Affairs* 50, no.1 (1996); Daniel Benjamin and Steven Simon, *The Age of Sacred Terror* (New York: Random House, 2002); Mia Bloom, *Dying to Kill: The Allure of Suicide Terror* (New York: Columbia University Press, 2005); Marc Lynch, "Al-Qaeda's Constructivist Turn," *Praeger Security International* (May 5, 2006); Brenda Shaffer, ed., *The Limits of Culture: Islam and Foreign Policy* (Cambridge, MA: MIT Press, 2006); and Monica Duffy Toft, Daniel Philpott, and Samuel Shah, *God's Century: Resurgent Religion and Global Politics* (New York: Norton, 2011).

45. Hedley Bull, *The Anarchical Society: A Study of Order in World Politics* (London: Macmillan, 1977).

46. Jeffrey T. Checkel, ed., *Transnational Dynamics of Civil War* (Cambridge, UK: Cambridge University Press, 2013), xiii.

47. Karen Ballentine and Jake Sherman, eds., *The Political Economy of Armed Conflict: Beyond Greed and Grievance* (Boulder, CO: Lynne Rienner, 2003).

48. Virginia Haufler, *Dangerous Commerce: Insurance and the Management of International Risk* (Ithaca, NY: Cornell University Press, 1997); Paul Collier and Anke Hoefler, "Greed and Grievance in Civil War," World Bank Policy Research Working Paper No. 2355 (May 2000); Ibrahim Elbadawi and Nicholas Sambanis, "How Much War Will We See? Explaining the Prevalence of Civil War," *Journal of Conflict Resolution* 46, no. 3 (2002): 307–34; James D. Fearon, "Why Do Some Civil Wars Last So Much Longer than Others?," *Journal of Peace Research* 41, no. 3 (2004): 275–301; Michael L. Ross, "What Do We Know about Natural Resources and Civil War?," *Journal of Peace Research* 41, no. 3 (2004): 337–56; Richard Snyder and Ravi Bhavnani, "Diamonds, Blood, and Taxes: A Revenue-Centered Framework for Explaining Political Order," *Journal of Conflict Resolution* 49, no. 4 (August 2005): 563–97.

49. Sam Gregory, "*Kony 2012* through a Prism of Video Advocacy Practices and Trends," *Journal of Human Rights Practice* 4, no. 3 (2012): 464–68.

50. Jeffrey Herbst, "War and the State in Africa," *International Security* 14, no. 4 (Spring 1990): 117–39.

51. Stephen M. Saideman, "Explaining the International Relations of Secessionist Conflicts: Vulnerability versus Ethnic Ties," *International Organization* 51, no. 4 (1997): 721–53;

Stephen M. Saideman, *The Ties That Divide: Ethnic Politics, Foreign Policy, and International Conflict* (New York: Columbia University Press, 2001); James D. Fearon and David Laitin, "Ethnicity, Insurgency, and Civil War," *American Political Science Review* 97 (February 2003): 75–90.

52. Idean Salehyan, *Rebels without Borders: Transnational Insurgencies in World Politics* (Ithaca, NY: Cornell University Press, 2009).

53. Lars-Erik Cederman et al., "Transborder Ethnic Kin and Civil War," *International Organization* 67, no. 2 (April 2013): 389–410.

54. David Malet, *Foreign Fighters: Transnational Identity in Civil Conflicts* (New York: Oxford University Press, 2013).

55. Mohammed Hafez, *Suicide Bombers in Iraq* (Washington, DC: United States Institute of Peace Press, 2007); Cerwyn Moore and Paul Tumelty, "Foreign Fighters and the Case of Chechnya: A Critical Assessment," *Studies in Conflict and Terrorism* 31, no. 5 (2008): 412–33; Thomas Hegghammer, "Should I Stay or Should I Go? Explaining Variation in Western Jihadists' Choice between Domestic and Foreign Fighting," *American Political Science Review* 107, no. 1 (February 2013): 1–15. But see Field, "Transnationalism and the New Tribe," 5, and J. Bowyer Bell, "Contemporary Revolutionary Organizations," 158–63, in Nye and Keohane, *Transnational Relations and World Politics*, for discussions of atypical "international volunteers" and "transnational individuals" such as Ché Guevara and diasporans in political and armed conflict.

56. Alexander Betts, *Protection by Persuasion: International Cooperation in the Refugee Regime* (Ithaca, NY: Cornell University Press, 2006).

57. Idean Salehyan and Kristian Skrede Gleditsch, "Refugees and the Spread of Civil War," *International Organization* 60 (Spring 2006): 335–66.

58. R. Gunaratna, "Sri Lanka," in Ballentine and Sherman, *Political Economy of Armed Conflict*.

59. Sidney Tarrow, *The New Transnational Activism* (New York: Cambridge University Press, 2005); Miles Kahler and Barbara F. Walter, eds., *Territoriality and Conflict in an Era of Globalization* (New York: Cambridge University Press, 2006).

60. Robin Cohen, *Global Diasporas: An Introduction* (Seattle: University of Washington Press, 1997).

61. Jennifer M. Brinkerhoff, *Digital Diasporas: Identity and Transnational Engagement* (New York: Cambridge University Press, 2009).

62. Matthew Evangelista, "The Paradox of State Strength: Transnational Relations, Domestic Structures, and Security Policy in Russia and the Soviet Union," *International Organization* 49, no. 1 (Winter 1995): 1–38; Thomas Risse-Kappen, *Bringing Transnational Relations Back In: Non-State Actors, Domestic Structures and International Institutions* (New York: Cambridge University Press, 1995); Yossi Shain and Aharon Barth, "Diasporas and International Relations Theory," *International Organization* 57, no. 3 (Summer 2003): 449–79; Rebecca K. C. Hersman, *Friends and Foes: How Congress and the President Really Make Foreign Policy* (Washington, DC: Brookings Institution Press, 2009).

63. Nina Glick Schiller, Linda Basch, and Cristina Szatnon-Blanc, "Transnationalism: A New Analytical Framework for Understanding Migration," *Annals of the New York Academy of Sciences* 645 (1992): 1–24; Olivier Roy, *Globalized Islam: The Search for a New Ummah* (New York: Columbia University Press, 2004).

64. Tarrow, *New Transnational Activism*.

65. Paul Hockenos, *Homeland Calling: Exile Patriotism and the Balkan Wars* (Ithaca, NY: Cornell University Press, 2003).

66. Maria Koinova, "Diasporas and Secessionist Conflicts: The Mobilization of the Armenian, Albanian and Chechen Diasporas," *Ethnic and Racial Studies* 34, no. 2 (2010): 333–56.

67. Hazel Smith and Paul Stares, *Diasporas in Conflict: Peace-Makers or Peace-Wreckers?* (New York: United Nations University Press, 2007).

68. Gabriel Sheffer, *Modern Diasporas in International Politics* (London: Croom Helm, 1986); Fiona B. Adamson, "Crossing Borders: International Migration and National Security," *International Security* 31, no. 1 (Summer 2006): 165–99. State efforts to curtail immigration appear to have less influence on migration flows than economic conditions do, indicating that migration patterns are also tied to the global market economy as much as they are to regimes (Wayne A. Cornelius and I. Salehyan, "Does Border Enforcement Deter Unauthorized Immigration? The Case of Mexican Migration to the United States of America," *Regulation and Governance* [2007]: 139–53).

69. Michael Barnett, *Empire of Humanity: A History of Humanitarianism* (Ithaca, NY: Cornell University Press, 2013); Thomas Davies, *NGOs: A History of Transnational Civil Society* (New York: Oxford University Press, 2014).

70. Martha Finnemore and Kathryn Sikkink, "International Norm Dynamics and Political Change," *International Organization* 52, vol. 4 (Autumn 1998): 887–917; Richard Price, "Reversing the Gun Sights: Transnational Civil Society Targets Land Mines," *International Organization* 52, no. 3 (1998).

71. Ann M. Florini, *The Third Force: The Rise of Transnational Civil Society* (Washington, DC: Carnegie Endowment for Peace, 2000).

72. Thomas Olesen, *International Zapatismo: The Construction of Solidarity in the Age of Globalization* (New York: Zed Books, 2005).

73. Mark I. Lichbach and Paul Almeida, "Global Order and Local Resistance: The Neoliberal Institutional Trilemma and the Battle of Seattle," unpublished manuscript, University of California Riverside Center for Global Order and Resistance, 2001; John D. Clark, *Worlds Apart: Civil Society and the Battle for Ethical Globalization* (Bloomfield, CT: Kumarian Press, 2003).

74. Margaret Keck and Kathryn Sikkink, *Activists beyond Borders: Advocacy Networks in International Politics* (Ithaca, NY: Cornell University Press, 1998).

75. Price, "Reversing the Gun Sights."

76. Marlies Glasius, *The International Criminal Court: A Global Civil Society Achievement* (New York: Routledge, 2006).

77. Ruth Reitan, "Coordinated Power in Contemporary Leftist Activism" in Olesen, *Power and Transnational Activism*; Rodney Bruce Hall, *Reducing Armed Violence with NGO Governance* (New York: Routledge, 2013); Charli Carpenter, *"Lost" Causes: Agenda Vetting in Global Issue Networks and the Shaping of Human Security* (Ithaca, NY: Cornell University Press, 2014).

78. Robyn Eckersley, *The Green State: Rethinking Democracy and Sovereignty* (Cambridge, MA: MIT Press, 2004).

79. Marjo Lindroth, "Indigenous-State Relations in the UN: Establishing the Indigenous Forum," *Polar Record* 42, no. 222 (2006): 239–48.

80. Amitav Acharya, "Norm Subsidiarity and Regional Orders: Sovereignty, Regionalism and Rule Making in the Third World," *International Studies Quarterly* 55, no. 1 (2011): 95–123.

81. William Casebeer and Troy Thomas, "Deterring Violent Non-State Actors in the New Millennium," *Strategic Insights* 1, no. 10 (December 2002), describe such actors as "violent nonstate actors (VNSAs)," while Oded Lowenheim, *Predators and Parasites: Persistent*

Agents of Transnational Harm and Great Power Authority (Ann Arbor: University of Michigan Press, 2007), calls them "persistent agents of transnational harm (PATHs)," and Oren Barak and Chanan Cohen, "The 'Modern Sherwood Forest': Theoretical and Practical Challenges," in *Nonstate Actors in Intrastate Conflicts*, eds. Dan Miodownik and Oren Barak (Philadelphia: University of Pennsylvania Press, 2013), employ the term "violent transborder nonstate actor (VITNA)" and argue that they require a universal ideology.

82. Janice E. Thomson, *Mercenaries, Pirates, and Sovereigns: State-Building and Extraterritorial Violence in Early Modern Europe* (Princeton, NJ: Princeton University Press, 1994); Sarah Percy, *Mercenaries: The History of a Norm in International Relations* (New York: Oxford University Press, 2007).

83. Deborah D. Avant, *The Market for Force: The Consequences of Privatizing Security* (Cambridge, UK: Cambridge University Press, 2003); P. W. Singer, *Corporate Warriors: The Rise of the Privatized Military Industry* (Ithaca, NY: Cornell University Press, 2010).

84. Mats R. Berdal and Monica Serrano, *Transnational Organized Crime and International Security: Business as Usual?* (Boulder, CO: Lynne Rienner Publishers, 2002); Phil Williams, "Transnational Organized Crime and the State," in *The Emergence of Private Authority in Global Governance* (New York: Cambridge University Press, 2002), ed. Rodney Bruce Hall and Thomas J. Biersteker; Roy Godson, "Transnational Crime, Corruption, and Security," in Brown, *Grave New World*, 237–42, 250; Max G. Manwaring, *A Contemporary Challenge to State Sovereignty: Gangs and Other Illicit Transnational Criminal Organizations in Central America, El Salvador, Mexico, Jamaica, and Brazil* (Carlisle Barracks, PA: Strategic Studies Institute US Army War College, 2007); Peter Andreas, *Smuggler Nation: How Illicit Trade Made America* (New York: Oxford University Press, 2013).

85. Lowenheim, *Predators and Parasites*; Martin N. Murphy, *Small Boats, Weak States, Dirty Money: Piracy and Maritime Terrorism in the Modern World* (New York: Columbia University Press, 2010); Stig Jarle Hansen, *Al-Shabaab in Somalia: The History and Ideology of a Militant Islamist Group* (New York: Oxford University Press, 2013).

86. Barak and Cohen, "'Modern Sherwood Forest.'"

87. Mary Kaldor, *New and Old Wars: Organized Violence in a Global Era*, 2nd ed. (Stanford, CA: Stanford University Press, 2007).

88. David M. Hollis, "Cyberwar Case Study: Georgia 2008," *Small Wars Journal* (2011).

89. Bruce Hoffman, *Inside Terrorism* (New York: Columbia University Press, 1998); Max Abrahms, "Why Terrorism Does Not Work," *International Security* 31, no. 2 (Fall 2006).

90. Madeline Gruen, "Innovative Recruitment and Indoctrination Tactics by Extremists: Video Games, Hip-Hop, and the World Wide Web," in *The Making of a Terrorist: Recruitment, Training and Root Causes*, ed. J. F. Forest (Westport, CT: Praeger Security International, 2005); Marc Lynch, Deen Freelon, and Sean Aday, *Syria's Socially Mediated Civil War* (Washington, DC: United States Institute of Peace, 2014).

91. Marc Sageman, *Understanding Terror Networks* (Philadelphia: University of Pennsylvania Press, 2004); Lorenzo Vidino, "Homegrown Jihadist Terrorism in the United States: A New and Occasional Phenomenon?" *Studies in Conflict and Terrorism* 32, no. 1 (2009): 1–17.

92. Hafez, *Suicide Bombers in Iraq*; Marc Sageman, *Leaderless Jihad: Terror Networks in the Twenty-First Century* (Philadelphia: University of Pennsylvania Press, 2008).

1

Knights of Columbus Catholic Recreation Clubs in Great Britain, 1917–19

LUKE FLANAGAN

This chapter analyzes the work of the Knights of Columbus, an international fraternal Roman Catholic order, during the First World War. Its focus is the order's establishment of Catholic recreation clubs in Great Britain in the latter stages of the conflict. It argues that the Knights of Columbus was an early example of a transnational organization seeking to influence state policies, one that remained constrained by the nationalist exigencies of a period of major interstate war and by the communication technologies of the era. Accordingly, national governments wanted to limit the Knights' activities because the respective states wished to control their war efforts, including welfare services. Furthermore, the political opportunity structure meant that the founders of the Knights of Columbus, Irish diasporans, were predisposed to use the organization as a vehicle to integrate into American society rather than to foster transnational relationships. While the order had expanded into Canada in the late nineteenth century, the overarching Knights' leadership was reluctant to occupy a transnational space, wishing instead to portray the order as patriotic.

The Knights' leadership, based in the United States, was wedded to the characterization of the order as an American organization. While it did not discourage the Canadian Knights from administering a welfare program, the leadership did not actively support one either, at least until the entry of the United States into the war in 1917. The crux of the Knights' dilemma was the preservation of its American identity. When the order expanded to Canada, it acquired new identities and different loyalties. Canadian loyalties were grounded in both state and empire. The benefit of this context for the Canadian Knights was the ability to form partnerships with like-minded organizations in Britain. However, as this chapter demonstrates, transnational coordination proved more difficult between the American and Canadian Knights. The result was that the Knights' war effort was fragmented into two separate welfare programs—American and Canadian.

From a broader conceptual standpoint, the Knights showed complex transnationalism, defined by David Malet and Miriam J. Anderson in the introduction to this volume as "the increasing number, scope, interactions, and influence of transnational actors on diplomatic and governance processes where states have invited as participants, been forced to respond to, or have become reliant upon the expertise of transnational actors and where transnational actors increasingly interact directly with each other." In this case, the state became reliant on religious actors to deliver recreation and welfare services to soldiers stationed abroad. While the state provided some funds and a national framework of authorization and/or recognition, the Knights provided the operational vision for the services in Europe. However, as shown in the latter portion of the chapter, although the contemporary Knights displayed an increasingly transnational character over time, the order continued to be constrained by its history as an American organization.

Origins and Organizational Structure

The Knights of Columbus was established in New Haven, Connecticut, in 1882 by Fr. Michael J. McGivney, assistant pastor of St. Mary's Church. The organization was founded upon three guiding principles: charity, unity, and fraternity.[1] The Knights was the product of second-generation members of the Irish diaspora who still experienced prejudice toward their ethnicity and religion. As Christopher Kauffman has noted, Irish immigrants to the United States had been caricatured as "rowdy drunks." The Knights of Columbus, in name and practice, attempted to reverse this image by developing a reputation of respectability.[2] The term "knights" conveyed a commitment to struggle against nativism and anti-Catholicism as "Catholic gentlemen," while "Columbus" was designed to tap into the sentimental attachment to Christopher Columbus as the discoverer of America. The Columbus name was seen as being central to its raison d'être. It sought to display pride in America's Catholic heritage and claim the "discovery of America as a Catholic event."[3] The Knights was thus a vehicle for the Irish minority to profess its loyalty to the state and reinforce its integration into both American and Canadian society.[4]

Patriotism and loyalty to the state was, and remains, integral to the Knights' doctrine. Writing in the *Tablet*, an international Catholic newspaper published in London since 1840, Shane Leslie describes the basis of the Knights' ethos as such: "They support the Pope and the [American] Republic. Their charters are two. The one [that] was dispensed at the Declaration of Independence—the other is the Sermon on the Mount."[5] The patriotism of the Knights was formalized in 1900 with the establishment of the fourth degree of membership. The three initial degrees encompassed the principles of charity, unity, and fraternity. The addition of patriotism as the fourth degree aimed to demonstrate the mutual compatibility of religion and commitment to the nation-state. The Knights define patriotism as such: "Members of the Knights of Columbus, be they Americans, Canadians, Mexicans, Cubans, Filipinos, Poles, or Dominicans, are patriotic citizens. We are proud of our devotion to God and country, and believe in standing up for both. Whether it is in public or private, the Knights remind the world that Catholics support their nations and are amongst the greatest citizens."[6] The fourth degree came to be the highest level of seniority within the order, which demonstrated the importance of patriotism as the central pillar of "Columbianism." As Jennifer M. Brinkerhoff notes in chapter 4, diasporans are often socialized into or strategically adopt the values of their country of residence, which enables them to more effectively influence the foreign policy of their state.

Operationally, the Knights of Columbus is a mutual-benefit society similar to the Freemasons or the Rotarians. It offers financial aid to members and their families through an insurance system. The insurance program was initiated to protect widows and orphans from financial ruin following the death of the main breadwinner.[7] The organizational structure of the Knights is both transnational and domestic in makeup. It maintains its headquarters in New Haven with a supreme knight as leader of the Supreme Council, the order's global governing body. The Supreme Council comprises seventy-five state councils, which govern the order at the subnational level—for example, US states or Canadian provinces. The constituents of the Supreme Council assume a similar role to shareholders: to select the executive governance of the order. The Supreme Council delegates elect the twenty-one-member Board of Directors to terms of three years.[8] At the local level, the individual state councils are divided into districts. These districts comprise groupings of local councils. The local councils are described as the "basic unit of the Knights," which carries out the work of the order at the community or parish levels.[9]

According to Kauffman, the organizational structure was intended to "reflect the democratic features of the American system of government."[10] The annually convened Supreme Council is envisaged as the legislative branch, while the Board of Directors is the executive. The state councils, districts, and local councils address matters of local concern in a way that reflects the principles of the order.[11] At the time of the First World War, the organizational structure was not dissimilar to its current form. The main difference was that the executive function of the Board of Directors was, until the 1950s, vested with a Supreme Committee of the Supreme Council.[12] The Knights' hierarchy was reluctant to extend the order beyond the confines of the United States. Maurice Francis Egan and John B. Kennedy argued that the "Knights strictly applied, as a brake on their own development, Washington's counsel to avoid entangling alliances."[13] The American Knights were concerned that their Canadian counterparts' support for the war would call into question their loyalty to the United States at a time when the country remained officially neutral.

In 1897, the Knights of Columbus established its first chapter in Canada with the opening of the Montreal council. The Canadian branch, however, was not afforded a role in the executive governance of the order, although Canadian councils were given representation on the Supreme Council. Owing to Canada's small representation—19,000 members out of a total of 350,000 at the time war was declared in 1914—the orientation of the Knights remained fundamentally American: "The executive board being practically American, and operating an American corporation, the country's [i.e., the US] course in foreign relations was bound to be faithfully reflected in the Order's activities."[14] The expansion into Canada created a tension between an evolving transnational character and a rigidly American organizational and operational structure. At the outset of the war, the American neutrality of the order prevented their Canadian counterparts from providing welfare services to Canadian soldiers:

> No action could possibly be taken to benefit the troops of any side of the conflict while the United States remained a neutral observer. The Supreme Board had no objections to interpose against the action of Canadian Knights, either individually or collectively, in their capacity as Canadian citizens loyal to the British crown. In fact, everything they did for their country, whether on active or home service, was warmly applauded as an exhibition of the patriotism which is one of the first principles of Columbianism. But it was not until the United States had entered the war that the Supreme Board could give its consent and moral support to the war relief work inaugurated by the Canadian Knights.[15]

The staunch commitment to the American state undermined the Knights' ability to cooperate with other Catholic partners, including the Canadian Knights. As will be shown, the Canadian Knights cooperated with the Catholic Women's League (CWL) in Britain to deliver their welfare program. It was the shared attachment to the British Empire that aided this cooperation. The absence of the United States underscored the tension between the national and transnational identity of the Knights. The commitment to patriotism acted as a restraint on transnational action. It was the differences in national and, in the case of the Canadian Knights, imperial loyalty that caused a schism in the

Knights of Columbus and effectively carved out distinct national organizations. In effect, the Supreme Council allowed the Knights of Columbus to be franchised as a brand and set of values that could be utilized by Catholics in state-specific contexts. The emergence of nationally distinct chapters of the Knights could be said to be an unintended consequence of the Supreme Council's reluctance to expand the order's presence transnationally. Its commitment to the order's American identity allowed the Canadian Knights to effectively operate separately from the central governing structure.

In many ways, the Knights filled a void left by the organizational deficiencies of the Catholic Church in both the United States and Canada. At the time of the war, the church in these jurisdictions was so loosely organized that it lacked the ability to act as a coordinated body. In the case of Canada, Terence J. Fay has argued: "There was no Canadian church with ready-made policies. There were dioceses linked to the Holy See, but geographically they were grouped together only by their commitment to Canadian Catholicism. The bishops remained independent of one another. In canon law, they were only responsible to the Holy See in Rome. A Canadian bishop was able to deal with particular problems in his own way—with or without the support of their colleagues."[16] Canada did not have a permanent body until the creation of the Canadian Conference of Catholic Bishops in 1943.

There was a similar situation in the United States. Until 1917, there was no national structure. The war, however, was the core catalyst for national organization. Following the US entry into the war in the same year, the National Catholic War Council (NCWC) was created in order to provide a collective national response to the war effort.[17] The NCWC comprised fourteen archbishops and operated through an Administrative Committee of four bishops. The Administrative Committee was itself divided into two subcommittees: the Committee on Special War Activities and the Knights of Columbus Committee on War Activities.[18] The inclusion of the Knights in the structural makeup of the NCWC was a central influencer of the order's ability to become a transnational actor during the war. The formation of an organized Catholic authority allowed the order to supplement the state provision of welfare and recreation services. In both the United States and Canada, the Knights became, with the approval of the respective national governments, official providers of spiritual, welfare, and recreational services to both Catholic and non-Catholic soldiers.

The Knights had already proven adept at administering to soldiers during a conflict. In 1916, when US soldiers assembled on the Mexican border during the Mexican Revolution, the Knights established fifteen recreation clubs to service the religious needs of Catholic soldiers.[19] Through their work in the Mexico conflict, the Knights became the Catholic counterpart to the Young Men's Christian Association (YMCA), which had forty-two recreation centers and 376 secretaries on the US-Mexico border.[20] When the United States joined the war in 1917, the Knights expanded their work beyond the US. However, by joining together in the NCWC, the Knights had ensured that they were institutionally committed to being an American organization for the primary benefit of American soldiers. The Canadian Knights were left to fund and operate their own recreation clubs.

How the Knights were organized and how the organization interacted with other actors was integral to the success of its transnational activities during the war. The Knights were not the only Catholic organization to provide recreational centers to soldiers. The CWL had begun such a program in Britain in 1915. The formation of a strategic partnership between the CWL and the Canadian Knights to fund and operate Canadian-oriented centers in Britain was the core transnational transaction. The American Knights, on the other hand, saw no need for transnationalism to deliver their social club program in Britain. Their continued focus on patriotism from an American standpoint and superior resources, in terms of finances and personnel, did not require an operational partnership. By working with the CWL, the Canadian Knights could maximize their lesser resources; transnationalism provided the bridge for it to operationalize the recreation club concept and provide Canadian soldiers of all faiths and creeds with a temporary reprieve from the horrors of war.

Everybody Welcome, Everything Free: The American Knights

When the United States joined the war, the Knights of Columbus, owing to its success in Mexico, came to the forefront as the eminent Catholic welfare organization. The order, however, required the sanction of the US government to administer to American soldiers. This was granted in April 1917.[21] It was designated by the War Department as the official agency for looking after the morale and social welfare of the Roman Catholics in the army and navy.[22] The requirement for official sanction is one way in which the Knights' war work stilted the transnationalism of the American order. With that sanction, the Knights' core remit was the welfare of American soldiers. All fundraising was directed to achieve that objective and aimed at an American audience. Announcing a nationwide appeal for $3 million to fund the establishment of recreation clubs in both camps and at the battlefield, Supreme Knight James A. Flaherty outlined the envisaged structure and function of the centers:

> The purpose will be to afford clean and wholesome recreation to all enlisted men in both [army and navy], regardless of creed. It will have for its purpose the maintenance of suitable places for the saying of Mass in each of the twenty-two cantonments in the United States, where the new National Army is being trained, as well as at the expansion camps of the Regular Army. Priests will also be furnished in units where the regimental chaplain is not a Catholic, and they

will be supported during their ministry, both while with the troops in the United States, and when on active service in Europe.[23]

Although the Knights of Columbus was a Catholic organization, its commitment that the centers would be for all soldiers "regardless of creed" broadened the appeal for funds beyond Catholicism. Still, it continued to be constrained by a national agenda. It is here where the rationale for the establishment of the NCWC can be found. The NCWC was about more than the pooling of resources; it was about patriotism and commitment to the country at a time of war. By coming together as a united organization, Catholics pledged their loyalty "to the country, its Government and its supreme Executive."[24] An extract of the letter presented to President Woodrow Wilson by Cardinal James Gibbons, the bishop of Baltimore, outlines the commitment to the war cause:

> Standing firmly upon our solid Catholic tradition and history from the very foundation of this nation, we reaffirm in this hour of stress and trial our most sacred and sincere loyalty and patriotism toward our country, our Government, and our flag. Moved to the very depths of our hearts by the stirring appeal of the President of the United States and by the action of our national Congress, we accept wholeheartedly and unreservedly the decree of that legislative authority proclaiming this country to be in a state of war. . . . Our people now, as ever, will rise as one man to serve the nation. Our priests and consecrated women will once again, as in every former trial of our country, win by their bravery, their heroism, and their service, new admiration and approval. We are all true Americans, ready, as our age, our ability, and our condition permit, to do whatever is in us to do, for the preservation, the progress, and the triumph of our beloved country.[25]

For America's Catholics, the NCWC was about national and religious unity. The language in Gibbons's letter aligned with the Knights' mandate. The staunch support of the country's war objectives spoke to the Knights' commitment to the state. The Knights had already received government recognition, but with the establishment of the NCWC it received religious recognition. In August 1917, the Knights of Columbus was declared by a general convention of Catholics "as the body representing the Church in the recreational welfare of the soldiers in the camps."[26] The NCWC and the strong patriotic language of American bishops encased the Knights firmly within a national context and undermined the scope for any transnational organization like that of its Canadian counterpart. The NCWC gave the Knights an outlet to demonstrate its patriotic commitment to the nation. The Knights, as an institution, sought to embody that in their principles. The war gave them the opportunity to put those principles into practice.

The NCWC also became the core channel for the disbursement of funds to the Knights' recreation club program. This was a central reason for the national compartmentalization of the Knights' war effort. The coming together of the American Catholic hierarchy in a single institution ensured that funds were collected and distributed nationally. Funding for the program was conducted by the individual state councils.[27] The NCWC was designated an official government agent in welfare work by the US War Department in August 1918. This designation brought in "thirty six million dollars, most of which went to the work of the Knights of Columbus and the NCWC overseas units."[28] Official designation also brought the NCWC and the Knights under the auspices of another national institution, the United War Work Campaign (UWWC), established at the behest of President Wilson in 1916.

The UWWC put the state more firmly in control of welfare provision by bringing the Knights' funding efforts together with six other welfare organizations—the YMCA, the Young Women's Christian Association, the Jewish Welfare Board, the War Camp Community Service, the American Library Organization, and the Salvation Army. In a letter to Raymond B. Fosdick, chairman of the US Government Commission on Training Camp Activities, Wilson said: "It is my judgment that we shall secure the best results in the matter of the support of these agencies if these seven societies will unite their forthcoming appeals for funds, in order that the spirit of the country in this matter may be expressed without distinction of race or religious opinion in support of what is in reality a common service."[29] The UWWC placed an emphasis on cooperation and coordination between the seven organizations under the direction of the Fosdick Commission. This cooperation between America's welfare organizations showed that, from the government's standpoint, the most effective way of providing welfare services was through the pooling of resources with similar and like-minded organizations.

American Knights Recreation Clubs in Britain

Between April 1917, when the United States declared war, and July 1918, an estimated one million American soldiers passed through England on their way to the front lines, with a further million expected by the end of 1918.[30] Recreation clubs in Britain were located in areas where the concentration of American soldiers was high, often cities and towns with significant strategic importance, such as naval ports. There were clubs in Glasgow, Edinburgh, Invergordon, Liverpool, Cardiff, and Plymouth.[31] The purpose of the clubs reflected the duality of the Knights' endeavors. While each club had a chapel for the celebration of Mass by Catholic soldiers, they also served as recreation clubs for all American soldiers. The slogan "Everybody Welcome, Everything Free" characterized both the ethos and function of the clubs. There was no single model that the clubs followed, but most were equipped with canteens and reading rooms, while some had gymnasiums and beds. The club in Glasgow, for example, was described as "really a hotel." Beds were also available at the London club.[32]

The clubs were staffed by secretaries, informally known as Caseys, and Catholic chaplains. Both the secretaries and chaplains were sent from the United States. It is estimated that the Knights provided 1,134 secretaries for service in the US at training camps, while a further 1,075 were dispatched to France, Britain, Italy, and Dalmatia.[33] As well as administering the clubs, the secretaries also visited hospitals throughout Britain to distribute cigarettes, chocolate, chewing gum, fruit, postcards, and reading matter to US servicemen.[34] Every service and product was available to all US soldiers regardless of creed and was provided free. The role of the chaplains was to attend to the spiritual welfare of Catholic soldiers. As the war went on, the availability of Knights' chaplains in Britain became more restricted. It is estimated that over half of the 1,075 chaplains dispatched overseas went to France.[35] Some clubs relied on British chaplains and local priests to fulfill their religious functions. In the absence of any great number of Knights of Columbus chaplains, the London office arranged with the different British chaplains throughout England and Scotland to look after the spiritual welfare of the men in the service.[36] It was also noted that the Westminster Catholic Federation, a British lay organization formed in 1905, had placed its services at the disposal of the Knights and the NCWC. Such cooperation was seen to reflect the bond shared between Catholics around the world.[37]

The use of British chaplains and priests reflected the duality of the Knights' mission—welfare and religion—and how it interacted with other actors overseas. The universality of Catholic beliefs and values meant that the religious aspect of the Knights' work could be delegated to other religious actors, a fact that the Canadian Knights would also draw upon. The use of external chaplains and priests reflected the balance between the order's principles of faith and patriotism. While the initial objective was to furnish the needs of Catholic soldiers, the commitment to serve the nation came to the forefront as the core function of the order's war work. As was reported in the *Tablet*, "the American Government recognized [the Knights'] endeavours primarily to see to [the religious] provision, and secondarily to provide amusements for men who were exposed to the danger of nostalgia."[38] To be clear, Catholicism guided the war work of the order; it believed that it was "following the example of the Good Samaritan" in tending to the welfare of all soldiers.[39]

The Good Samaritan perspective galvanized the Knights as they sought to ease the horror and drudgery of war. Those men who did not require or desire spiritual welfare were instead offered practical welfare, through free products and services. This was the Knights' primary contribution to the war; whether in the United States or overseas, the Knights' clubs allowed the soldiers to take a break from the war and get a temporary glimpse of normality through spiritual-ity, socialization, and a feeling of home. As Egan and Kennedy argued, the welfare of the Knights was more than materialism: "Even when the secretaries had nothing to give, they were cordially welcomed by officers and men because their presence had some emotional value and their relief workers were the visible examples of the interest and affection of the people at home, more vivid than the written word and more graphic than photographs."[40] Beyond the free goods, the Knights were seen to be handing out "big fistfuls of friendship" to help ease the effects of war.[41]

The welfare work of the Knights, whether in wartime or peacetime, typified the duality of the Knights' purpose. On the one hand, Catholicism was the foundation and the guiding philosophy, while the nation was the focus on the other. Through their war work, the Knights proved their ability to act beyond the borders of the home nation, but they could not achieve this without interaction with Catholic partners. However, the order's commitment to patriotism restricted the transnational scope of its work. It was essentially an American organization. Its national posture split its war efforts as the Canadian Knights established their own similar but structurally distinct recreation club program.

Everybody Welcome: The Canadian Knights

The genesis for the Canadian program began in mid-1917 shortly after the United States entered the war. The organization of the Canadian program was swift. An initial per capita levy of one dollar per member was applied at the annual convention of the Ontario Knights of Columbus in May 1917. A further $80,000 was raised following a fundraising drive.[42] The initiation of the Canadian program exposed flaws in the Knights' national structure in that country. Like in the United States, there was no central authority either in the Catholic Church or the Knights in Canada. While individual Knights councils were seen to be the primary channel to raise funds, a national war committee was established to better coordinate the welfare program.[43] According to Duff Crerar, the Canadian Knights saw their war work as an excellent opportunity to increase their public visibility and silence critics decrying the lack of Catholic support for the war effort.[44]

Mark G. McGowan has argued that the Canadian Knights "imported wholesale" the principles first outlined by their American counterparts.[45] Patriotism was, as in the United States, a central part of the Canadian Knights' ethos, though it was "altered to suit the British North American context."[46] This was important because Canada provided a complex national landscape in terms of its bilingual character and constitutional status within the British Empire. At the time of the war, Canada was a self-governing dominion of Britain. Its foreign policy was administered from London, and when Britain declared war Canada, as a constituent unit of the Empire, was automatically at war. There was also no single Canadian citizenship—all Canadians were British subjects.[47] From a patriotic standpoint, Canada had dual loyalties. It was a committed member of the empire, yet at the same time there was an emergent and strengthening attachment to Canada as an object of loyalty and belonging. How the war affected these loyalties is a key focus of the scholarly literature. While some argue that the war helped Canada to develop a greater sense of nationhood, others have argued that Canada's national development was not so clear-cut.[48]

As well as being able to draw upon the imperial link to aid the welfare program, the Canadian Knights also attempted to reconcile the diasporan tensions in Canadian national identity. McGowan has argued that the Knights felt that the English-speaking Catholics of Canada could transcend the divide between Canada's two peoples because they were "united to Protestant Canada by language, and shared a common faith with French Quebec."[49] The order sought to rise above the fissures in Canadian society by positioning itself as both Catholic and Canadian.[50] By fully supporting the war effort, the Canadian Knights caused their unifying purpose to be undermined, because the war was seen as an imperial endeavor. The Knights' commitment to the war effort favored the English Canadian perspective of enthusiastic commitment to the empire.

Whether the Knights were successful in bridging the divide between English and French Canadians is a matter of debate.[51] Tensions over conscription certainly had a hand in preventing the Knights from establishing a permanent administrative body in Canada.[52] Although funds were raised by the individual provincial councils, in order to increase fundraising the Ontario Council sought incorporation from the Canadian government. Letters patent incorporating the Canadian Knights were issued on October 20, 1917, which empowered the Knights to "erect, equip and conduct Catholic Army Huts for Canadian Soldiers, which were to serve the two-fold purpose of chapels for Catholic soldiers and recreation huts for all soldiers, irrespective of creed."[53]

Although the centers were specifically established for the benefit of Canadian soldiers, the imperial connection helped the Canadian Knights to overcome the practical obstacles of establishing the program outside of Canada, especially in Britain. Interaction with others was at the forefront of its mission. The fact that other Catholic organizations had already established recreation clubs made this task easier. The CWL had opened its first hut in March 1916 in central London at the site of what is now Westminster Cathedral's conference center. A prefabricated structure staffed by local CWL members and equipped with a twenty-four-hour canteen, the facility was established for the benefit of "troops passing through London."[54] CWL huts were not just for the benefit of British soldiers and were not confined to Britain; the CWL also operated huts in Europe. In 1917, the CWL established the Services Committee to "plan and organise the work of the growing number of huts."[55] The CWL hut program was important because it offered the Knights an opportunity to further their own ambitions and establish specifically Canadian huts in Britain and Europe.

The Canadian Catholic Army Huts (CAH) program was different in scope from its American counterparts. The slogan "Everybody Welcome" reflected the same sentiments of inclusivity: "No distinction was made regarding the creed or race of those benefited."[56] However, a nominal charge was applied for the services and goods supplied. Those who could not pay were still served. Egan and Kennedy noted that normally charged-for items, mainly meals and beds, were "provided gratis to as great an extent as they were sold, largely thanks to the generosity of the CWL in the localities where the Canadian huts operated."[57] Despite "big fistfuls of friendship," the "everything free" aspect of the American centers did place a strong emphasis on the quantity of goods that were given away, and accordingly accounts of their work often contained figures detailing these gifts. The following quote is a typical example: "A million cigarettes are expected to arrive this week from the States. Thousands of pounds of candy, athletic goods [and] games of every description are also on the way from the New York headquarters."[58] The absence of the "everything free" commitment and the partnership with the CWL gave the Canadian Knights' program a different character from that of the American Knights. Moreover, as the following case studies will show, the partnership with the CWL gave the Canadian huts an added morale function that complimented the mix of patriotism and Catholicism.

When the CWL began opening huts in areas with a high concentration of Canadian soldiers, the Knights considered it wrong that Canadian Catholics "should depend upon an English society and English money for the erection of Canadian Huts."[59] A hut at Bramshott Camp in Hampshire, southern England, where Canadian soldiers had been based since late 1915, was built by the CWL and opened in March 1917 to specifically serve the needs of the Canadians.[60] The CWL built and funded the hut but was reimbursed by the Knights' CAH fund. Huts were typically equipped with study rooms; writing desks; billiard rooms; separate rooms for cadets, noncommissioned officers, and private soldiers; and canteens where refreshments were sold for one penny per item.[61] This was the Knights' main contribution to conflict: It was there to ease the experience of war through recreation. It was there to help soldiers disconnect from conflict by creating "real Canadian homes for Canadians."[62]

The CAH program demonstrated a dual context. It was inclusive but underpinned by the Catholic ethos of both the Knights and the CWL. The strong emphasis on patriotism was coupled with a desire to provide for the spiritual needs of Catholic soldiers in a comfortable and familiar environment.[63] The interaction with the CWL was instrumental in creating the home environment. In an article published in the *Tablet*, Fr. Joseph Bampton, rector of Farm Street Church in London, gave his perspective on how CWL personnel influenced morale in the huts. In short, it was their compassion that gave the huts their feeling of home:

> In our women [the war] has brought out the qualities with which God endowed woman to fit her to be the helpmeet of man—the devotion, the self-sacrifice, the patience, the endurance, the tenderness, the gentleness, the thoughtfulness, the solicitude, the tactfulness, the sympathy. There may be difference of opinion as to this or that other sphere of woman's activities. On this there can be none. Woman is always in her element when she is soothing pain and relieving distress and solacing misery and ministering comfort, and working deftly with her quick comprehension in such matters, and her unerring taste and nimble fingers to provide the necessaries which keep men fit for their work. Above all, woman is in her right place in the home. It is often the mother, the wife, the sister, who more than anyone else keeps the home together, and makes home what it is.[64]

In this case, gender roles associating women with the private sphere were mobilized to support the war effort. This is in stark contrast to the way in which women's peace advocates have mobilized gender identity as a unifying discourse to demand access to peace negotiations, as discussed by Miriam J. Anderson in chapter 9 of this volume, and the explicitly feminist objectives promoted by the Women's International League for Peace and Freedom (WILPF), as outlined by Catia Cecilia Confortini in chapter 2.

The Canadian Knights' CAH program was about inclusivity and forgetting the stress of war. As well as the established adage that it was a "home," the hut was seen to provide a place where soldiers could "forget the exigencies of army discipline and where we can hear the treasured sound of a woman's voice."[65] This quote underscores the effect of the CWL believed to have been had on the men. Just the opportunity to see and interact with women was considered to be a boost to morale.

The Knights were not content with relying on the CWL and its resources to provide recreational huts for Canadian soldiers. After all, the CWL was an English organization with no presence in Canada at that time. However, the Knights needed the CWL to fulfill its transnational mission. What subsequently emerged was a formal partnership between the Knights and CWL: "The Knights provided the 'Capital,' while the CWL provided the 'Labour.'"[66] The commonality of purpose and values between the Knights and the CWL—Catholicism, charitable works, and patriotism—led the CWL to be seen as the Knights' female counterpart, particularly when it was established in Canada in 1920.[67] The English CWL motto "Charity Work Loyalty" showed a more understated commitment to God and patriotism than the Canadian motto "Love of God and Canada." After the war, a proposal was made to open a British branch of the

Knights. The Catenian Association, a British lay order, suggested that it be merged into a British Knights of Columbus. This proposal was not enacted. The characterization of the order as embodying American society and/or values, or at the very least those of the New World, may have hindered its extension into Britain.[68] Still, it was the reach of the CWL in England that allowed the Canadian Knights to expand its CAH program on a transnational scale.

Contemporary Observations

A century later, the organizational structures of the Knights are considerably more transnational than in the First World War period. The various national interests are represented through direct channels to the order's hierarchy. Canada, for example, is represented by an assistant to the supreme knight for Canadian affairs; Mexico, the Philippines, and Poland all have similar representation. Members of the Board of Directors are elected to office and serve in a personal capacity. From a military standpoint, the Knights remain a primarily American order. Their current military activities remain welfare oriented. Their primary programs are funding the education of Catholic chaplains in the US Armed Forces; administering the "Serving Those Who Served" program, which fields Knights volunteers to Veterans Affairs medical centers in the United States; and the distribution of wheelchairs to US veterans. The fact that all of the order's fifty-two military councils and assemblies are based in US states or in countries with large numbers of US military personnel—for example, South Korea and Japan—can help to explain why the military focus of the order is on America.

In 2013, the order established the Military Overseas Europe Special District to oversee the military councils in Britain, Germany, and Italy. These councils are situated to serve US servicemen and -women based in those countries. The order has, however, taken some steps to reconcile the transnational character of its membership in the administration of its military work; in 2009, a Canadian version of the Knights' military prayer book *Armed with the Faith* was published that included prayers in both English and French.[69] There is still a tension between the American focus of the order's work and its transnational makeup. As of 2013, the Knights had 1,843,587 members and 14,606 councils worldwide.[70] As a proportion of population, growth in membership was highest in Poland, with 23 percent growth in the same year.

The largest Knights jurisdiction is also outside of the United States: Quebec maintains the most members, with 99,505.[71] For four years to 2013, Quebec also placed first for charitable donations. In 2013, Quebec councils donated nearly $10.7 million. Ontario was second with $7.9 million, followed by Texas and California.[72] These figures reveal that the Knights have established a broader transnational footprint in recent years. However, the order's overall organizational and operational posture, particularly in terms of its military work, remains decidedly American.

Conclusion

The case of the Knights of Columbus presents a mixed picture of the salience of transnationalism in the provision of Catholic welfare and recreation services during the First World War. Religion provided the core motivation for its transnational mission, which aided the formation of formal and informal partnerships. However, the patriotic ethos of the Knights and their organization according to national loyalties acted as a restraint on transnationalism and fractured the structural and operational posture of the order into two separate operations—American and Canadian. It is the Canadian example that can offer the clearest insights into the transnational character of the Knights.

In contrast to WILPF, which also operated in a similar period (analyzed in the following chapter by Confortini), the Knights of Columbus remained a largely nationally oriented organization. Unlike WILPF, which consciously sought to transcend nationalism, the Knights used their organization as a vehicle for national integration and patriotism.

The Canadian Knights showed that it was difficult to operate in isolation; it was necessary to obtain internal agreement within the organization and the sanction of national governments to fulfill its mission. It was external interactions that allowed it to achieve its objectives beyond borders. The Canadian Knights were able to draw on the imperial link and form a transnational partnership with another nonstate actor—the British CWL. The CWL's existing welfare program provided a readymade infrastructure to which the Knights could contribute. Overall, the Knights' influence on conflict was important yet understated. The order's patriotic ethos meant that it fervently supported the course of action chosen by the state. It supported the war effort. The CAH program's huts, designed to elicit images of home and provide a reprieve from the horrors of conflict, served to ease the impact of conflict through relaxation and recreation. The Canadian Knights and the CWL showed that imperialism was an important factor in facilitating transnational action. The attachment to a broader political unit allowed transnationalism to occur in partnership with organizations that shared the same philosophy (Catholicism) and loyalty (the British Empire).

The Knights of Columbus entered the transnational sphere around the time the term "transnational" was coined. At the time, they utilized existing state-based actors to achieve their objectives and maximize their resources. A century on, the Knights continue their mission. However, the evolution of conflict means a transnational approach is all the more important if the organization is to continue its mission of "charity, unity, fraternity and patriotism" in the modern world.

Notes

1. "Our Principles," Knights of Columbus, http://www.kofc.org/en/about/principles/index.html.

2. Christopher J. Kauffman, *Faith and Fraternalism: The History of the Knights of Columbus, 1882–1982* (New York: Harper & Row, 1982), 262.

3. Ibid., 16.

4. See James Trepanier, "Battling a Trojan Horse: The Ordre de Jacques Cartier and the Knights of Columbus, 1917–1965," unpublished MA diss., 2007, 23, http://www.collections canada.gc.ca/obj/thesescanada/vol2/002/MR34115.PDF.

5. Shane Leslie, "America and the War," *Tablet*, November 27, 1915, 6, http://archive .thetablet.co.uk/article/27th-november-1915/6/america-and-the-war.

6. "Our Principles."

7. Ibid.

8. Kauffman, *Faith and Fraternalism*, 375.

9. "Our Principles."

10. Kauffman, *Faith and Fraternalism*, 23.

11. "Our Principles."

12. Maurice Francis Egan and John B. Kennedy, *The Knights of Columbus in Peace and War*, vol. 1 (New Haven, CT: Knights of Columbus, 1920), 57.

13. Ibid., 340.

14. Ibid.

15. Ibid., 341.

16. Terence J. Fay, *A History of Canadian Catholics: Gallicanism, Romanism and Canadianism* (Kingston and Montreal: McGill-Queen's University Press, 2002), 267.

17. Michael Williams, *American Catholics in the War: National Catholic War Council* (New York: Macmillan, 1921), vii.

18. Ibid.

19. Administrative Committee of Bishops, *Handbook of the National Catholic War Council* (Washington, DC: Administrative Committee of Bishops, 1918).

20. Kauffman, *Faith and Fraternalism*, 191.

21. Ibid., 190.

22. "Catholic War Work in America," *Tablet*, March 2, 1918, 22, http://archive.thetablet .co.uk/article/2nd-march-1918/22/catholic-war-work-in-america.

23. Ibid.

24. Administrative Committee of Bishops, *Handbook*, 7.

25. Ibid.

26. Ibid.

27. See Egan and Kennedy, *Peace and War*, 230–34.

28. "An Inventory of Records of the National Catholic War Council at the American Catholic History Research Center and University Archives," Catholic University of America, http://archives.lib.cua.edu/findingaid/ncwarcouncil.cfm.

29. Committee on Public Information, *United War Work Campaign* (Washington, DC: Government Printing Office, 1918), 4.

30. "Catholic War Work," *Tablet*, 17.

31. Ibid., 12.

32. Ibid.

33. Kenneth Steuer, "Service for Soldiers: American Social Welfare Agencies in World War I," in *Personal Perspectives: World War I*, ed. Timothy C. Dowling (Santa Barbara, CA: ABC-Clio, 2006), 205–58.

34. "Catholic War Work," *Tablet*, 12.

35. Steuer, "Service for Soldiers," 215.

36. "Catholic War Work," *Tablet*, 12.

37. Ibid., 13.

38. Ibid.

39. Ibid., 5.

40. Egan and Kennedy, *Peace and War*, 1.

41. "Catholic War Work," *Tablet*, 5.

42. I. I. E. Daniel and D. A. Casey, *For God and Country: War Work of the Canadian Knights of Columbus* (no publisher, 1922).

43. Egan and Kennedy, *Peace and War*, 342; Duff Crerar, *Padres in No Man's Land: Canadian Chaplains and the Great War* (Montreal and Kingston: McGill-Queen's University Press, 1995), 81.

44. Crerar, *Padres*, 81.

45. Mark G. McGowan, *The Waning of the Green: Catholics, the Irish, and Identity in Toronto, 1887–1922* (Kingston and Montreal: McGill-Queen's University Press, 1999), 177.

46. Ibid.

47. Randall Hansen, "The Politics of Citizenship in 1940s Britain: The British Nationality Act," *Twentieth Century British History* 10, no.1 (1999): 67–95.

48. See Philip Buckner, "The Long Goodbye: English Canadians and the British World," in *Rediscovering the British World*, eds. Philip Buckner and R. Douglas Francis (Calgary: University of Calgary Press, 2005): 181–208.

49. McGowan, *Waning*, 178.

50. Ibid.

51. See Trepanier, *Battling a Trojan*.

52. McGowan, *Waning*, 179.

53. Daniel and Casey, *For God*, 17.

54. "Services Committee—Feature: History of CWL Services Committee," Catholic Women's League, http://www.catholicwomensleague.org/services-history.html.

55. Ibid.

56. Egan and Kennedy, *Peace and War*, 342.

57. Ibid.

58. "The Knights of Columbus," *Tablet*, January 4, 1919, 12 http://archive.thetablet.co.uk/article/4th-january-1919/12/the-knights-of-columbus.

59. Daniel and Casey, *For God*, 22–23.

60. "CWL Annual Report of 1917–18," Catholic Women's League, 1918.

61. "Ye Old Trench Club," *Chevrons to Stars: The Official Organ of the Canadian Training School, Bexhill*, October 1917.

62. Daniel and Casey, *For God*, 23.

63. For more on Canadian social clubs in Britain, see Cozzi 2011; Cozzi 2009; Vance 2011, 88–91.

64. Joseph Bampton, "The Catholic Women's League and Catholic Huts," *Tablet*, November 25, 1916, 31, http://archive.thetablet.co.uk/article/25th-november-1916/31/the-catholic-womens-league-and-catholic-huts.

65. Ibid.

66. Daniel and Casey, *For God*, 23.

67. McGowan, *Waning*, 181.

68. "Catholic War Work," *Tablet*, 5.

69. "Supporting Those Who Serve and Those Who Have Served," Knights of Columbus, http://www.kofc.org/un/en/military/history.html.

70. "Helping 'Nos Chers Conscrits': The Knights of Columbus Catholic Army Huts and French-Canadian Nationalism, 1917–26," *Journal of Canadian Studies* 47 (2013): 246–67.

71. Knights of Columbus, 2011, 2.

72. Knights of Columbus, 2013, 6.

2

Transnational Feminist Praxis in the Women's International League for Peace and Freedom in the Aftermath of the Second World War

CATIA CECILIA CONFORTINI

This chapter uses the example of the Women's International League for Peace and Freedom (WILPF) to highlight traces of transnational feminist praxis prior to the 1970s, a time often marked as the beginning of the transnational feminist movement.[1] I understand transnational feminist praxis to "involve shifting the unit of analysis from local, regional, and national culture to relations and processes across cultures" and trying to understand the local in relation to larger, cross-national processes.[2] Following in the footsteps of historians of the women's peace movement who challenge the tendency of some transnational feminist theorists to discount earlier women's organizing as hegemonic, Euro-centric, and compromised by Western orientalist and imperialist policies,[3] I "supply a historical dimension" to contemporary transnational feminism through the example of WILPF.[4]

I see WILPF as a site where global processes and local practices came into contact and confrontation and where they informed and shaped each other.[5] In its Western liberal self, WILPF embodied transnational feminism, if in an imperfect, incomplete way. Although WILPF was a geographically and ideologically limited transnational social movement,[6] its praxis in fact made possible its participation in later, broader, and perhaps more critical transnational organizing of the kind described and theorized by transnational feminist scholars and outlined in the introduction to this volume.[7] I focus on the decade immediately following the Second World War as a period of particular significance, as feminist organizing has been considered "in abeyance,"[8] while the US-dominated postwar international liberal order was taking shape.[9] Though WILPF was situated in, as well as limited by, this context, its theoretically informed practices were feminist and transnational. Following Gramscian and feminist traditions,[10] I understand theory to be indivisible from practice. Hence, I use the term "praxis" to express the interplay between the two. I argue that, like other international women's movements born in the late nineteenth and early twentieth centuries in the United States and Europe,[11] WILPF was transnational in ways that their critics underestimate. It called itself "international," but it was practicing transnational politics in a world already characterized by power asymmetries, about and in which it held ambiguous and multifaceted positions. This case demonstrates that this organization practiced an important form of transnational feminism: While still Western and liberal in origin, WILPF engaged in bilateral and multilateral flows of ideas, relationships, and counterhegemonic learning even in a "non-receptive political environment."[12]

This chapter is divided into three sections. The first offers a genealogy of WILPF, pointing at significant transnational feminist dimensions in its origins and organizational structure. The second section delves further into WILPF's feminist transnational praxis, focusing on the 1940s and 1950s, using examples drawn from some of its most important areas of work, and highlighting its interactions with states and other transnational actors. Finally, I conclude with some remarks on the significance of this organization for feminist and nonfeminist transnational organizing after the Second World War and for complex transnationalism in general.

A Transnational Feminist Genealogy of WILPF:
Ideology and Organization

In the narrow sense of "movement of tangible and intangible items across state boundaries when at least one actor is not an agent of a government or intergovernmental organization,"[13] WILPF was a transnational organization. Founded along the principles of liberal internationalism in 1915 as the International Committee of Women for Permanent Peace (its name was changed and the organization institutionalized in 1919), WILPF was composed of women from belligerent and neutral countries aiming to stop the First World War.[14] From governments, they demanded plans to establish a system conducive to peace "based on principles of justice" and women's full share of "civil and political rights and responsibilities on the same terms as men."[15]

Transnational feminism offers, however, a broader, more critical account of transnationalism, rejecting feminist identity politics that construct women as a unified category (thus erasing differences among them) and arguing that such politics results in a facile universalism that sees Western white women as the parameter against which all other women are measured and inevitably perceived as different and inferior. Rather, Western white women wishing to engage in a transnational feminist politics of solidarity need to recognize that their privileges in the world system are always linked to another woman's oppression and exploitation, in the context of multiple, intersecting, and discrete "scattered hegemonies."[16]

WILPF was mostly composed of upper-class Euro-American women, some of whom did not even identify as feminist, who articulated their work often in identity terms (working for peace as women). It partnered with international liberal governance institutions, the League of Nations first and subsequently the United Nations (UN), where it was granted consultative status in 1948. Some transnational feminist theorists might discount WILPF as a Eurocentric organization, embedded in a global hegemonic political economic system, with little in common with the transnational feminist movements of the 1980s and 1990s.

Transnational feminism, however, also rejects facile dichotomies. A sharp distinction between organizations and movements based on identity politics versus those based on political resistance may be just one of those dichotomies. Some movements may claim both identity and resistance as bases for actions at different moments and for different purposes.[17] In WILPF's case, identity politics coexisted along with political practices and objectives uncovering a transnational feminist core. WILPF's origins in the suffrage and social work movements of the progressive era, for example, situated the group in an already transnational framework.[18] Jane Addams, presiding over the meeting at The Hague and later WILPF's first international president, had established Hull House, a coeducational settlement house in Chicago in the late 1800s, itself a small experiment in transnationalism. In some of her numerous writings, Addams offered a sharp social-justice-focused analysis of the immigrant condition in urban centers in both Great Britain and the United States.[19] WILPF also owed its origins to socialist and pacifist movements, both arguably transnationally organized.[20] Emily Greene Balch, WILPF's first international secretary, was a passionate pacifist and socialist whose writings consistently denounced US immigration and economic policies, imperialism, and militarism.[21] Since its origins, then, the organization navigated uneasily between socialism and liberal internationalism.

Moreover, although dominated by Euro-American members, WILPF started with "an optic or gaze that [began] with a world without borders,"[22] while not "assum[ing] away the importance of the global and local, or the nation-state system form."[23] WILPF was organized through membership in national sections, each entitled to send representatives to an international congress held every three years and serving as the organization's highest decision-making authority.[24] The international congress elected an international president and an executive committee of individual members. A secretariat was in charge of WILPF's day-to-day operations and was based in Geneva, the site of the League of Nations.[25] WILPF was a "centri *fugal* not a centri *petal* [*sic*] organisation"[26]: The work of all sections was to be based upon the statements and resolutions passed by the international congress,[27] but national sections could participate in WILPF's decision-making process through study groups and committees. The executive committee, meeting once a year, carried out policies, if possible in consultation with sections. The international governing bodies as a whole came to be referred to as "the International," a structure that remains to this day largely unchanged.

Sections were structured along their own set of governing rules and employed different methods for the selection of candidates to the international congress. The biggest sections could be organized into local branches. Internally, communications between the International and national sections were maintained by officers' circular letters, UN representatives' reports, and an international magazine. Some national sections also published their own literature for communication with their members and with the International.[28] But internal communication was also conducted through informal networks of friendships and travels, personal relationships that had inevitably political implications and consequences. Likewise, communication with external entities, other transnational organizations, and states was maintained via a series of formal channels (e.g., participation at international conferences, accreditation with UN agencies, letters, and communiqués), as well as informal or ad hoc contacts with representatives of state, international, or transnational institutions.

WILPF's formal organizational structure was thus open enough to allow the employment of a variety of methods to advance specific political objectives. Unlike the Knights of Columbus, described by Luke Flanagan in chapter 1, whose loyalty to the American state created an obstacle to transnationalization of the organization, WILPF's members' allegiance, since its very beginning, was not to their country but to the organization itself. National sections, however, operated with varying degrees of autonomy from the International, a practice that was sometimes decried by WILPF's international officers.[29]

WILPF's founders described their organization as "international": As the introduction of this volume explains, the term "transnational" was not widely in currency at the time. Its officers sometimes employed the words "global" or "globalism" to indicate broader aspirations to transcend political boundaries and a vision of WILPF as "a body based on the conception of the oneness of the world"[30] and not one of several "loose confederations of nationally based units" (as described in this volume's conclusion). As an organization for peace whose members were almost exclusively women,[31] with multi-issue political analysis and prescriptions and the aspiration to have global reach, WILPF saw itself as unique. Since 1919, its constitution had proclaimed that "every nation, free or subject, and every self-governing dominion may be represented in the League." The same constitution declared that "any minority in a country which claims the status of a separate nationality may also form a National Section."[32] Although designed for minorities inside European states, this principle was significant, as it implicitly affirmed the rights to self-determination of national minorities in colonies or former colonies, as well as aboriginal and indigenous people. Since the beginning, WILPF's structure and practices revealed attempts to abandon the modernist legacy of "colonial discourses and hegemonic First World formation that wittingly or unwittingly lead to the oppression and exploitation of many women" and to engage in struggles to challenge "extralocal processes" that shaped local oppressive practices and contributed to violence and oppression.[33]

Up until the Second World War, WILPF continued to grow, and by 1937 it counted members in twenty-nine sections, mostly (but not exclusively) in North America and Europe.[34] During this time, WILPF took "consistently more radical positions" than other women's organizations in many areas of its work, speaking out against imperialism and fascism while navigating uneasily between bourgeois liberalism and socialism.[35] During the war, German Jewish exile Gertrude Baer, like other political exiles (including those, albeit in all other ways different, described in chapter 5 by Ariel Ahram and John Gledhill), maintained "cross-borders political networks" and kept the organization functioning in New York City. Through her and a few others' staunch determination and dedication, two hundred WILPF women from thirteen countries met again in Luxembourg in 1946 to decide whether the organization should continue or dismantle.

WILPF's Transnational Feminist Praxis in the Postwar Moment

Robert Latham calls the immediate aftermath of the Second World War a "liberal moment," when the destruction of the old world order gave rise to an opportunity for the creation of a new one, within the macrohistorical fabric of liberal modernity.[36] A brief period of unique "openness to pluralism and tolerance for experimentation" and no global hegemon or power gave way to US hegemony,[37] which soon shaped the future for the international order based on a symbiotic relationship between liberalism and militarism.[38]

This liberal moment marks a crucial turning point for the study of critical social movements and nongovernmental organizations (NGOs) to ascertain the possibility of resistance to the hegemonic forces of liberal-order making. WILPF, like other NGOs, the UN, its agencies, and liberal states, operated within that system, which shaped their forms, purposes, and ideologies. James Richardson characterizes liberalism as having multiple facets and comprising an "egalitarian, social, or inclusive" strand, as well as a "liberalism of privilege" that underpinned Eurocentrism, racism, and oppression.[39] The women who met in Luxembourg realized that the liberal internationalist ideology upon which the organization itself was founded had failed to prevent the Second World War, and they wrestled with how to reconcile their belief in peace with their experiences of war and occupation. They even debated at length whether their organization was worth carrying forward.[40] Their eventual decision to continue working as WILPF expressed more the women's will to keep searching for ways to achieve a world of peace and justice than certitudes about methods or ideologies.

In fact, as I have argued elsewhere, WILPF's understanding of peace as expressed in its policies on disarmament, decolonization, and the conflict in Israel/Palestine underwent several changes between 1945 and 1975. These policy changes reflected the gradual development of a critique of the historical and political context of liberalism. In turn, this shift represented a different understanding of peace, one that expanded the boundaries of the historical and ideological context that had shaped the organization. Eventually, WILPF's critique of militarism, racism, and the international economic order became more explicitly informed by feminist theory and activism.[41] In this self-reflexive aspect too, the Euro-American women's organization embodied a transnational feminist ethos: It viewed itself as a never completed project, ready to revisit itself continually and provide for "self-critique" of its policies and assumptions, of the very narratives in which they were embedded.[42]

Emerging from the ruin of a devastating world war, WILPF was already thinking transnationally—beyond and through the nation-state, beyond and through local politics—seeing the intersections of multiple forms of injustice as obstacles to a world of "peace and freedom." In the remainder of this chapter, I am going to illustrate some transnational aspects of WILPF's praxis in the context of the liberal moment, paying particular attention to the ways in which WILPF women scrutinized and wrestled with their own assumptions about race and the non-Western "other" as they affected their political practices in regard to membership and WILPF's engagement in transnational networks.

Membership and the Question of Race:
Developing Communication, Expanding Influence

Through the work of its sections and the interactions between national sections and the International, WILPF was uniquely positioned to engage in, or be in coalition with, local struggles while also playing a role in an international political system where local struggles could be made intelligible for international liberal institutions. Perhaps this represented a watering down or homogenization of local needs and aspirations. Another way of interpreting WILPF's praxis, however, is seeing it as expanding the limits of the liberal order and making political links between local struggles possible.[43] WILPF's attempts to reach out beyond its European and North American confines and beyond the confines of its members' identities as primarily white and middle-to-upper-class women is important, then, to understand both the limits of liberalism and the possibility that liberal groups at times transcend these limits. WILPF was an organization that navigated within the international system according to the parameters of liberalism, yet it was guided by principles, rules, and behaviors that were sometimes at odds with liberal norms and policies.

As early as 1946, women in WILPF were concerned about the limits of an organization whose membership had been decimated during the war. Though at the 1946 congress representatives from what soon was to become the other side of the Iron Curtain were present (namely, Czechoslovakia, Hungary, Poland, and Yugoslavia), their sections had already been (or were soon to be) dismantled. Personal contacts among friends remained, and they informed some of the positions of the organization in the years to come, including its cautious skepticism toward the Marshall Plan and its opposition to the North Atlantic Treaty Organization (NATO). Personal forms of communication with the world outside the organization, therefore, shaped the women's political views and their policies toward institutions ostensibly charged with the maintenance of international order and peace. Weakened WILPF sections existed also in Australia and New Zealand. A new section had recently formed in Brazil (but was short-lived), and a Japanese section was soon to be admitted.

The women made it a priority to resume outreach activities toward women's groups outside their primary constituencies and geopolitical reach. Their aim was for the organization to become "genuinely global"[44] and extend its membership to women in all parts of the world, not only nominally but also substantially. This included seeking to nurture the creation of new sections in what we would now call the global South, while supporting the continuation of old but struggling ones. For example, in 1937 the International Congress had asked the US section to "develop work" in Latin America.[45] When WILPF met in 1946, Heloise Brainerd, chairman of the Committee on the Americas, reported continuous work with women's groups in nearly all countries in the region "to help all the Latin American women it can reach to solve their own political and social problems and those of the Western Hemisphere"[46] and to ensure Latin American women's participation in inter-American politics. The establishment of new sections in Brazil and Cuba had been the outcome of these efforts, which capitalized on a vibrant Latin American women's movement.[47] The committee and the US section had also engaged in coalitions with Latin American women against US imperialism in Latin America,[48] in support of migrant workers (particularly Mexicans in the United States and African Americans working in US Navy and US Army base construction projects in the Caribbean), and for the national control of natural resources (in particular the nationalization of Mexican oil and land owned by US companies). In a later occasion, they expressed concern about "the conduct of an American corporation operating in Central

America," the infamous United Fruit Company.[49] Organizational outreach and expansion were, therefore, viewed as forms of communication across national sections, which facilitated the formulation of more genuinely transnational feminist policies, and extending WILPF's influence in the emerging transnational women's movement.

Around this time the US section also spearheaded the Inter-American Congress of Women, which was eventually held in 1947 in Guatemala City. Sixty-eight delegates from eighteen countries participated in the congress, which concluded with the establishment of the Inter-American Federation of Women.[50] When reporting about the conference at the 1949 WILPF Congress, Brainerd remarked: "Liberal women everywhere were heartened to go on with their struggles against reactionary forces, knowing that they were not as isolated as they had supposed."[51] Brainerd asked that the Committee on the Americas be restructured to include more Latin American women "in the *planning*" of its work in the region (emphasis mine).[52]

Other efforts to seek a broader membership were also under way. By the early to mid-1960s, WILPF counted several new sections in all continents, but it never became a mass or widespread organization. As it is often the case for transnational social movements (including feminist ones), it continued to have difficulties recruiting members outside a limited geopolitical area and from the poor or working classes. Concerns about this problem gave rise to internal debates about the organization's racism and classism. At the 1946 congress, Gertrude Bussey of the US section stated: "It is hard for people who look as most of us in this group look to accept the fact that the white race is not naturally superior. We may theoretically accept this fact on the basis of both science and religion, but actually there is usually hidden in the back of our minds some vestige of prejudice which is likely to reveal itself in action."[53]

A "Report on Race Relations" by British member G. R. McGregor-Wood at the International Congress in 1953 illustrates the ambivalence of WILPF's racial politics. McGregor-Wood started by summarizing contemporary scientific consensus about "racial groups" and highlighted that "racial discrimination [was] irrational" because no intellectual or emotional differences existed between them and "all races [were] potentially equal."[54] Basing her report on the 1952 UNESCO Statement on Race and Race Differences, as well as her personal contacts with some women and men from African countries under British administration, McGregor-Wood condemned colonialism, missionary zeal, and economic exploitation and expressed some sympathy for aspirations to "self-government." She also spoke, however, of the impossibility of "responsible co-government" in the British colony of Kenya due to "the extreme backwardness of the Kenya natives."[55] She remarked: "When the negro and asiatic becomes [sic] educated, receives fair wages and lives in a decent hygienic house he will find that as a person the scales will not be unduly weighted against him and white people generally will begin to realize the rich gifts he has to give to the world family."[56] On the one hand, the author of this report expressed confidence in the possibility of transforming a racist world for the better through structural and personal changes; on the other hand, she could not distance herself enough from colonial assumptions and liberal paternalist arguments that justified the continued subjugation of people in the countries of the British Empire.

Yet the women of WILPF knew that awareness of racism would not necessarily translate into policy changes unless that awareness brought about a willingness to continuously scrutinize their own actions and be self-reflexive, a trait that feminist critique has identified as necessary to the development of a politics of solidarity.[57] Gertrude Baer (at the time WILPF's representative to the UN Economic and Social Council [ECOSOC] and director of the international office in Geneva) summed up this urge as follows:

> It seems sometimes that WILPF, too, might do a little more to help maintain flexibility in a world which is growing increasingly uniform, dull and inflexible. This very inflexibility of thought and action is a real threat to Freedom since Freedom derives from and grows and develops in differentiation. Therefore we want constant revision and re-shaping of what we are doing. Sterility is the death of all movement. But it has, alas, crept into our own work, our own International Center.[58]

WILPF women were willing to subject their unstated assumptions about race, colonial relations, and the international economic system to a self-reflexive process through attentive listening and the search for a broad spectrum of voices, particularly those not represented in their geographically and sociopolitically limited organization, and through a variety of means. Their membership outreach was never really only about membership; rather, through "less formal networks of interactions across national borders and between diverse peoples"[59] and in "an amalgamation of fundamentally local bilateral and intimate interactions,"[60] WILPF women were engaging in a learning process and questioning their own complicity in oppressive systems of marginalization and exclusion. In other words, they were engaging in the kind of reflexive process that transnational feminist scholars find necessary in order for Western white women to be able to practice a politics of solidarity.

Transnational Interactions on Women's Rights and Decolonization

Prior to the Second World War, one strategy that WILPF employed to ensure that its deliberations and policies were informed by a broad spectrum of experiences and forms of knowledge had been the engagement in direct forms of political protest, which often offered the opportunity to participate in transnational coalitions and cooperative interaction with other NGOs. Coming out of the war in a world dominated by Cold War rivalries, suspicions, and paranoia, WILPF did not engage systematically in cooperative issue- or campaign-based efforts with other women's organizations until at least the 1960s. WILPF justified its retrenchment from a politics of protest in terms of political strategy. Gertrude Bussey and Margaret Tims, WILPF members and authors of an important biography of WILPF commissioned by the UK section in 1965, commented: "The mass protests, manifestoes and petitions of the 1930s were no longer adequate, although they were still being used by some organizations. The need now was not so much to protest when an international crime had been committed, as to anticipate the crisis and offer an alternative, practicable policy."[61]

It would be a mistake, however, to think of WILPF as isolated from other nongovernment actors at this time. Several WILPF sections, even as the war was raging, maintained close links and engaged in joint programs (coalitions) with other peace and social justice organizations on locally based initiatives.[62] This had been the case of the Australian and New Zealand sections, which had remained more isolated from other WILPF groups during the war but closely cooperated with local peace groups.[63] I have already mentioned the US section's interactions with Latin American groups. Several branches in the US section also engaged in activism for racial justice together with African American women and organizations, through networks that had formed during WILPF's 1926 trip to Haiti.[64]

While at the international level WILPF did not participate in transnational coalitions, it nevertheless engaged in network politics during the 1940s and 1950s.[65] Internationally, in this period WILPF maintained loose forms of association with umbrella organizations and entertained regular contacts and conversations with international civil servants at the UN headquarters in Geneva and New York. It participated in UN-sponsored NGO conferences across the world, consciously seeking to develop better-informed decisions on matters of international peace. Sometimes WILPF members participated as observers at other organizations' meetings. Upon Baer's insistence, however, official attendance at these meetings was at this time discouraged. The 1949 Congress had, in fact, established a policy of nonaffiliation with "any other international organization," though the policy did not "apply to national or international coordinating organizations," and national sections were "at liberty to cooperate to the fullest possible extend [sic] with such other organizations as are working in harmony with their aims."[66] WILPF refused, for example, to send representatives to a meeting of the Women's International Democratic Federation in 1957, which Baer considered too closely associated with Soviet Russia.[67]

WILPF's (and Baer's) independence became evident in the discussions around the establishment of the Commission on the Status of Women (CSW) in 1946. Originally set up as a subcommission of the Commission on Human

Rights, it was made into an independent commission upon the insistence of several women's groups.[68] Unlike other women's lobbyists, Baer staunchly opposed the creation of a separate commission, believing that it would become a lesser entity in the UN human rights system, effectively establishing women's rights as a separate (and lesser) category of rights.[69] It is now widely recognized that the mechanisms for the enforcement of women's rights were, in fact, far less effective than general human rights mechanisms,[70] at least until the addition of the Optional Protocol to the Convention on the Elimination of Discrimination against Women in 1999. The separation of functions, however, may have afforded the CSW with some degree of flexibility and innovative potential.[71]

When Baer became WILPF's first representative at the UN, she started issuing a regular and very detailed circular letter on her work there. Her intention was to foster a "two way link" between the work of national sections and the International.[72] She asked that sections report their activities and give their input to her so that their work could be mutually informed. Baer was also indefatigable in her efforts to have WILPF represented at the largest possible number of international governmental agencies' meetings.

For the purposes of this chapter, WILPF's engagement with the Trusteeship Council, the UN body established to supervise the administration of colonial territories ostensibly to "guide" them toward independence,[73] was significant. Shifts in WILPF's relationship with it show the openness of the organization and its conscious attempts at being more critically transnational and feminist. WILPF closely followed the work of the council, and in the 1940s and 1950s it trusted that its five administering authorities were making "a genuine effort . . . to develop the territory and to improve existing conditions" of people under their administration. But (WILPF admitted) political, economic, social, and educational "advancements" were limited at best.[74]

Progressively, however, WILPF became increasingly disillusioned about the intentions of colonial powers. Attendance at the First Asian-African Conference in Bandung in 1955, the First All-African People's Conference in Accra in 1959, and the Second UN Conference of Nongovernment Organizations on the Eradication of Prejudice and Discrimination in the same year was instrumental in WILPF's reassessment of its policies toward decolonization and independence movements in what became known as the third world. By the end of the 1950s, some WILPF leaders had become more clearly sympathetic to (particularly, but not exclusively, nonviolent) independence struggles. They considered it a mistake of the West to view revolutionary movements in new countries as "Communist-inspired" and to support dictators and colonial powers "rather than supporting the struggles for freedom and independence."[75]

In the 1940s and 1950s, other interaction and networking means included official and unofficial "fact-finding" trips.[76] WILPF often set up such missions to areas of conflict. For example, it was one of the first organizations to investigate the effects of the US occupation of Haiti in 1926, with a multiracial group led by Emily Greene Balch. The group subsequently issued a scathing condemnation of the US intervention and its paternalist racist practices, which they judged responsible for Haiti's appalling poverty.[77] In 1927, a WILPF delegation visited China and Indochina to assess the political situations there and seek contacts with women's groups. The delegation urged WILPF to support the Kuomintang as the legitimate government of China.[78] After the Second World War, WILPF immediately urged the UN to admit the People's Republic of China and to recognize the communist government as China's legitimate representative on the Security Council.

Fact-finding missions, like Orientalist travels, had, of course, ambivalent implications.[79] Sometimes these trips resulted in the confirmation of previously held positions and ideas. Ultimately, however, they offered WILPF the occasion to increase its knowledge about local and global interconnections. Sometimes trips and direct contacts with groups of women working on local issues resulted in significant policy changes for WILPF. This was the case of a 1958 trip to the Middle East by Haitian member Madeleine Bouchereau, which planted the seeds for the establishment of a Lebanese section in 1962 and marked the beginning of radical shifts in WILPF's policies toward the conflict in Israel/Palestine.[80] It would only be in the 1970s that WILPF would more explicitly denounce colonialism and neocolonialism as forms of violence; link colonialism, capitalism, and militarization to each other and to violations of women's rights[81]; and condemn Israel's policies toward Palestinians and its occupation of the West Bank and Gaza. These shifts, however, evolved out of WILPF's transnational feminist praxis, its search for relations of solidarity coupled with a consciousness and openness to critiques of the limits of this organization of Western, white, liberal women. WILPF women's engagement with questions of race, membership, decolonization, and transnational interactions helps us understand the nuances and multiple configurations of Eurocentrism, its inadequacy as a label that too easily dismisses transnational mutual influences, and WILPF's imperfect and ongoing attempts to transcend Eurocentric perspectives.

Conclusion

I have argued in this chapter that WILPF embodied transnational feminism even in the hostile climate of the mid-1940s to late 1950s: As the liberal order was taking shape, WILPF's praxis was already, if imperfectly, transnational and feminist. An organization always ideologically at the border between liberalism and socialism, WILPF continued its trajectory of pushing its own boundaries even during the liberal moment. WILPF's story not only reveals the possibilities for transnational organizations and social movements to challenge and transcend the ideological contexts in which they are embedded, but it also highlights the need to take transnational feminism seriously as inviting a praxis of "flexible, practical relations of solidarity,"[82] coming from diverse local or global struggles against oppression. At the same time, WILPF's story challenges a monolithic view of white, Western liberal women's organizations as invariably ethnocentric and inevitably tied to colonial legacies.

Looking back at this time allows us to see WILPF as an evolving, dynamic organization, responding to its times and transforming itself and the world around it while practicing a transnational feminist ethos. WILPF's transnational networking of the 1940s and 1950s made later participation in transnational coalitions possible, as trips, conferences, and UN meetings nurtured conversations and contacts across the ideological and geopolitical spectrums of local and international peace organizing. WILPF became progressively more involved in transnational coalitions with other women's organizations, participating, for example, in women's antimilitarist and disarmament movements (from Women Strike for Peace in the 1960s to Women's Pentagon Action and the women's peace encampments of the 1980s), stressing the human and developmental costs of arms manufacturing and use. The organization's story reflects, therefore, developments in transnationalism, but it also highlights continuities in transnational feminist organizing.

Between 1975 and 1995, WILPF women attended and often played leadership roles in the organization of the UN women's conferences, as well as in alternative conferences with women and organizations that rejected the UN framework. In fact, unlike most of its Western counterparts, WILPF sided with third world women in expressing the need for the conferences to confront imperialism, racism, and the impact of the international economic system on the lives of women. It rejected the idea that women's oppression could be isolated from other forms of oppression and that any women's issue could be considered "apolitical" or that "political" issues should not be within the purview of UN women's conferences.[83]

WILPF's intense networking represents an instance of complex transnationalism, defined as "the increasing number, scope, interactions, and influence of transnational actors on diplomatic and governance processes where states have invited as participants, been forced to respond to, or have become reliant upon the expertise of transnational actors and where transnational actors increasingly interact directly with each other." The organization's efforts ultimately culminated in the formation of a coalition of women's organizations that pressured the UN Security Council to issue, in October 2000 and for the first time since its creation, a resolution (number 1325) that recognizes women's roles as agents in armed conflicts and peacebuilding processes, their diverse needs during conflict and postconflict transitions and reconstruction, and their right to participate in all phases of peace processes.[84] In chapter 9 of this volume, Miriam J. Anderson discusses the links between transnational feminist networks, local women's

peace advocacy groups, and these new global norms in favor of women's participation in peace negotiations. The first in a series of resolutions collectively
constituting the UN's "Women, Peace and Security agenda," Resolution 1325
represented a breakthrough for women, not the least because it was "both the
product of and the armature for a massive mobilization of women's political
energies."[85] The continuing relevance of this organization and other transnational feminist peace and justice organizations is manifested in the many postconflict and peacebuilding initiatives by state and nonstate actors that, even if
incompletely, attempt to include women and a gender perspective in their
operations.[86] Though the women, peace, and security agenda disillusioned activists on many fronts (not the least because it reflects a limited understanding of
gender relations),[87] it is also evidence that women's and WILPF's transnational
organizing had a profound influence on the UN peace and security system itself.

Notes

1. See, for example, Nadje Sadig Al-Ali and Nicola Pratt, eds., *Women and War in the Middle East: Transnational Perspectives* (London: Zed Books, 2009); Manisha Desai, "Transnationalism: The Face of Feminist Politics Post-Beijing," *International Social Science Journal* 57, no. 184 (June 2005): 319–30; Richa Nagar and Amanda Lock Swarr, "Introduction: Theorizing Transnational Feminist Praxis," in *Critical Transnational Feminist Praxis*, ed. Richa Nagar and Amanda Lock Swarr (Albany: State University of New York Press, 2010); and Caren Kaplan and Inderpal Grewal, "Transnational Practices and Interdisciplinary Feminist Scholarship: Refiguring Women's and Gender Studies," in *Women's Studies on Its Own: A Next Wave Reader in Institutional Change*, ed. Robyn Weigman (Durham, NC: Duke University Press, 2002): 66–81.

2. M. Jacqui Alexander and Chandra Talpade Mohanty, "Introduction: Genealogies, Capitalist State Practice, and Feminist Movements," in *Feminist Genealogies, Colonial Legacies, Democratic Futures*, ed. M. Jacqui Alexander and Chandra Talpade Mohanty (New York: Routledge, 1997), xix.

3. For example, Ellen Carol DuBois and Katie Oliviero, "Circling the Globe: International Feminism Reconsidered, 1920 to 1975," *Women's Studies International Forum* 32, no. 1 (January 2009), Special Issue on Circling the Globe: International Feminism Reconsidered, 1910 to 1975: 1–3; Leila J. Rupp, *Worlds of Women: The Making of an International Women's Movement* (Princeton, NJ: Princeton University Press, 1997); Mrinalini Sinha, Donna Guy, and Angela Woollacott, *Feminisms and Internationalism* (Oxford, UK: Wiley-Blackwell, 1999); Kaplan and Grewal, "Transnational Practices"; Antoinette Burton, *Burdens of History: British Feminists, Indian Women, and Imperial Culture, 1865–1915* (Chapel Hill: University of North Carolina Press, 1994); Aili Mari Tripp, "The Evolution of Transnational Feminisms," in *Global Feminism: Transnational Women's Activism, Organizing, and Human Rights*, ed. Myra Marx Ferree and Aili Mari Tripp (New York: NYU Press, 2006): 51–75; Nupur Chaudhuri and Margaret Strobel, eds., *Western Women and Imperialism: Complicity and Resistance* (Bloomington: Indiana University Press, 1992).

4. DuBois and Oliviero, "Circling the Globe," 1.

5. Desai, "Transnationalism," 319–30.

6. Louis Kriesberg, "Social Movements and Global Transformation," in *Transnational Social Movements and Global Politics: Solidarity beyond the State*, ed. Jackie Smith, Charles Chatfield, and Ron Pagnucco (Syracuse, NY: Syracuse University Press, 1997).

7. Chandra Talpade Mohanty, "Cartographies of Struggle: Third World Women and the Politics of Feminism," in *Third World Women and the Politics of Feminism*, ed. Chandra Talpade Mohanty, Ann Russo, and Lourdes Torres, (Bloomington: Indiana University Press, 1991): 1–50; Inderpal Grewal and Caren Kaplan, "Introduction: Transnational Feminist Practices and Questions of Postmodernity," in *Scattered Hegemonies: Postmodernity and Transnational Feminist Practices*, ed. Inderpal Grewal and Caren Kaplan (Minneapolis: University of Minnesota Press, 1994): 1–36; Kaplan and Grewal, "Transnational Practices"; Tripp, "Evolution of Transnational Feminisms," 51–75.

8. Verta Taylor, "Social Movement Continuity: The Women's Movement in Abeyance," *American Sociological Review* 54, no. 5 (October 1989).

9. Robert Latham, *The Liberal Moment: Modernity, Security, and the Making of Postwar International Order* (New York: Columbia University Press, 1997).

10. Antonio Gramsci, *Quaderni del carcere*, ed. Valentino Gerratana, (Milan: Einaudi, 2007), notebooks VIII and IX; Brooke A. Ackerly, *Political Theory and Feminist Social Criticism* (New York: Cambridge University Press, 2000); Brooke A. Ackerly, *Universal Human Rights in a World of Difference* (New York: Cambridge University Press, 2008); Catherine Eschle and Bice Maiguashca, *Making Feminist Sense of the Global Justice Movement*, (Lanham, MD: Rowman & Littlefield, 2011).

11. Cecelia Lynch, *Beyond Appeasement: Interpreting Interwar Peace Movements in World Politics* (Ithaca, NY: Cornell University Press, 1999); Harriet Hyman Alonso, *Peace as a Women's Issue: A History of the U.S. Movement for World Peace and Women's Rights* (Syracuse, NY: Syracuse University Press, 1993); Rupp, *Worlds of Women*; Kimberly Jensen and Erika Kuhlman, *Women and Transnational Activism in Historical Perspective* (Dordrecht, Netherlands: Republic of Letters, 2009); Karen Garner, *Shaping a Global Women's Agenda: Women's NGOs and Global Governance, 1925–85* (Manchester, UK: Manchester University Press, 2013).

12. Taylor, "Social Movement Continuity," 761.

13. Joseph S. Nye and Robert O. Keohane, "Transnational Relations and World Politics: An Introduction," *International Organization* 25, no. 3 (1971): 329–49.

14. Catia Cecilia Confortini, *Intelligent Compassion: Feminist Critical Methodology in the Women's International League for Peace and Freedom* (New York: Oxford University Press, 2012); Rupp, *Worlds of Women*.

15. WILPF, Resolutions, 1919, http://www.wilpfinternational.org/resolutions-from-wilpfs-triennial-congresses/; WILPF, Resolutions, 1915, ibid.

16. Grewal and Kaplan, *Scattered Hegemonies*.

17. See, for example, Eschle and Maiguashca, *Making Feminist Sense of the Global Justice Movement*.

18. See Rupp, *Worlds of Women*; Jo Vellacott, "Women, Peace and Internationalism, 1914–1920: Finding New Words and Creating New Methods," in *Peace Movements and Political Cultures*, ed. Charles Chatfield and Peter Van Den Dungen (Knoxville: University of Tennessee Press, 1988), 106–24; Jo Vellacott, "A Place for Pacifism and Transnationalism in Feminist Theory: The Early Work of the Women's International League for Peace and Freedom," *Women's History Review* 2, no. 1 (1993): 23–56; Ellen DuBois, "Woman Suffrage: The View from the Pacific," *Pacific Historical Review* 69 (2000): 539–51; Corinne A. Pernet, "Chilean Feminists, the International Women's Movement, and Suffrage, 1915–1950," *Pacific Historical Review* 69 (2000): 663–88; Francisco O. Ramirez, Yasemin Soysal, and Suzanne

Shanahan, "The Changing Logic of Political Citizenship: Cross-National Acquisition of Women's Suffrage Rights, 1890 to 1990," *American Sociological Review* 67 (1997): 735–45; Allison Sneider, "'The New Suffrage History: Voting Rights in International Perspective,'" *History Compass* 8, no. 7 (July 1, 2010): 692–703; and Caroline Daley and Melanie Nolan, *Suffrage and Beyond: International Feminist Perspectives* (New York: NYU Press, 1994).

19. Jane Addams, *Peace and Bread in Time of War* (Urbana: University of Illinois Press, 2002); Jane Addams, *20 Years at Hull-House* (New York: Macmillan, 1912; Philadelphia: Addams Publications, 2013), http://digital.library.upenn.edu/women/addams/hullhouse/hullhouse.html.

20. Lynch, *Beyond Appeasement*; James Hinton, *Labour and Socialism: A History of the British Labour Movement, 1867–1974* (Amherst: University of Massachusetts Press, 1983); James T. Kloppenberg, *Uncertain Victory: Social Democracy and Progressivism in European and American Thought, 1870–1920* (New York: Oxford University Press, 1988).

21. Kristen E. Gwinn, *Emily Greene Balch: The Long Road to Internationalism* (Champaign: University of Illinois Press, 2010). Addams and Balch were, respectively, the first (1931) and second (1946) American women to be awarded the Nobel Peace Prize.

22. Peggy Levitt and Sanjeev Khagram, "Constructing Transnational Studies," in *The Transnational Studies Reader: Intersections and Innovations*, ed. Sanjeev Khagram and Peggy Levitt (New York: Routledge, 2007), 5.

23. Ibid., 4.

24. Cecelia Lynch observed in *Beyond Appeasement* that several interwar peace movements had similarly rigid structures.

25. After the Second World War and with the establishment of the UN, a second international hub was created in New York. Today it is a US-incorporated nonprofit organization with tax-exempt status and hosts two WILPF projects, PeaceWomen (focusing on the UN's Women, Peace and Security agenda) and Reaching Critical Will (following international disarmament questions).

26. WILPF, *Xth International Congress of the Women's International League for Peace and Freedom* (Luxembourg: WILPF, 1946), Swarthmore College Peace Collection, 47.

27. WILPF, "WILPF Constitution, By-Laws and Rules of Order," (Geneva: WILPF, 1929), Swarthmore College Peace Collection.

28. Although some details were modified in subsequent versions of the International Constitution, and on occasions efforts at "world membership" were made, WILPF's basic structure remains the same. Today it maintains this essentially liberal framework and formal decision-making procedures along nation-state lines, unlike other newer women's groups, which have opted for more flexible, horizontal structures.

29. WILPF, *XIth International Congress of the Women's International League for Peace and Freedom* (Paris: WILPF, 1949), Swarthmore College Peace Collection.

30. WILPF, *Xth International Congress*, 50.

31. Some sections or branches admitted men as members but never as leaders.

32. Emily Greene Balch, *WILPF 1915–1938: A Venture in Internationalism* (Geneva: Maison Internationale, 1938): 11.

33. Grewal and Kaplan, "Introduction: Transnational Feminist Practices," 2; Nancy A. Naples, "The Challenges and Possibilities of Transnational Feminist Praxis," in *Women's Activism and Globalization: Linking Local Struggles and International Politics*, ed. Nancy A. Naples and Manisha Desai (New York: Routledge, 2002), 265.

34. Rupp, *Worlds of Women*, 16–18.

35. Ibid., 31–33.

36. Latham, *Liberal Moment*.

37. Siba N. Grovogui, *Beyond Eurocentrism and Anarchy: Memories of International Order and Institutions* (New York: Palgrave Macmillan, 2006).

38. Latham, *Liberal Moment*.

39. J. L. Richardson, *Contending Liberalisms in World Politics: Ideology and Power* (Boulder, CO: Lynne Rienner, 2001), ch. 1.

40. Confortini, *Intelligent Compassion*.

41. Ibid.

42. Brooke A. Ackerly and Jacqui True, "Studying the Struggles and Wishes of the Age: Feminist Theoretical Methodology and Feminist Theoretical Methods," in *Feminist Methodologies for International Relations*, ed. Brooke A. Ackerly and Maria Stern, (New York: Cambridge University Press, 2006), 241–60.

43. Mohanty, "Cartographies of Struggle."

44. WILPF, *Xth International Congress*, 50.

45. Ibid., 59.

46. Ibid., 58.

47. Tripp, "Evolution of Transnational Feminisms."

48. WILPF, *Xth International Congress*, 59; Gwinn, *Emily Greene Balch*.

49. WILPF, *XIth International Congress*, 93. The report of the committee's chairman did not mention the United Fruit Company by name.

50. The Inter-American Federation of Women is not to be confused with the Inter-American Commission of Women, which was founded in 1928 at the Sixth International Conference of American States (www.oas.org/en/cim/history.asp). By contrast, the Inter-American Federation of Women was an NGO and, to my knowledge, short-lived.

51. WILPF, *XIth International Congress*, 91.

52. WILPF, *Xth International Congress*, 61.

53. Ibid., 144.

54. WILPF, *XIIth International Congress of the Women's International League for Peace and Freedom* (Paris: WILPF, 1953), Swarthmore College Peace Collection, 251.

55. Ibid., 252.

56. Ibid., 253.

57. For example, Ackerly, *Political Theory and Feminist Social Criticism*.

58. Gertrude Baer, *WILPF Work at Geneva, October 1950–May 1951*, Reports 1949–1951 (WILPF, 1951), WILPF SCPC Accession, University of Colorado–Boulder Archives, 6.

59. DuBois and Oliviero, "Circling the Globe," 1.

60. Rumi Yasutake, "The First Wave of International Women's Movements from a Japanese Perspective: Western Outreach and Japanese Women Activists during the Interwar Years," *Women's Studies International Forum* 32, no. 1 (January 2009), Special Issue on Circling the Globe: International Feminism Reconsidered, 1910 to 1975: 19.

61. Gertrude Bussey and Margaret Tims, *Pioneers for Peace: Women's International League for Peace and Freedom 1915–1965* (London: WILPF British Section, 1980), 203.

62. Mary K. Meyer, "The Women's International League for Peace and Freedom: Organizing Women for Peace in the War System," in *Gender Politics in Global Governance*, ed. Mary K. Meyer and Elisabeth Prügl (Lanham, MD: Rowman & Littlefield, 1999), 107–21.

63. Bussey and Tims, *Pioneers for Peace*, 187.

64. Melinda Plastas, *A Band of Noble Women: Racial Politics in the Women's Peace Movement* (Syracuse, NY: Syracuse University Press, 2011); Joyce Blackwell, *No Peace without*

Freedom: Race and the Women's International League for Peace and Freedom 1915–1975 (Carbondale: Southern Illinois University Press, 2004).

65. Sanjeev Khagram makes a distinction between transnational coalitions (where actors and movements formulate and implement campaigns in a coordinated manner for strategic purposes along campaign goals) and transnational networks (where actors and movements at the core share normative concerns but do not necessarily act in coordinated ways). Sanjeev Khagram, *Dams and Development: Transnational Struggles for Water and Power* (Ithaca, NY: Cornell University Press, 2004). See also Margaret E. Keck and Kathryn Sikkink, *Activists beyond Borders: Advocacy Networks in International Politics* (Ithaca, NY: Cornell University Press, 1998).

66. WILPF, *XIth International Congress*.

67. International Executive Committee, WILPF, *Decisions and Summary of Records*, Circular Letters, October 1956–December 1957 (WILPF, 1957), WILPF SCPC Accession, University of Colorado–Boulder Archives.

68. Felice Gaer, "Women, International Law and International Institutions: The Case of the United Nations," *Women's Studies International Forum*, 32, no. 1 (January 2009), Special Issue on Circling the Globe: International Feminism Reconsidered, 1910 to 1975: 61.

69. Bussey and Tims, *Pioneers for Peace*, 199, 200. Baer firmly believed in the indivisibility of human rights, and in this vein she also opposed the establishment of two separate human rights covenants (which became the Covenant on Civil and Political Rights and the Covenant on Economic, Social and Cultural Rights).

70. Laura Reanda, "Human Rights and Women's Rights: The United Nations Approach," *Human Rights Quarterly* 3, no. 2 (May 1, 1981): 11–31.

71. Gaer, "Women, International Law and International Institutions," 61–62.

72. Bussey and Tims, *Pioneers for Peace*, 198.

73. Sylvanna A. Falcón, *Power Interrupted: Antiracist and Feminist Activism inside the United Nations* (Seattle: University of Washington Press, 2016), 42–47.

74. Gertrude Baer, *LOWUN with a Study of the Trusteeship System*, Circular Letters/Reports Re: WILPF and UN 1949/1961–69 (WILPF, 1949), WILPF Second Accession, University of Colorado–Boulder Archives.

75. WILPF, *XVIIIth International Congress of the Women's International League for Peace and Freedom* (New Delhi: WILPF, 1970), Swarthmore College Peace Collection.

76. Bussey and Tims, *Pioneers for Peace*, 35.

77. Plastas, *Band of Noble Women*, 114–19; Gwinn, *Emily Greene Balch*, 136–40.

78. Bussey and Tims, *Pioneers for Peace*, 62.

79. Billie Melman, *Women's Orients: English Women and the Middle East, 1718–1918: Sexuality, Religion and Work* (Ann Arbor: University of Michigan Press, 1992).

80. Confortini, *Intelligent Compassion*; Catia Cecilia Confortini, "How Matters: Women's International League for Peace and Freedom's Trips to the Middle East, 1931–1975," *Peace and Change* 38, no. 3 (July 1, 2013): 284–309.

81. Confortini, *Intelligent Compassion*.

82. Fred Pfeil, "No Basta Teorizar: In-Difference to Solidarity in Contemporary Fiction, Theory, and Practice," in Grewal and Kaplan, *Scattered Hegemonies*, 225.

83. Confortini, *Intelligent Compassion*, epilogue.

84. Carol Cohn, Helen Kinsella, and Sheri Gibbings, "Women, Peace and Security," *International Feminist Journal of Politics* 6, no. 1 (March 2004): 130–40; Felicity Hill, "How and When Has Security Council Resolution 1325 (2000) on Women, Peace and Security

Impacted Negotiations Outside the Security Council?," MA thesis, Uppsala University Programme of International Studies, 2004; UN Security Council Resolution 1325, 2000.

85. Carol Cohn, "Feminist Peacemaking," *Women's Review of Books* 21, no. 5 (February 2004): 8.

86. Transnational women's networks' engagement and influence in this area is well documented in Miriam J. Anderson, *Windows of Opportunity: How Women Seize Peace Negotiations for Political Change* (New York: Oxford University Press, 2016).

87. Cynthia Cockburn, "Snagged on the Contradictions: NATO and UNSC Resolution 1325," *Notowar: Cynthia Cockburn's Weblog*, 2011, http://www.cynthiacockburn.org/notowar/thinking-aloud-talks.html.

3

Governing Conflict through Transnational Corporations

The Case of Conflict Minerals

VIRGINIA HAUFLER

Efforts to bring an end to violence in the Democratic Republic of the Congo (DRC) and elsewhere have focused to a surprising extent on the role of transnational market actors. Activists and policymakers have lamented the trade in so-called conflict minerals—that is, mineral resources that can be sold for money to buy weapons and pay soldiers. From 2000 to now, a variety of actors—the United Nations (UN), the Organisation for Economic Co-operation and Development (OECD), regional security organizations, individual states, industry trade associations, business organizations, and transnational activist organizations—all have adopted a common frame for addressing resource conflicts by regulating international supply chains. The processes by which these actors create new regulatory institutions illustrate the rise of complex transnationalism in security affairs.

In this chapter, I explore the creation of transnational business regulation for conflict minerals to demonstrate how transnational actors impact war and contentious politics. My primary focus will be on one particular actor—the transnational corporation (TNC), which is one of the most powerful and significant transnational actors challenging the role of the state in a global era. TNCs are in some ways the quintessential transnational actor: They operate through nonstate mobilizing structures, are perceived to be beyond the state, and identify themselves as transnational in terms of their organization, operations, and identity.[1] Like other transnational actors discussed in this volume, such as the Women's International League for Peace and Freedom, they have been contributors to peace promotion for many decades. However, unlike many of the other transnational actors discussed here, TNCs bring significant resources to bear on issues of war and peace.

In the last two decades, the private sector has become much more visible as an actor in security affairs, particularly in conflict prevention. The question of how to regulate the behavior of corporations in conflict zones and unstable countries has been the subject of extensive debate and negotiation. One focus of attention has been the role of private security firms in the developing world, which is discussed in Matthew LeRiche's chapter in this volume. The other main focus has been on companies in the extractive sector—primarily oil, gas, and mining but also including other commodities such as timber. The fear is that privately held resource wealth can undermine security, as illustrated also by the land rights conflicts discussed in Kate Macdonald's chapter.[2]

I provide here a case study of how particular minerals became associated with conflict and how TNCs interacted with other actors to develop a conflict minerals regulatory system. In this chapter, I look at how TNCs are organized into global supply chains, how they respond to demands by other actors (particularly activist nongovernmental organizations [NGOs] and states) to do something to restrict the use of mineral wealth to finance war, the way they communicate about the issue of conflict minerals, and what impact they have on peace and conflict. In the conclusion, I reflect on the larger picture of transnational business regulation today and how it is a part of the evolution of complex transnationalism.

Multiple forms of global governance exist today that are an essential element of complex transnationalism, as defined in this volume. TNCs are both the targets of much of this governance and direct participants in governance processes. The state finds itself responding to the actions of corporations, both as indirect contributors to ongoing violence and as partners in establishing new standards, rules, and regimes. This can be seen in the case of conflict minerals regulation. In civil conflicts, natural resources are a primary source of revenue for rebel forces and a common source of grievance in relations between TNCs and communities, as Macdonald discusses in her contribution to this volume. In response, for almost two decades now, external actors have tried to change the costs and benefits of fighting by limiting the ability of rebels to sell those resources in legitimate global markets. Activists have drawn attention to oil and gas revenues, sales of illegal timber, and a range of high-value minerals as an incentive for rebel leaders to continue fighting. These "conflict commodities" have been the object of a number of global interventions to reduce their utility for rebel finance, spawning an extensive debate over the role of economic factors in civil conflict.[3]

To discuss transnational business regulation as an element in complex transnationalism, I look at the five minerals named by policymakers and activists as contributing to rebel support.[4] Today there exist a wide variety of governance schemes that seek to identify minerals sourced from regions of conflict and therefore likely to support rebels, and that have put in place mechanisms to reduce or eliminate them in world markets. I focus on (1) the organization of corporate actors in global supply chains; (2) how TNCs interact with a wide array of other actors in developing and implementing governance processes; (3) the communication of new norms throughout the supply chain through industry interactions and to the public via reporting mechanisms; and (4) the impact of these schemes on conflict. In the conclusion, I discuss how conflict minerals governance is a contemporary manifestation of transnationalism.

Conflict minerals schemes use the way in which modern industries are organized into international supply chains as a way to put constraints on rebel activity. Each scheme is dominated by a different set of actors—states, corporations, international organizations, NGOs—but all of them require action by TNCs to restrict rebel access to global markets. Some are hybrid or multistakeholder initiatives, while others are purely industry efforts, and still others constitute traditional forms of state regulation. Participants communicate indirectly through the media and directly through negotiation, reporting, and legislation. The schemes themselves reflect normative developments within the discourse on business and conflict, which has reshaped a decade of conflict-prevention initiatives to incorporate a role for the private sector.[5]

The issue of conflict minerals brings into a play a wide range of actors that are transnational—nonstate actors that mobilize politically and/or economically across borders and beyond the state. This issue area also brings into play the way in which modern business is organized into extensive global supply chains linking core producers and buyers with numerous other companies—smaller suppliers, brokers, financiers, transportation firms, and others. Even small and seemingly local firms are indirectly transnationalized through their participation in these global networks. The supply chain is also the site of activist mobilization and ultimately of transnational regulation itself.

In the following section, I discuss the organization of transnational business governance as one aspect of complex transnationalism. I highlight fragmentation in governance—in hard and soft law—as key dimensions of variation in governance outcomes. I then report on the evolution of interaction among TNCs and other actors in the regulation of conflict minerals, resulting in the creation of multiple governance initiatives. Within this interaction, different participants communicate through media, negotiation, public reporting, certification schemes, and legislation. The effort to end conflict through controlling markets in this way has uneven effects on local violence but is considered by many to be an innovative way to engage in peace promotion. In the conclusion,

I discuss how the debate over conflict minerals is a response to the growing transnationalism of actors, governance, and conflict itself.

The Organization of Transnational Business Governance

Recent analyses of global governance focus on institutions that complement or
compete with traditional forms of public authority and view the private sector as
both the subject of regulation and a provider of regulatory governance.[6] The
character of this new global governance, whether by states or nonstate actors,
can be described in terms of hierarchy, participation, comprehensiveness, and
other features. Here, I focus on two significant dimensions of governance: fragmentation or concentration and hard or soft governance mechanisms.

Fragmentation

Transnational governance seeks to regulate the behavior of firms in order to
solve a public problem. While states are not absent from these new forms of
global governance, they are not the central authority, and private actors play a
powerful role.[7] There is no single, central authority in global governance, no
comprehensive organization governing across issue areas, and no single set of
potential participants. Therefore, transnational business governance can vary
along a number of different variables, which has posed significant challenges to
analyzing it. One aspect that we can examine is the degree of fragmentation in
the governance of a specific issue area. Fragmention in the organization of transnational business governance can be defined by two variables: political jurisdiction and market scale.

Governance schemes that are truly global in scope, and that apply across
multiple political jurisdictions, are more centralized and less fragmented. These
are characteristic of our traditional view of an international organization, such
as the UN. Transnational governance initiatives in which nonstate actors are
influential also can be global in scope, applying across borders and reaching into
every country, such as the Forest Stewardship Council. Some are more selective,
covering only a particular region instead of the entire globe—for instance, the
voluntary carbon market in the European Union (EU).[8] Some may be rooted in
a particular nation and yet have transnational or extraterritorial reach, in which
the standards set in one market have influence beyond that state, such as the
sustainability standards set by the Dutch UTZ Certified coffee certification system, which covers coffee producers worldwide.

We can distinguish between this political geography and the economic
geography defined by markets. Transnational business governance can target a
broad market that cuts across industries, as in the case of fair trade initiatives, or
they can apply much more narrowly to a particular sector, supply chain, or product. The ability to segment the market in this way creates the possibility for high

levels of fragmentation within an issue area when market transactions are the object of governance.[9] Global initiatives that cover more than one sector or segment require a more centralized form that brings everything under one umbrella, while individual, narrowly tailored initiatives that target a single sector or product will make fragmentation of governance possible and indeed likely.

This raises the important conceptual problem of how we define an issue in order to determine whether governance in that area is truly fragmented. When we see multiple governance schemes, is it because there are multiple issues? Or is this a single issue area with more than one segment? The definition of issue area poses difficult problems methodologically because issue boundaries are constructed by the most interested participants in any governance effort. Charli Carpenter argues that issue emergence—the construction of a problem and its acceptance as an international issue—occurs prior to the activity that can produce governance, before transnational activism occurs.[10] Social movements and activists who campaign for regulatory change strategically define a problem and frame a solution, and it becomes an issue when their frame is widely adopted.[11] Corporations can respond by attempting to narrow the definition of the issue, reframing it in ways that are easier for them to manage and control. Many issues are essentially given to us as preexisting constructs, while others are constantly debated, redefined, and understood in multiple ways by the actions and discourse of socially concerned people.

In the case of conflict minerals, there is relative consensus by most participants on cause and effect relationships across all minerals implicated in conflict, whether or not each mineral is currently included in a governance scheme. There is also general consensus on the broad outlines of regulatory solutions. All of these conflict minerals could in theory be regulated in one comprehensive system, or they could be regulated individually or through some intermediate mix. In other words, the separate minerals do not necessarily constitute separate issue areas. If we expand our view to include all conflict commodities—for instance, to include timber—then we would have to wrestle further with the quesiton of whether this is one or multiple issue areas, since debates over non-mineral commodities involve a wider variety of causal understandings and regulatory proposals. Currently, for conflict minerals alone, the existence of a variety of regulatory outcomes reflects fragmentation of governance and not the existence of multiple issue areas.[12]

Hard and Soft Governance Mechanisms

For some, the distinction between hard and soft law hinges on whether or not it is legally binding: Hard law is legally binding, and soft law is voluntary. This implies a clear-cut distinction between them, but in reality the lines between them are not so evident, and the two can coexist and overlap.[13] Some voluntary standards that are not backed by state authority and are not part of law are nonetheless enforceable, and violations can lead to significant costs. A more complex definition is provided by Kenneth Abbott and Duncan Snidal, who look at the degree of precision, obligation, and delegation that particular standards entail.[14] Hard law has all three characteristics—precise rules, binding obligations, and delegation to others for adjudication of disputes. Any weakening of these three characteristics produces soft law. Note that their definition applies both to state-based regulation and voluntary standard-setting and does not rely on state authority as part of the definition of hard law. Voluntary initiatives can include precise rules, binding obligation, and delegated dispute resolution; state-backed regulations can be imprecise, without binding obligations, and lack outside adjudication. The boundaries between the two are fuzzy, and yet they point to some important distinctions in the nature of governance systems.

In this chapter, I use the terms "hard" and "soft" to designate particular mechanisms that are used to govern transnational supply chains that are the object of the conflict minerals governance schemes. A "supply chain" (also called a value chain or commodity chain) refers to the step-by-step process by which material, labor, and technology are combined to produce, distribute, and market goods and services on a global basis.[15] While a supply chain can be contained completely within a vertically integrated firm, it can also be disaggregated across producer and consumer firms located around the globe. Many of the problems that require transnational governance are due to the lack of accountability in a system in which different firms participate at different stages in a long and geographically extensive system of cross-border exchange relationships.

The transnational nature of a supply chain makes it particularly difficult to regulate from source to market. It requires standards, rules, and systems to operate across multiple jurisdictions. The targets of regulation can be located at any point in the supply chain, from raw material suppliers to processors to distributors and retailers. The supply chain has become a target of regulatory efforts in part because of the asymmetrical power that other firms in the chain potentially can bring to bear. Unlike a pure market-exchange relationship, the supply chain embeds firms within an ongoing contractual relationship in which major producers and major buyers have significant leverage over others and can provide incentives or enforcement of rules and standards.

Negotiations to develop a new governance scheme require participants to establish the contours of the issue they want to solve, the targets of their regulatory action, and the rules and standards of behavior they want them to adopt. Beyond that, one of the key decisions they make is the mechanisms they want to use to make all this "stick." The most common mechanism and often the simplest to adopt is to implement some form of transparency requirement (that is, information disclosure).[16] Transparency mechanisms vary in the degree to which they entail precise rules, binding obligations, and third-party adjudication. The softest transparency mechanism is simply self-reporting by firms about their own behavior, with the expectation that concern for a firm's reputation will lead them to adopt higher standards. This is typically purely voluntary, with imprecise obligations, no binding obligation, and no delegation to third parties. A stronger form of transparency would require firms not just to disclose what they are doing in general but also detail who they are doing it with and where their material and products come from. In other words, standards of "due diligence" provide information about the supply chain itself and entail more precision and obligation. A harder form of transparency requires that the information be audited and certified by a third party and that the standards be upheld throughout the supply chain through chain-of-custody arrangements. When any element of this is required by law—self-reporting, due diligence, or certification and auditing—the governance system becomes a form of hard law.[17] In the rest of this chapter, I look at this range of options (reporting, due diligence, certification, and law) as a way to identify choices between hard and soft forms of governance.

Transnational Supply Chains and Conflict Minerals

The conflict minerals arena is a particularly interesting area to explore for understanding contemporary transnationalism. First, it reflects the degree to which outside actors—international organizations, international NGOs, and other states—intervene today in domestic conflicts that would have been ignored in the past. Second, the regulatory mechanisms proposed rely on the existence of transnational supply chains, which are a key element of the modern global economy. As David Malet and Miriam J. Anderson note in their introduction, this was facilitated by the reduction of transaction costs for acting transnationally, in this case a reduction in the costs of contracting and communicating business on a worldwide basis. The emergence of transnational supply chains in the modern era and the increasing dependence of the world economy on them created the opportunity to link local conflicts to global markets. This led in turn to increasing concern about how civil wars might arise from economic competition and greed rather than from intergroup grievances. While there have always been exchanges between firms located within a common industry but in different countries, the number, extensive reach, and complexity of twenty-first-century supply chains is unprecedented. Third, the nonstate actors involved, both activists and firms, are more transnational in their activities than in the past. Both direct contention and relationship-building between transnational advocacy coalitions and TNCs constitute a new form of "private politics" that operates at both local and transnational levels.[18]

The conflict minerals issue is also interesting from the standpoint of understanding the creation of new global governance institutions. This is a brand-new issue area, starting from a clean slate, with no preexisting national or international legislation that has to be taken into account. It is also an arena in which traditional efforts at intervention by governments and international organizations, such as sanctions, had failed to bring about peace. These failures led to a crisis of confidence in old forms of governance, and many observers recognized the need for innovation.

Should we expect to see centralized hard-law institutions for all conflict minerals? The first institution—the Kimberley Process Certification Scheme for Rough Diamonds—was a centralized and hard-law institution that could have become a model for future efforts. The major participants in that institution-building exercise created an epistemic consensus on the links between the minerals trade and conflict and focused on regulating the minerals supply chain to end the violence. Many of the same activists and policymakers remained engaged in this issue over time as it expanded to other minerals, and some of the same states participated in multiple regulatory efforts. Transparency and certification became focal points for policy solutions. The targets of governance were narrowly defined as minerals from conflict regions within specific states, which limited the number of states and firms that would be affected. Despite all of this, what we see today is fragmentation in governance, with a mix of hard- and soft-law institutions at global, regional, and national levels.

Issue Creation and Consensus

Both the concept of conflict minerals and the necessity to intervene to ensure they do not enter world markets are relatively new ideas. They grew out of rising international concern about the link between natural resources and weak governance, propelled by transnational activists committed to ending the bloodshed in the Great Lakes region of Africa in the 1990s. The period immediately following the end of the Cold War was not one of peace, as many had hoped. States in the former Soviet orbit broke apart violently, particularly in the Balkans. Clients of both the United States and the USSR in Africa and Central America were cut adrift. Civil wars and state failures spiked upward in the 1990s, with the horrors of genocide in Rwanda, child soldiers in Sierra Leone, and seemingly everlasting civil war in Angola. Long-running and brutal conflicts in Africa spilled across national borders and engulfed entire regions.

The pressures for the international community to respond to these conflicts grew acute. Policymakers tried a variety of ways to intervene and end the bloodshed—peacekeeping, the imposition of sanctions, and humanitarian intervention all became common in the 1990s.[19] The continuation of violence despite international attention stimulated a growing debate within the security and humanitarian communities over state failure, civilian victims, and human rights. Leaders in the international community, including UN secretary-general Kofi Annan, began to discuss the "responsibility to protect" citizens even from their own governments and the need to intervene in sovereign state affairs for humanitarian causes.[20] Different arenas of activism and policy concern overlapped in this debate, blurring the lines between issue areas: conflict prevention, anticorruption, human rights, environmental harm, management of natural resources, and others. In many of these, the business community became one focus of attention. Activists demanded that the private sector adopt better practices that would prevent harm to individuals, communities, and the environment. The discourse on corporate social responsibility became common, even among business leaders. These trends form the backdrop to the effort to create transnational business governance for conflict minerals.

Many observers of conflicts began to identify economic factors as a feature of these "new wars" of the post–Cold War years.[21] Empirical and policy-oriented research analyzed a number of mechanisms by which trade and investment can contribute to the political economy of conflict by creating conditions that sustain the continued use of violence.[22] The idea of a "resource curse" drew attention to the correlation between resource wealth and various forms of state failure, from poverty to violence.[23] Weak governance is exacerbated by the acquisition, especially sudden, of resource wealth as both governing elites and rebels fight to gain control of revenues.

This attention led to proposals to prevent the extensive revenues from natural resource development from getting into the "wrong" hands—for example, rebels, paramilitaries, corrupt politicians, and bureaucrats. Two broad approaches have been applied: targeted international sanctions on commodities (and finance) and regulation of the supply chain. The failure of targeted sanctions to achieve their goals laid the groundwork for experimentation in other areas. Participants quickly converged on the idea of identifying the origins of minerals in order to label some as legitimate (from government-controlled territory) and some as illegitimate (areas controlled by rebels). This would require both controls within the borders of producing countries and controls on the supply chain that links producers and consumers.

We can date the first steps in constructing conflict minerals as an issue area to the initial outcry against "conflict diamonds"—rough diamonds from regions of conflict, whose sale financed bloodshed in Angola and Sierra Leone. Global Witness, a London-based NGO, issued groundbreaking investigative reports in 1998 and 1999 highlighting the role of oil and diamonds as a source of finance for bloodshed. Ian Smillie, a Canadian humanitarian, investigated the role of rough diamonds in the ongoing violence in Sierra Leone.[24] A coalition of European groups, financed in part by the EU, launched the Fatal Transactions campaign to publicize the trade in conflict diamonds. Major human rights organizations, including important gatekeepers such as Amnesty International and Human Rights Watch, joined a transnational campaign against what they called "blood diamonds." The aim of this campaign was to affect consumer buying preferences by linking diamonds with bloodshed, which would threaten the reputation of the

diamond industry as a whole. Other natural resources also came in for attention—timber, oil, and other minerals—but the diamond campaign caught the
public's attention most prominently.

From 1998 to 2000, the conflict diamond campaign generated increasing
attention within the diamond industry and in the international community.
Concerns about the resource curse animated activists in Europe and the United
States, and transnational campaigns pressed for more transparency about the
source of minerals consumed in the West. Conflict minerals, or more particularly
conflict diamonds, rose to the top of the international agenda. Activists, policymakers, and industry all agreed on the appropriate governance mechanism—
certification of the diamond supply chain to identify rough stones from conflict
regions.

From the end of the Cold War to the turn of the century—a relatively short
span of time in international relations history—we saw the creation of a new
international agenda about conflict prevention and natural resources, born in
part out of the contention between humanitarian activists and corporate leaders. Larger debates about the role of business in conflict prevention had emerged
by this time. A number of prominent NGOs made the case that business should
become more directly involved in peacebuilding, given its natural interest in a
peaceful system that would benefit commerce.[25] Secretary-General Kofi Annan
launched the UN Global Compact in 2000, and one of its first activities was a
Policy Dialogue on Business in Zones of Conflict. The participants in the dialogue, drawn from industry, government, three UN agencies, and NGOs,
included a number of representatives from the diamond industry.[26]

This was the political and normative environment within which transnational business governance for diamonds and then other conflict minerals
emerged. Major industry players and governments—both producer states and
consumer states—were open to negotiating with a variety of private actors to
manage the natural resource pipeline and ensure these resources did not finance
corruption and violence.

The Kimberley Process Certification Scheme

By 2000, various systems of information disclosure had become common touchstone proposals to regulate natural resources to prevent conflict and corruption.
Over the next decade, transnational actors would slowly build up the number
and type of governance systems for the main conflict minerals. Each succeeding
initiative both built upon and differed in significant ways from the others. All
entailed some form of information disclosure—certification, reporting, or due
diligence. But only the negotiations over diamonds led participants to create a
highly centralized governance system, with strict and specific certification rules,
backed by public authority. Some initiatives include purely private actors, some

include both public and private participants, and some are more traditional public governance organizations. The main participants are the transnational activists; industry representatives from both ends of the supply chain—producers and buyers, along with industry sector associations; the main producer and consumer states; the UN and other international organizations; and the conflict-affected states themselves.

The "sanctions decade" of the 1990s came to a close with increasing evidence that targeted "smart" sanctions had failed. These sanctions included bans on trade in commodities such as minerals, timber, and oil that were identified with conflict. As evidence of sanctions violations mounted, the UN established a panel of experts to review the sanctions experience in Angola, which produced a devastating indictment of sanctions-busting by individuals, firms, and governments.[27] Even prior to the report being published, however, the UN Security Council began experimenting with diamond certification along with sanctions. It worked with the diamond industry to develop a system within Angola to certify that diamond exports were from conflict-free zones. Nevertheless, there was rising impatience among those concerned about the violence and bloodshed, seeing the failure of traditional measures to end conflict or prevent the horror of genocide in Rwanda and child soldiers in Sierra Leone.

The ongoing bloodshed generated media attention and galvanized activism on behalf of the victims. Global Witness published widely noted investigative reports in 1998 and 1999 that put companies on a par with governments in facilitating the ongoing conflict in Angola, focusing especially on oil companies and banks. Smillie investigated, identified, and publicized the links between rough diamonds and war in Sierra Leone. Other activists and NGOs began to identify rough diamonds as a major source of war finance, including the Fatal Transactions campaign in Europe and increasing activism among groups in the United States that began lobbying Congress for a ban on conflict diamonds.

The structure of the industry and the political interests of major producer and consumer states shaped the resulting governance systems. The diamond industry had been highly organized into a cartel maintained by De Beers, a South African firm that signed long-term supply contracts with all diamond producers, promising to buy up any excess stones in order to maintain the price. This was the longest-running cartel in history, lasting from 1888 to around 2000.[28] Different stages of the diamond value chain were also highly organized in associations for diamond bourses, jewelers, and others. However, the conflict diamond issue arose at a time when De Beers faced challenges in maintaining the cartel. Conflict diamonds in Africa were flooding the market, and the collapse of the Soviet Union and establishment of a new Russian government undermined control of the market. New producers were entering the market, and Africa itself was no longer the central source of rough diamonds. The leadership of De Beers began to shift strategy toward becoming a consumer-oriented company. The diamond industry, including De Beers, recognized the threat to the market that the blood diamond campaign posed and quickly proposed developing a certification system of some sort.

Just as the industry was highly concentrated, so too were the major producer and consumer states, which stimulated their interest in this issue. South Africa, along with Botswana, took leadership in responding to the conflict diamond debate. They did not want to see their major export market collapse due to consumer flight or further sanctions. The United States dominated the consumer market, and Congress was considering restrictions on conflict diamonds. The US was interested in ending civil conflict abroad but not through direct intervention as it had done in Somalia and elsewhere. The major producer and consumer states agreed on the idea of developing a certification system to identify legitimate stones, undermine rebel activity, and preserve diamond markets along with national sovereignty.

In 2000, the UN General Assembly unanimously passed a resolution condemning the role of diamonds in financing conflict and supporting the institution of a global certification regime. The UN defines conflict diamonds as "diamonds that originate from areas controlled by forces or factions opposed to legitimate and internationally recognized governments, and are used to fund military action in opposition to those governments, or in contravention of the decisions of the Security Council."[29] The conflict areas of concern initially were in Sierra Leone, Angola, and Liberia. The Security Council had already applied sanctions against the UNITA rebels in Angola, including an embargo on trade in diamonds in 1998 (and oil in 1999), but the evident failure of these sanctions—which did nothing to stem the flow of commodities or to bring the warring parties to the negotiating table—helped spur the blood diamond campaign.

Transnational activism, industry concern, and producer and consumer state interest all came together in a common response to the problem. The diamond industry itself proposed a voluntary system to identify rough diamonds from conflict zones and certify them as "conflict free." In 2000, South Africa hosted negotiations in Kimberley among industry representatives, diamond-producing states, consumer states, and two of the NGOs most active in the conflict diamond campaign, Global Witness and Partnership Africa Canada. This launched what became known as the Kimberley Process, with the goal of developing a global certification system. The negotiations, although difficult, reflected a surprising amount of consensus among the participants on what to do. Within the year, the World Federation of Diamond Bourses and the International Diamond Manufacturers Association created the World Diamond Council with a mandate to develop a tracking system for the export and import of rough diamonds and to represent the industry in future negotiations. Within one year, negotiations had established the outlines of the certification system, and by 2003 the Kimberly Process Certification Scheme (KPCS) was launched.

Under the KPCS, rough diamonds (diamonds that are uncut or minimally cut and unpolished) would be packaged together in a parcel with a forgery-resistant certificate that documents that the stones do not come from designated conflict zones—that is, rebel-held or contested territory. The industry would develop a system of warranties to track the rough diamonds internally within states, from the mineral source to the border. All member states are required to ensure that exports and imports of diamonds are in sealed containers, properly certified, and do not come from nonparticipant states. States also would establish the KPCS standards in domestic law. Member states would be subject to regular peer review and monitoring and could have their membership revoked. The Kimberley Process participants include almost the entire diamond industry. There is only one transnational governance initiative for rough diamonds, providing highly centralized regulation of the diamond trade. The system is detailed, specific, and backed by state authority.

For the first few years, the KPCS was counted as a major success and provided a strong model and focal point for other similar initiatives. However, it is currently confronting significant challenges that have weakened its influence as a model for how to deal with conflict commodities. In 2006, the government of Zimbabwe took over the Marange diamond region—potentially one of the richest sources in the world. It has controlled the region through violence and repression, leading to calls for Zimbabwe's membership in the KPCS to be revoked. However, under the terms of the Kimberley Process, conflict diamonds come from rebel-held or contested territory and not from territory that a government controls by violence and human rights abuses. The Kimberley Process members are divided on whether to certify Marange diamonds as conflict-free and over whether to expand the KPCS definition of conflict diamonds to include human rights violations. Some industry players refuse to buy from Zimbabwe, and both Ian Smillie and Global Witness have walked away from the KPCS. Zimbabwe argues that it has met the conditions of membership and that the definition of conflict diamonds should not be broadened to include human rights. Other African states support Zimbabwe on this and have resisted attempts by the EU, the United States, and others to renegotiate the KPCS to include human rights violations. To do so might open them up to challenges and undermine their sovereignty. The rift among Kimberley Process members over these issues has weakened the authority and legitimacy of the KPCS in the last few years.

Transparency and Due Diligence for Conflict Minerals

The first stage of the conflict minerals governance story was the creation of the Kimberley Process. The next stage focused on other conflict minerals found in the DRC, which suffers from rebel violence in particular regions of the country. Global Witness continued to be one of the most visible campaigners, arguing that other conflict commodities needed to be regulated, but new NGOs such as the Enough Project in the United States also brought attention to conflict minerals and pursued a different strategy. The second stage involved debates over initiatives to establish standards of "due diligence" and "responsible sourcing." The most significant of the efforts at this stage are two that are in some sense opposites: the voluntary OECD Due Diligence Guidance for Responsible Supply Chains of Minerals from Conflict-Affected and High-Risk Areas (hereafter the OECD Due Diligence Guidance) and the Section 1502 provisions of the Dodd-Frank Wall Street Reform and Consumer Protection Act. In addition to these two major efforts, there are certification provisions in UN sanctions, supply chain initiatives sponsored by industry groups, regional certification proposals for the Great Lakes region and specific producer countries, and legislation under consideration in the EU.

From the beginning, activists pointed to other minerals (and other commodities) as contributors to conflict, but it was the diamond campaign that proved initially successful. The other minerals identified as contributing to rebel violence came to be known as "3TG": tin, tantalum, tungsten, and gold. The DRC and its neighbors are a source of these strategic minerals, and the trade in minerals is one of the sources of financial support for the rebels.[30] None of these mineral industries is organized in the same way as the diamond sector. Tin is used as a solder in electronics, and the supply chain includes major electronics industry players. The tin industry at the producer end is not tightly organized, and in 2005 the tin market was in real disarray. Many of the main mineral producers today are based in China and Malaysia where there is little concern over the conflict minerals issue. The International Tin Research Institute (ITRI), a tin industry association based in England, nevertheless has been a leading player on conflict minerals governance in recent years. Tantalum, which is processed from coltan, is a vital component for modern equipment, including cell phones and GPS systems. It is not a large industry, and sources of tantalum are widely dispersed internationally. Some of the leading firms are Chinese, although they obtain the mineral from outside the country; Brazil currently is the leading producer of tantalum.[31] Tungsten is classified as a rare mineral; it is widely dispersed, but currently China dominates production.[32] Gold is the only one of the 3TG minerals that is global and well organized, with South Africa and recently China as major producer countries. Barrick Gold and Goldcorp are major industry players.

Activists, led by some of the newer players, strategically chose to target the vulnerable consumer end of the supply chain, focusing on the electronics industry and minerals such as coltan and gold used in cell phones and other electronic devices. By 2004, the electronics industry had formed the Electronic Industry Citizenship Coalition (EICC) to develop a general code of conduct for corporate social responsibility in supply chain sourcing. Along with the Global eSustainability Initiative (GeSI), it identified tin smelters as a choke point in the supply chain and established a Conflict Free Smelter program.[33] ITRI participates in this program and has also assisted in establishing a conflict-free tin initiative and traceability program in Rwanda and the DRC. The EICC and the GeSI collaborated in creating an Extractives Working Group, which developed a reporting template for users up and down the supply chain for gathering information relevant to due diligence and responsible sourcing.

In 2012, slowly following the lead of the tin industry, the World Gold Council began developing its own system of due diligence for conflict gold. The tantalum industry and the tungsten sector have made no similar move. Instead, it is the electronics firms that use the minerals that are leading the push for ways to identify conflict minerals and ensure the electronics supply chain is "conflict free." Firms such as Hewlett-Packard and Apple have global brand names and are sensitive to claims that they are promoting bloodshed. While the conflict minerals campaign has not been as startlingly effective as the blood diamond campaign was a decade ago, the choice to target electronics firms instead of mining companies has slowly produced results.

Shortly after the EICC and the GeSI began their investigation of whether the mineral smelters could be leveraged effectively, the International Conference on the Great Lakes Region (ICGLR, a regional organization) adopted a Protocol on the Illegal Exploitation of Natural Resources in 2006.[34] It was pushed in part by increasing attention by UN sanctions committees to the role of natural resources in conflict. In 2007, the UN Security Council issued a statement recommending that its peacekeeping missions, especially the one established in the DRC in 1999, help states prevent the illegal exploitation of natural resources, and it called for strengthening sanctions and expert groups. In other words, at the same time as industry began exploring soft-law options, producer states and the UN were exploring hard-law alternatives.

Toward the end of the decade, we saw another tipping point similar to the one in 2000 that preceded the establishment of the Kimberley Process. In 2009, the OECD convened a series of meetings with the ICGLR and other actors to develop guidance on supply chain due diligence. These meetings included representatives of civil society, such as the Enough Project, Global Witness, and International Alert; industry players from the DRC, ITRI, and major mining and electronics firms; interested governments; and international organizations. The latter included the UN Group of Experts on the DRC, along with the UN Stabilization Mission in the DRC (MONUSCO). The negotiations created the OECD Guidance on Due Diligence standards, adopted in 2011. The guidance encourages voluntary annual reporting and due diligence in supply chain management for tin, tungsten, tantalum, and gold.[35] In addition, the UN Group of Experts itself issued due-diligence guidelines, which were designed to be complementary to the OECD and ICGLR efforts, along with complying with DRC law.

Around the same time, the UN Expert Group on the DRC produced a report that recommended the UN Security Council adopt due-diligence guidelines that explicitly referenced the OECD Guidance. The Security Council approved the report, and these guidelines now apply to all sanctions on natural resources. The ICGLR, partly in response, is beginning to implement its own regional certification system, working with the OECD, ITRI, the NGO Partnership Africa Canada, and the German consultants GIZ. The participants in each of these schemes varied, and yet a variety of transnational actors participated in multiple negotiations and contributed to more than one governance effort.

The most dramatic and far-reaching changes came with the unprecedented action taken by the US government. Activist groups such as the Enough Project and Global Witness targeted the US Congress in an effort to pass conflict minerals legislation. Rep. Jim McDermott proposed legislation for a number of years, and the issue was taken up by Senators Sam Brownback, Dick Durbin, and Russ Feingold in 2009. They succeeded in attaching what became Section 1502 of the Dodd-Frank legislation. It requires companies to identify whether any products they make depend on gold, tin, tantalum, or tungsten.[36] If so, they have to determine whether their source is in a conflict-affected area of the DRC and publish this information, and the company must file a report describing the due diligence it undertook to trace its materials.[37] If it cannot be sure about the source, it can say so but must then investigate further. Trade in conflict minerals is not forbidden, unlike the KPCS, but the expectation is that this transparency will reduce or eliminate the willingness of processors and consumers to buy conflict minerals. Needless to say, business groups such as the US Chamber of Commerce and the National Association of Manufacturers have condemned the regulations, and many citizens of the DRC argue it amounts to an informal trade embargo.[38] In response, some individual firms are seeking to establish "closed" pipelines, such as by buying mines in peaceful areas of the DRC.

Following the passage of Dodd-Frank and the publication of implementation rules by the SEC in 2012, the participants in both international and transnational business governance systems explicitly adjusted their terms to fit with both the US regulations and the OECD Guidance. The UN Group of Experts Guidelines for sanctions, the OECD Due Diligence Guidance, the Conflict Smelter Scheme, and new conflict minerals due-diligence standards put forth by the World Gold Council in 2012 all have published claims saying they are—or will be—in conformity with Section 1502 of the Dodd-Frank regulations. The Conflict Smelter Scheme standards also incorporate the OECD Guidance for any smelters obtaining materials from the DRC region. There is an ongoing effort to make the different systems compatible.[39] Given that Section 1502 reports are only now being submitted, we do not yet have evidence on the impact this is having on the conflict.[40]

Partly in response to the US legislation, the EU also began to consider legislation in this arena. They modeled their proposals on the OECD Guidelines. They also took up the perspective reflected in the Conflict Smelter program, seeing the smelters as a more effective means to identify the source of minerals than a broader company-based process. The idea is that any firm using minerals from a certified smelter could be accepted as having a conflict-free pipeline, without needing to do extensive research and tracking itself. The weakness in this approach, as many have pointed out, is that the existing system for managing the minerals from field to smelter is a weak one that does not identify the source of individual stones. It is a "bag and tag" system that is simple and cost-effective but not airtight.

Conclusion: Transnational Corporations in War and Peace

TNCs today are key players in global efforts to reduce conflict and promote peace. They participate in new forms of governance, such as those designed to restrict the use of mineral resources to finance rebel violence. Furthermore, these new forms of transnational governance designed to address the problem of civil conflict demonstrate the increasing transnationalism of security itself, as local conflicts that would have been ignored in the past become the subject of international attention. These transnational initiatives also reflect both the negative and positive impact of the globalization of markets on conflict, as they target international trade and supply chains as contributors to instability. In this conclusion, I briefly recap the organization of TNCs into supply chains, how TNCs interact with other actors in regulatory governance, and the way they communicate their interests. I conclude with a discussion of TNCs in conflict prevention and peace promotion and what it means for the evolution of complex transnationalism in the arena of security affairs.

First, in looking at market actors, we need to recognize the significance of how production is organized today. The growth in number and scope of international supply chains has reshaped markets and created new opportunities for power and leverage within them. How they are organized, and which firms are privileged within the supply chain, varies across industry sectors. This has implications for policy outcomes. The major supplier and consumer corporations are transnational organizations that own assets and conduct business across sovereign borders. Today they also are central nodes in larger globe-spanning networks in which both local and transnational firms participate through contractual relationships (instead of ownership) in a transnational supply chain. The major players in these networks are clearly transnational actors, with other firms acting as "satellites" around them. For instance, De Beers is an international corporation with affiliates—and mines—in more than one country. But it is also deeply tied to other firms within the diamond industry, including both national and transnational firms in the cutting, polishing, distribution, and retail sectors.

The development of the Kimberley Process is striking for how highly organized and transnational the diamond industry was, largely due to a unique history as one of the most durable international cartels that has ever existed in modern times. Although the cartel was beginning to weaken by the time the "blood diamond" campaign began, the industry still remained highly organized through formal associations and informal networks. They viewed the conflict diamond campaign as a crisis for diamond markets, which solidified consensus on developing a certification system. Firms producing the other 3TG minerals are in less concentrated industries, characterized by more complicated processing systems and supply chains in which other unrelated industries, such as the electronics sector, have significant influence. The firms themselves tend to produce, process, or distribute a wider range of minerals, and an increasing number of them are Chinese firms that are only beginning to become transnational. The greater diversity of organization and interests inhibited the development of a sense of immediate crisis for the 3TG minerals and weakened the consensus needed to support a comprehensive centralized and hard-law governance system.

This case illustrates the degree to which TNCs today interact with transnational NGOs. They are often engaged in contentious debates over the appropriate role and accountability of the business community, especially in zones of conflict. They also increasingly collaborate in creating new regulatory schemes, with the potential for them to develop a common sense of identity and purpose, as Malet and Anderson speculate in their introduction.[41] Transnational NGOs played a critical role in establishing conflict minerals on the international agenda. Like the companies they target, these NGOs have different organizational characteristics that can limit their reach. For instance, some of the lead NGOs in the blood diamond campaign were closely tied to their home country and were only transnational in limited ways. This was the case for Partnership Africa Canada, which is based in Canada and operates in only a handful of countries in Africa. Others are highly transnational organizations with global reach, such as Amnesty International. Both national and international NGOs were effective in organizing larger transnational coalitions to press their campaigns both at home and abroad. These campaigns could garner the support of literally hundreds of organizations and many thousands of consumers.[42]

Transnational campaigns decrying the link between minerals and rebel violence propelled transnational business governance forward. The imposition of sanctions by the UN in the 1990s as a means to resolve conflict in Africa was perceived to have failed by the turn of the new century. Activist campaigns condemned states for their failures and turned instead to the private sector. The blood diamond campaign they launched posed an existential threat to the diamond market and created the crisis conditions needed for change. Compare this to the 3TG minerals, where the campaign did not rise to the level of an existential threat. Activist groups chose instead to target the end users in the electronics industry instead of mineral producers because they were more sensitive to reputational threat.

Transnational NGOs have been a critical voice in defining the issues and proposing remedies. They were able to take something that has been in existence for centuries—rebels using local natural resources to finance rebellion—and link it to foreign markets and foreign responsibility to end the bloodshed. These transnational NGOs do not, however, have the capacity on their own to regulate international supply chains or end the conflict itself. They must work through states and firms to bring about the restrictions on the trade in minerals that they view as vital to ending conflict.

The conflict minerals case also tells us something about the changing relationship between security issues and market instruments. Since the end of the Cold War, civil war and rebellion in often remote areas have gained the attention of the international community. Discourse now speaks as much of human security as national security and the responsibility of the international community to protect individuals even from their own governments. This is being extended to include a business responsibility for protecting the innocent. Most significantly, we see public and private policymakers utilizing natural resource markets and transnational supply chains as an instrument to manage violent conflict through transnational business governance institutions.

The kinds of global governance initiatives I have discussed for conflict minerals have been created to regulate other industries and other issues—for example, sustainable forestry, socially responsible labor standards, fair trade schemes, and others. Conflict minerals, however, are a new issue area for regulation, one in which there is no competition from preexisting domestic regulations. The interactions among transnational actors and states have been on the whole marked by significant cooperative behavior instead of fierce competition. Both state and nonstate actors have achieved a degree of consensus about cause and effect regarding conflict minerals, although they disagree on the appropriate policy tools to address it. They have all adopted the same understanding of the problem and have chosen policy solutions from among a limited set of options—certification, transparency, and due diligence.

Competitive pressures between the various schemes have been few, and instead they have undergone a process of mutual adjustment. The question of convergence and divergence that animates much debate over the increase in transnational business regulation has been less important in this area than in others. The interaction of hard and soft law has been uneven, and we cannot identify an evolution toward either end of the hard law–soft law spectrum. Given the consensus among states, it is not surprising to find that hard law and soft law are complementary in this case.[43] In this chapter, I have focused narrowly on the issue of conflict minerals governance. However, there has been a much broader effort to engage TNCs in conflict prevention and peace promotion. The focal point in this effort has been the UN Global Compact, which is a partnership between UN agencies, transnational business, nonprofits, and member governments. Over the course of fifteen years, the UN Global Compact has supported the development of conflict-sensitive business practices for individual companies and promoted multistakeholder governance processes such as the ones I discussed here. It recently created the Business4Peace platform to continue to support these initiatives, especially at the local level in countries challenged by rebel violence. All of these efforts have shifted expectations about the appropriate role for business in conflict prevention and reshaped the discourse on how to think about companies as part of peacebuilding initiatives.

Frank Biermann, Philipp Pattberg, and Harro van Asselt discuss what they call the "global governance architecture" as "a patchwork of international institutions that are different in their character (organizations, regimes, and implicit norms), their constituencies (public and private), their spatial scope (from bilateral to global), and their subject matter (from specific policy fields to universal concerns)."[44] What they describe are characteristics of complex transnationalism in the arena of global governance. Transnational business regulation for conflict commodities is characterized by multiple levels of governance, different jurisdictions with no official or formal relations among them and with a diversity of specialized and flexible governance processes.[45] This fragmented system with both hard and soft governance balances the desire of Western states to manage risk in the developing world without intervening directly in the sovereign affairs of other states. It also responds to the demands of activists to do something about the bloodshed and abuse of states at war with themselves and the interest of firms in maintaining their markets without damaging their reputations. They illustrate the way in which transnational forces lead to diversity, not homogeneity, and facilitate the expansion and reorganization of transnational actors.

Notes

1. David Malet and Miriam J. Anderson introduce this definition in this volume's introduction.

2. In her chapter in this volume, Macdonald looks on TNCs as a source of conflict instead of as an instrument for peace.

3. Mats Berdal and David M. Malone, eds., *Greed and Grievance: Economic Agendas in Civil Wars* (Boulder, CO: Lynne Rienner Publishers, 2000); Paul Collier and Anke Hoeffler, "Greed and Grievance in Civil War," in *World Bank Working Paper Series* (Washington, DC: World Bank, 2000); Macartan Humphreys, Jeffrey D. Sachs, and Joseph E. Stiglitz, eds., *Escaping the Resource Curse* (Cambridge, UK: Cambridge University Press, 2007); Pauline Jones Luong and Erika Weinthal, "Rethinking the Resource Curse: Ownership Structure, Institutional Capacity, and Domestic Constraints," *Annual Review of Political Science* 9, no. 1 (2006): 241–263.

4. In addition to the five minerals named by activists and targeted by the new governance schemes I discuss here, there are many other gemstones that have supported rebel groups but are too scarce or insignificant to become an object of international attention.

5. Virginia Haufler, "Corporations in Zones of Conflict: Issues, Actors and Institutions," in *Who Governs the Globe?*, eds. Deborah Avant, Martha Finnemore, and Susan Sell (Cambridge, UK: Cambridge University Press, 2010): 102–30.

6. Avant, Finnemore, and Sell, *Who Governs the Globe?*; Rodney Bruce Hall and Thomas J. Biersteker, eds., *The Emergence of Private Authority in Global Governance* (Cambridge, UK: Cambridge University Press, 2002); Martin Hewson and Timothy J. Sinclair, eds., *Approaches to Global Governance Theory* (Albany, NY: SUNY Press, 1999); Matthew Hoffman and Alice Ba, eds., *Contending Perspectives on Global Governance: Coherence, Contestation and World Order* (London: Routledge, 2005); Wolfgang Reinicke, Thorsten Benner, and Jan Martin Witte, "Innovating Global Governance through Global Public Policy Networks: Lessons Learned and Challenges Ahead," *Brookings Review* 1(2003).

7. Avant, Finnemore, and Sell, *Who Governs the Globe?*

8. Jessica F. Green, "Private Standards in the Climate Regime: The Greenhouse Gas Protocol," *Business and Politics* 12, no. 3 (2010): 1–39.

9. Rabih Helou, "An Industry of Standards: How Voluntary Standards Emerge, Compete and Segment International Policymaking," PhD diss., Department of Government and Politics, University of Maryland, 2014.

10. Margaret E. Keck and Kathryn Sikkink, *Activists beyond Borders: Advocacy Networks in International Politics* (Ithaca, NY: Cornell University Press, 1998); Charli Carpenter, "Studying Issue (Non)-Adoption in Transnational Advocacy Networks," *International Organization* 61, no. 3 (2007): 643–67.

11. Robert D. Snow and David A. Benford, "Framing Processes and Social Movements: An Overview and Assessment," *Annual Review of Sociology* 26, no. 1 (2000) : 611–39; Dennis Chong and James N. Druckman, "Framing Theory," *Annual Review of Political Science* 10, no. 1 (2007): 103–26.

12. Activists may launch campaigns about different minerals individually but with clear understanding that they are part of a larger category of "conflict minerals" and an even larger category of "conflict commodities." This creates a future agenda for further advocacy and regulatory action.

13. Gregory Shaffer and Mark A. Pollack, "Hard vs. Soft Law: Alternatives, Complements, and Antagonists in International Governance," *Minnesota Law Review* 94 (2009–10): 706–801.

14. Kenneth Abbott and Duncan Snidal, "Hard and Soft Law," *International Organization* 54, no. 3 (2000): 421–56.

15. Gary Gereffi, John Humphrey, and Timothy Sturgeon, "The Governance of Global Value Chains," *Review of International Political Economy* 12, no. 1 (2005): 78–104.

16. Thomas N. Hale, "Transparency, Accountability, and Global Governance," *Global Governance: A Review of Multilateralism and International Organizations* 14, no. 1 (2008): 73–104; Aarti Gupta, "Special Issue: Transparency in Global Environmental Governance," *Global Environmental Politics* 10, no. 3 (2010).

17. The "new governance," as it is often called, is not based on traditional command-and-control regulations but uses incentives instead of demands, requirements for transparency as a means to shape behavior, and delegation of services to NGOs. See, for instance, Burkard Eberlein and Dieter Kerwer, "New Governance in the European Union: A Theoretical Perspective," *JCMS: Journal of Common Market Studies* 42, no. 1 (2004): 121–42.

18. David P. Baron 2001. "Private Politics, Corporate Social Responsibility, and Integrated Strategy." Journal of Economics & Management Strategy 10 no. 1:7-45.

19. Martha Finnemore, *The Purpose of Intervention: Changing Beliefs about the Use of Force* (Ithaca, NY: Cornell University Press, 2003); Michael Barnett and Thomas Weiss, *Humanitarianism in Question: Politics, Power, Ethics* (Ithaca, NY: Cornell University Press, 2008).

20. International Commission on Intervention and State Sovereignty, "The Responsibility to Protect" (Ottawa: International Development Research Centre, 2001); Gareth Evans and Mohamed Sahnoun, "The Responsibility to Protect," *Foreign Affairs* 81, no. 6 (November–December 2002); Robert Rotberg, ed., *When States Fail: Causes and Consequences* (Princeton, NJ: Princeton University Press, 2003): 99–110.

21. Mary Kaldor, *New and Old Wars: Organized Violence in a Global Era* (Oxford, UK: Polity Press, 1999); Mark Duffield, *Global Governance and the New Wars: The Merging of Development and Security* (London: Zed Books, 2001); Edward Newman, "The 'New Wars' Debate: A Historical Perspective Is Needed," *Security Dialogue* 35, no. 2 (2004): 173–89.

22. Michael Klare, *Resource Wars: The New Landscape of Global Conflict* (New York: Metropolitan/Hold Paperbacks, 2002); Berdal and Malone, *Greed and Grievance*; Karen Ballentine and Jake Sherman, eds., *The Political Economy of Armed Conflict: Beyond Greed and Grievance* (Boulder, CO: Lynne Rienner Publishers, 2003); Collier and Hoeffler, "Greed and Grievance in Civil War"; Humphreys, Sachs, and Stiglitz, *Escaping the Resource Curse*; Pauline Jones Luong and Erika Weinthal, *Oil Is Not a Curse: Ownership Structure and Institutions in Soviet Successor States* (Cambridge, UK: Cambridge University Press, 2010).

23. Terry Lynn Karl, *The Paradox of Plenty: Oil Booms and Petro-States* (Los Angeles: University of California Press, 1997); Michael Ross, "A Closer Look at Oil, Diamonds, and Civil War," *Annual Review of Political Science* 9 (2006): 265–300; *The Oil Curse: How Petroleum Wealth Shapes the Development of Nations* (Princeton, NJ: Princeton University Press, 2012); Jeff Colgan, *Petro-Agression: When Oil Causes War* (Cambridge, UK: Cambridge University Press, 2013).

24. Global Witness, *Rough Trade: The Role of Companies and Governments in the Angolan Conflict*, (London: Global Witness, 1998); Global Witness, *A Crude Awakening: The Role of Oil and Banking Industries in Angolan Civil War and the Plunder of State Assets* (London: Global Witness, 1999); Ian Smillie, Lansana Gberie, and Ralph Hazleton, *The Heart of the Matter: Sierra Leone, Diamonds, and Human Security* (Ottawa: Partnership Africa Canada, 2000).

25. Jane Nelson, *The Business of Peace: The Private Sector as a Partner in Conflict Prevention and Resolution* (London: Prince of Wales Business Leaders Forum, 2000).

26. The founding principles of the Global Compact contain three principles on labor, three on human rights, and three on the environment; an anticorruption principle was added later.

27. Robert R. Fowler, "Report of the Panel of Experts on Violations of Security Council Sanctions against Unita," (New York: UN Security Council, 2000).

28. Debora L. Spar, *The Cooperative Edge: The Internal Politics of International Cartels* (Ithaca, NY: Cornell University Press, 1994); Debora L. Spar, "Markets: Continuity and Change in the International Diamond Market," *Journal of Economic Perspectives* 20, no. 3 (2006): 195–208.

29. World Diamond Council, http://www.diamondfacts.org/.

30. They are generally listed as tin, tantalum, tungsten, and gold—the 3TG.

31. Research and Markets, *Global and Chinese Tantalum Industry Report 2011*, (Dublin, Ireland: Research and Markets, 2011).

32. Celia Taylor, "Conflict Minerals and SEC Disclosure Regulation," *Harvard Business Law Review Online* 2, no. 1 (2012): 105–20.

33. Resolve, *Tracing a Path Forward: A Study of the Challenges of the Supply Chain for Target Metals Used in Electronics* (Washington, DC: Resolve, 2010).

34. The member states are Angola, Burundi, the Central African Republic, the Republic of the Congo, the Democratic Republic of the Congo, Kenya, Uganda, Rwanda, Sudan, Tanzania, and Zambia.

35. "OECD Due Diligence Guidance for Responsible Supply Chains of Minerals from Conflict-Affected and High-Risk Areas," OECD, Paris, 2011.

36. The legislation actually names wolframite, cassiterite, and coltan, which are processed into tin, tungsten, and tantalum.

37. PwC, "A Closer Look: The Dodd-Frank Wall Street Reform and Consumer Protection Act; Impact on Disclosures Related to the Use of 'Conflict Minerals,'" 2011, http://www.pwc.com/us/en/financial-services/regulatory-services/publications/assets/closer-look-conflict-minerals-disclosures.pdf.

38. Taylor, "Conflict Minerals and SEC Disclosure Regulation."

39. Gisa Roesen and Estelle Levin, *Conformance and Compatibility Analysis: CFS, iTSCi, and the OECD Due Diligence Guidance* (Cambridge, UK: Estelle Levin, 2011).

40. Interestingly, a number of firms conducting due diligence discovered that some of their gold is sourced from North Korea, despite US sanctions.

41. Malet and Anderson argue that cooperation between NGOs and TNCs in areas where they have common interests may even promote a sense of solidarity. In the conflict minerals regulatory systems I discuss, that sense of solidarity is not widespread, though there are a few firms and NGOs that are committed to the same cause.

42. For conflict minerals, the final consumers may be individuals who buy gemstones or who buy the products that utilize the 3TG minerals. They can be viewed either as the extreme end of the international supply chain or, alternatively, as a participant in NGO activism when they commit to buying conflict-free minerals.

43. Shaffer and Pollack, "Hard vs. Soft Law."

44. Frank Biermann, Philipp Pattberg, and Harro van Asselt, "The Fragmentation of Global Governance Architectures: A Framework for Analysis," *Global Environmental Politics* 9, no. 4 (2009): 16.

45. Liesbet Hooghe and Gary Marks, "Unraveling the Central State, but How? Types of Multi-Level Governance," *American Political Science Review* 97, no. 2 (2003): 233–43.

4

Beyond the Conflict

Diasporas and Postconflict Government Reconstruction

JENNIFER M. BRINKERHOFF

iasporas are increasingly recognized as important nonstate actors who influence global politics as well as the politics and socioeconomic development of their countries of origin (COOs). When they choose to engage in their COOs or on behalf of people there, they become transnational actors, frequently leveraging their resources abroad (including relationships) to increase potential impacts on and in the COO. They self-identify as transnational and operate largely (though not exclusively) through nonstate mobilizing structures. Their pertinence to international relations cannot be overstated; they are potential participants in essentially every element of how and why state and nonstate actors interact in the global arena. Yet they continue largely to be ignored in theoretical and policy frameworks concerning international development, conflict mitigation, and postconflict reconstruction.[1]

Fiona Adamson and Madeleine Demetriou assert that the diaspora phenomenon is a function of both "non-state political entrepreneurs" *and* state elites, who may use the notion of diaspora to solicit support for political, material, or conflict agendas.[2] In this sense, diasporans become important actors in a "boomerang effect,"[3] whereby internal actors use diasporans to voice, promote, and engage what cannot be done within the borders of the homeland. This experience reinforces the porosity of national boundaries and at once confirms diasporans not only as agents but also as instruments of change, driven by complex interests within and outside of national regimes.

Most research on diaspora political engagement to date focuses on collective action to pursue political aims. What happens when those contestations are somewhat settled and the business of consolidating and moving on is initiated? While diasporans may organize groups to influence politics from afar, their contributions to government reconstruction are necessarily specific to individuals. When these individuals join postconflict governments, they enter into systems of entrenched interests. What happens when nonstate actors transition to become state actors? Do their initial agendas—those that may have attracted international attention in the first place—dissipate? How might they retain their transnational influence and adhere to their original aims? Is succumbing to the state's status quo inevitable, or might they bring new understandings, both technical and normative, to postconflict governance processes? What are the prospects for lasting change?

This chapter specifically examines diaspora participation in postconflict or fragile state government reconstruction. Conflict-affected countries tend to be limited-access orders, characterized by personal relationships forming a dominant coalition providing "only limited access to organizations, privileges, and valuable resources and activities."[4] Theory related to limited-access orders, and neoinstitutional theory more generally, tends to radically underplay the role of individual agency in fomenting change.[5]

I explore diaspora postconflict government reconstruction through illustrations from the Chadian and Zairean diasporas. These examples are illustrative; more extended and additional case studies are needed to corroborate their suggestive conclusions. Nevertheless, potential implications for understanding transnationalism can be identified. Diasporans are at once agents and instruments of other actors, whether for promoting change or protecting the status quo. Though they are not sufficiently recognized in our conceptions of transnationalism, individuals matter. Their motivations, personal histories, and associated social networks impact their potential efficacy as well as the public orientation of their contributions. Diasporans may bring particular characteristics and potential comparative advantages vis-à-vis other external actors deriving from the diaspora identity and experience.[6]

The chapter proceeds as follows. I begin by reviewing diaspora experience and what it suggests for potential advantages for diasporans as reformers. I then review the potential importance of diaspora political reformers in rebuilding governments after conflict. Following, I present two illustrations of diaspora political reform efforts: Djimé Adoum and his efforts to promote good governance in his homeland of Chad and Zairean American professionals' efforts through the All North American Conference on Zaire (ANACOZA) to support regime change and good governance in the former Zaire and nascent Democratic Republic of the Congo (DRC). Finally, I summarize the parameters of these transnational actors in terms of how they organize, interact with other transnational actors, communicate, and influence conflict or peace. I conclude with what they can contribute to our understanding of transnationalism.

The Diaspora Experience: Potential Advantages as Reformers

Scholars have long noted a relationship between the likelihood of entrepreneurial behavior and social marginalization. Nonacceptance in the societies in which they live gives individuals the freedom to be creative in initiating and responding to change. Everett Einar Hagen asserted that the "withdrawal of status" results in the emergence of "individualism and self-reliance as key personality attributes, which in turn favor creativity and entrepreneurial activity."[7] In the diaspora context, migrants may face fewer social sanctions from mainstream society than their native-born counterparts when they initiate entrepreneurial activities.

Literature suggests diasporans' potential to embrace and promote liberal values, which can be reinforced through their activities targeted to the COO.[8] Yossi Shain argues that diasporas can both "humanize" and "Americanize" US foreign policy, combating isolationist tendencies and reflecting American values of freedom and democracy.[9] Diasporans may come to share civic and other values of the country of residence (COR), learned through exposure and/or social pressure or consciously sought. US-based diasporas, in particular, are believed to embrace American values of pluralism, democracy, and human rights (though this assumption does not hold across or within all diasporas). Transnational political activism may be targeted to recreating in the COO "the discourses and institutional practices of probity and respect for civil rights learned in the United States."[10] From an instrumental perspective, Shain argues that diasporans' influence on COR foreign policy will be most effective when it corresponds with COR national interest and values.[11] Diasporans may use the language of liberal values to influence international public opinion and build political support for their agendas.

This is not to imply that diasporans completely replace their cultural values with those of the COR. The diaspora experience yields a hybrid identity, combining elements of identity and experience from both the COO and the COR.[12] The maintenance of cultural affinity and shared values with the COO may, in fact, yield additional advantages to the emergence and success of diaspora entrepreneurs, particularly with respect to institutional reform.

Avner Greif argues that potential institutional elements (rules, beliefs, norms, and organizations) only become actual institutions when individuals are motivated to follow them.[13] The hybrid identities that diasporas represent may serve to inform creative combinations of old and new institutional elements, perhaps even packaging completely new institutions in language and values that correspond to cognitive beliefs consistent with existing norms. With their visceral understanding of targeted groups' identity, experience, and possibly even fears related to proposed changes, diasporans may be particularly suited to act as role models and introducers of institutional reforms.

Beyond the Politics of "Good Governance"

Political reform can incorporate policy change as well as changes in the practice of governance and administration. Can diasporans help to introduce responsive and efficient governance? And, specifically, can they help to rebuild governance capacity in postconflict countries? Since diaspora political activists tend to be among the more educated elite of their immigrant communities, they may have much to contribute to rebuilding governments in terms of expertise and possibly professional networks.[14] Governance and administrative systems are a particularly salient concern in war-torn societies as they are both part of the problem— due to their absence, insufficiency, or capture—and part of the solution, in their centrality to the viability of the state.[15] The good governance agenda, or more specifically calls to end corruption and patronage, are frequently used in the political efforts of diasporans seeking political reform in their COOs. The rhetoric resonates strongly with the international community and, as Shain argues, enhances these reformers' ability to influence international interventions.[16] But beyond the politics of the rhetoric, can diasporans contribute to rebuilding governance in fragile and postconflict states?

Broadly construed, good governance can be seen as incorporating and integrating three related components: effectiveness (administrative-economic governance), legitimacy (political governance), and security (security governance).[17] Rebuilding government is perhaps the greatest challenge and a precursor to the provision of these three governance components. The civil service is "the main agent delivering the state's obligations to the citizenry and encouraging the latter to accord legitimacy to the state."[18] Yet recruitment for civil service is no less politicized than the distribution of political office. For example, diasporans' experience in the Palestinian Authority has often been ineffectual; a RAND Corporation report credits this to the "overtly politicized and personalized decisionmaking process."[19] These processes tend to be characterized by cronyism on the one hand and threats and intimidation on the other.[20] The result may often be an oversized civil service, which nevertheless lacks capacity to make good on the provision of good governance.[21]

Despite immediate needs, a sole emphasis on effectiveness can impede the sustainability of governance systems, which require security and legitimacy as well. On the one hand, citizens may withdraw government support if immediate needs and longer-term material interests are not adequately addressed, either through lack of capacity, insufficient political will, or corruption. On the other hand, regardless of service delivery performance, the legitimacy challenge is exacerbated by continuing rivalries among social groups that were party to the conflict, particularly when there are strongly perceived "winners" and "losers," with the "losers" perceiving the winners as having captured the spoils of government. Parties to conflict, as well as international intervenors, often must strike a devil's bargain, where political representation and deal-making trumps the needs for effective government and public administration and a functioning economy.[22]

The participation of diasporans can complicate these fragile bargains and balances. Diaspora participation may be essential for the expertise that is needed but may also pose challenges to security and legitimacy. Beyond their participation in the patronage systems and power competitions alluded to above, even well-intentioned diaspora returnees may create or encounter returnee-specific challenges to their good-governance efforts. My review of migrant return and knowledge exchange programs identifies several challenges resulting from diaspora repatriation for rebuilding governments.[23] First, diaspora return may result in the emergence of a new political elite, which can give rise to new political tensions.[24] Those who do return may face resentment and blatant hostility for having escaped the worst of the conflict.[25] Depending on the length of their separation from the COO, they may be more or less effective at navigating political and cultural systems and reading associated cues. Their perceived relationship to the COO may even inspire a hubris that is not representative of the accuracy of their local knowledge.

Diasporas and Postconflict Governments

Following are two illustrations of diaspora efforts to contribute to postconflict government reconstruction. Both illustrations represent the elite of the diaspora and stated goals consistent with liberal values (for example, human rights, basic freedoms) endorsed and promoted by the international community. Each illustration begins with a brief review of the conflict setting.

Djimé Adoum in Chad

Chad's civil war first erupted in 1965, and in 1979 rebels managed to secure the capital and declare victory.[26] However, fighting among the rebel commanders (and perhaps the brutality and corruption of the established regime) eventually led to a coup d'état in 1990 spearheaded by Idriss Déby, who has remained president ever since (despite several coup attempts). President Déby legalized opposition parties in 1992. However, in 2005, he amended the constitution, consolidating central power and removing presidential term limits. He was legally reelected in 2006, though the opposition boycotted the election in protest of the constitutional amendments. Competing warlords and coup attempts (e.g., in February 2008 and most recently May 2013) continued to plague Chad.

Several efforts sought an end to these conflicts. An internal political accord was reached on August 13, 2007, aimed at reinforcing the democratic process in Chad. Approximately ninety-five political parties signed the accord, which called for a free and fair electoral process (including an electoral census, registration improvements, and an independent electoral commission), as well as a "suitable climate" for elections (for example, depoliticization and demilitarization of administration, freedom of speech, and an independent judiciary).[27] Civil society organizations and the armed opposition did not participate in these negotiations, and civil society leaders considered the August 13 agreement a failure to address the roots of the crisis and a strategy for avoiding a global dialogue.[28] In 2010, new elections were held and key opposition leaders were incorporated into the government.

Meantime, Chad remains one of the poorest and most corrupt countries in the world. It retains an "alert" status as a failed state (ranked fourth in 2012 by the Fund for Peace) and scores two out of ten on the Corruptions Perceptions Index 2011.[29]

Good Governance Reformer

Djimé Adoum is the son of an uneducated farmer and community leader in Chad. He was the first of his family to receive any education outside of the local madrassa. With his marriage to an American, he came to the United States and had the opportunity to continue his formal education, which culminated in a PhD in agricultural economics. After extensive related international consulting in Chad and elsewhere in Africa, he joined the US Department of Agriculture working in agricultural extension.

Adoum began his diaspora engagement with Chad as an advocate and activist for an inclusive peace process—including effective engagement of rebel groups in the political process—in order to ensure the sustainability of peace agreements. He started with a blog, widely read by the Chadian diaspora and within Chad, which sought to provide objective analysis of the events unfolding and options for peaceful resolution. He had already cofounded the Mid-Atlantic Chadian Association, a cultural organization. He spun off a contingent of those members who were interested in engaging more politically, creating GRANIT (Groupe de Réflexions et d'Analyses d'Intérêts Tchadiens) to advocate for peace and good governance in Chad. He then partnered with a nongovernmental organization (NGO), Caring for Kaela, to provide technical analysis of the Chadian situation and policy recommendations to international actors, such as the European Union (EU), US president Barack Obama's administration, and the United Nations (UN). He also participated in a high-level multistakeholder consultation with UN delegates and other government representatives.[30]

When the rebellion was weakened in 2010, Adoum was asked to join the Déby government as a technical expert (applying his PhD training), first as technical adviser on rural development and then as minister of agriculture and irrigation. The following describes Adoum's efforts to work, from inside the government, for good governance and sustainable development in Chad. During his tenure as technical adviser (eighteen months) and later as minister (eighteen months), Adoum introduced both technical agricultural innovations and good-governance reforms.

Adoum views his technical work as a pathway to promoting good governance with broad reach. By improving people's lives—and for the majority of people in Chad—Adoum hoped to give people a greater stake in peace. Adoum's good-governance contributions included empowering farmers through participatory processes, ensuring Chad owned its own development process while still working effectively with donors, speaking truth to power, and introducing accountability into management systems.

Participation and Empowerment

Adoum was the only presidential technical adviser to date to visit the field and, he claims, the only minister to do so. He brought his staff along and, together, they experienced the potential impact of their work, as producers delighted in the attention they received and perceived new hope for the future. In 2012, he described bringing fifty of his staff to the field to talk to local farmers, listen to their problems, and generate trust that they would return with solutions. The farmers reported never having seen such a thing.

Donors recognized his mission, describing Adoum as "someone who is trying to show that the population should own their own development."[31] Observers from the donor community marveled at his ability to connect with different audiences and stakeholder groups. As one put it, "he has an incredible ability to charm the public."[32]

As minister, to plan more strategically, Adoum organized a national forum: "I brought in a thousand people—the producers, government, technical folks from the different regions—and we talked for four days." He planned to use the output from those discussions "to design a new road map," which was finalized and approved a few months after Adoum left the ministry. He describes it as "a codebook basically, with the strategic framework, as well as programs, projects, activities that need to be undertaken."[33] The framework was the culmination of a massive participatory process, followed by significant technical input from the ministry, donors (notably the Food and Agriculture Organization [FAO]), and hired consultants. In addition to technical outcomes for the national planning, Adoum suggests regional participants were empowered in thinking about their own development and resilience: "Every delegation went away with at a minimum something much clearer, crisper" than what they came with. Farmer representatives confirm that the forum "allowed us to express ourselves," and, as of 2013, the results represented well their concerns.[34]

Donor Relations

Subsequent work mapped the priorities on a timeline, with performance indicators and a budget. This required close cooperation with the donor community, notably the FAO. Beyond "amicable relations," Adoum worked in partnership with donors, listening and gaining their expertise, while also educating the donors on the needs and constraints of the country.[35] As one FAO representative reported, during this process Adoum was "sending people from different divisions and departments of the government to participate and to analyze and defend the position so that we could see exactly why they have chosen this priority versus the other one, and take into account all the realities of the country."[36] Similar interactions led to project renewals, increased funding, and the return of some donors. He was instrumental in negotiating a project renewal with the EU for an early warning system and at twice the budget of its predecessor.[37]

He reinvigorated relations with donors to ensure they worked in partnership to maximize all resources available through coordinated efforts. He believes he inspired in them a belief that change was possible.[38] Before he began his role as technical adviser, there was no effective interface between donors and the government concerning agriculture investments. As minister, he brought donors with him to meet and discuss program options directly with the president.[39] Donors recognized that "he was bringing [donors] to have the space where they could express themselves, where they can present their plans. So he was not someone imposing what has to be done, but he was listening a lot and taking advantage of what you tell him to suggest now his own opinion."[40] Another donor reported that when Adoum was named minister, the international community celebrated.[41] That both the FAO and the UN Development Programme tried to hire him in some capacity following his tenure as minister is testament to his good relations with donors and the confidence they had in him technically, morally, and in terms of getting things done.

Speaking Truth to Power

According to Adoum, "I am in the business of telling." With other government officials—starting with President Déby himself, his staff, donors, and local farmers—Adoum stressed, no "business as usual" and "no more talk—we need action."[42] Donors, particularly, admired his straightforwardness with the government: "When he had an opinion to give to the government in this country, he was not hesitating. He was mentioning what could be the priority if you want to develop agriculture in the country and also to develop the livelihoods and the resilience of the communities."[43] Farmer representatives confirm his frankness as part of what made him an "extraordinary minister."[44]

Upon his arrival in the ministry, he sought to clean up shop to the extent he could and to establish a professional bureaucracy. He promptly fired people because he could see "these guys are not going to help me get anywhere. So I sent a decree to the president to sign it and I said, 'These guys are out.'"[45] Feeling the pressure to accomplish as much as he could during his short tenure, he wanted to have the most technically qualified staff.[46] He succeeded in hiring in top positions four professionals with technical credentials in agriculture. Adoum knew he could not rid the ministry of corruption in a mere three years (let alone eighteen months), but he reported that "people felt the heat from me."[47] Adoum introduced the integration of performance budgeting, insisting on project proposals with performance indicators and review. He even told the producers, "We're going to be investing this much money. You should see these results."[48]

Resistance

According to a donor observer, "when [Adoum] became minister of agriculture, [within] the ministry . . . I think everyone was against it."[49] Resistance derived both from the presidential appointment process, which lacks transparency, and notably because "he's seen as a foreigner. And the way, his openness, his frankness, his transparency, etcetera, was not very well appreciated by the staff, who had another way of working."[50] Adoum seemed to recognize this as he stated, "I was the minister, the lone camper."[51]

Adoum encountered resistance to all of the governance changes he tried to introduce. Starting with the participatory planning process, Adoum indicated that "it created some hard feelings. Because some people, they are not used to these kinds of things."[52] He encountered perceptions that "'it's so huge,' and 'oh, it's not going to work.'" He was direct and immediate in his response, telling the resisters: "Those of you who want to stay in the kitchen, it's going to be very hot. But if you can sustain [in] the heat keep in, and if you can't sustain [in] the heat you're out. And whether you are part of it or not part of it, it will happen. And so I'd rather you be a part of it, because when it happens you can say 'I was there. I contributed to it.'" When some of his staff threatened to withhold what they deemed a necessary input, Adoum did the work himself. Perhaps as an understatement, he concludes, "So we ruffled a lot of feathers." He added, "Then I used transparency. They're used to doing a few things, and if they find they don't want to, then nobody is being held accountable. I said, 'No. This time it has to be up to standard. If somebody looks at it, then they have to say procedurally it's good.'"

Naturally, he heard complaints when he fired senior staff upon his arrival at the ministry. "Around town," he said he knew people were saying, "He doesn't understand" how things work.[53] There was every expectation that he would hire family members or at least those from his same ethnoreligious background. Instead he hired the most qualified available people, none of whom, it turns out, shared that background.

Beyond elites, Chadians generally perceive diasporans as having escaped the struggle and its consequences. Some local civil social leaders sometimes resented Adoum's external advocacy and felt betrayed when he joined the government. On the other hand, direct beneficiaries of his work as technical adviser and later as minister viewed him—including his diaspora origins—favorably. The president of the National Council for the Rural Producers of Chad, speaking on behalf of local farmers, for example, reported Adoum's diaspora identity "was good because he was proactive. . . . He was practical. That's what we loved. . . . It was this behavior that we wanted. This is the behavior of the United States, this way of doing things that interests us very much."[54]

Resistance was potent enough to lead to his premature departure from the Ministry of Agriculture and Irrigation. Whether that decision came directly from President Déby or due to pressure from other stakeholders is unknowable. Adoum hypothesizes that he might have made other ministers look bad: "I don't know whether the politicians looked around and said, 'Well, this guy is running his mouth, he's in the field. Oh, he's making the rest of us look bad. So maybe get him out of here." Referring to his televised visits to the field, he adds, "And any time you look at the national TV, I'm [there] wearing my sombrero."[55] On the other hand, it may be that his tenure lasted longer than many ministers, especially strong ones. There is very high turnover within the government, particularly among high-performing or popular ministers.[56] Two months prior to the announcement, he sensed the decision would be taken "because I shook up the establishment. I went against people's established procedures . . . putting brakes on too many things."[57] This extended to his unwillingness to cooperate in patronage exchanges that included blatant corruption: "People in town were saying, 'Gee. This guy, he doesn't take anything. He doesn't facilitate anything. He doesn't understand the system.'"

ANACOZA in Zaire

The Zairean diaspora in the 1990s was no different from any other diaspora and shared many characteristics with other diasporas from COOs considered "failed" or "fragile" states. Worldwide, diasporans from Zaire came together on the Internet through Listservs and discussion groups to commiserate on the fate of their COO and to reflect on current politics and future prospects. One group in particular prided itself on its expertise in a variety of fields and emerged from cyberspace to discuss concrete proposals for then-Zaire's future. ANACOZA was incorporated as a nonprofit organization in the US state of Michigan on October 14, 1996, with the following purposes:

- To strengthen, encourage, and promote close relationships among Zairians and friends of Zaire;
- To monitor, disseminate, and advocate Zairian issues;

- To foster and encourage democracy in Zaire; and
- To rebuild Zairian democracy.[58]

According to one member, the less formally explicit aim of the group was "to kick [President] Mobutu [Sese Seko] out of power."[59] In three years, the nonprofit would be dissolved, with members divided—some disappointed and some profiting from newfound power and prestige.

Membership largely comprised Western-educated professionals in a variety of fields. Primary activities included a series of academic conferences, beginning in 1994, where members presented research reports and proposals related to the development (economic, social, and political) of Zaire. ANACOZA is credited with helping to convince the international community to shift its support from Mobutu to Laurent Kabila's "rebellion."[60] Its influence extended to how the war was portrayed in the international media, for example, using letter campaigns and other lobbying efforts.[61] ANACOZA member André Kapanga confirmed, "It was a strategy of ours to make [Kabila] acceptable to the American public."[62]

The question of who initiated contact between ANACOZA and Kabila remains murky. Some report that Kabila, from the bush near Goma, got wind of the group and understood it to have access to both political channels and money.[63] Others report that ANACOZA members, surprised at Kabila's rapid succession of victories over Mobutu's forces, decided to dispatch several members to investigate firsthand.[64] In any event, a meeting did take place in Goma, December 26–29, 1996, wherein the ANACOZA representatives declared their support on behalf of the organization. At this time, Mwana Mawapanga and Mwenze Kongolo offered their advisory services in finance and justice, respectively.[65] Indeed, Mawapanga, with a PhD in economics from Pennsylvania State University and formerly a lecturer on agriculture economics at the University of Kentucky, was to become Kabila's finance minister, and Kongolo, onetime president of ANACOZA, just shy of his law degree, and working for the Pennsylvania attorney general's office, was to become his minister of the interior.

The remaining history is well known. Kabila did garner support from the international community (or at least noninterference). ANACOZA members met, for example, with the US State Department in January 1996. According to transcripts from the meeting, they thanked the State Department for interfering with France's intention to intervene and shared impressions of Kabila from their visit in the bush, highlighting the local support they claimed he was already enjoying there.[66] International funding and support was attributed to the efforts of ANACOZA. On May 20, 1997, Kabila proclaimed himself president of the DRC and assumed its presidency in Kinshasa.

Kabila swooped into power long before he would have been able to consider government formation, which would be problematic in any case given the size, complexity, and history of Zaire. His most immediate challenge was finding talented administrators who had both technical expertise to run specific ministries and the ability to manage them. Kabila's first cabinet, announced July 1, 1997, largely comprised returnees from the diaspora. But diaspora members were viewed as high on idealism and lacking in experience or ability.[67] Overall the cabinet "represented a bewildering array of personal and professional experiences which precluded any possible idea of teamwork."[68] Five members of ANACOZA found a home in Kabila's new government. In addition to Nanga, minister of Finance (and later Agriculture), and Mwenze Kongolo, Minister of Interior (and later Justice), ANACOZA members took prime positions in diplomacy—Faida Mitifu, DRC Ambassador to the US, and André Kapanga (former professor at Illinois State University, teaching French as well as diplomacy and African politics) became ambassador to the UN.

Despite skepticism about Kabila, hopes from the diaspora were high but cautious. Many were interested in returning, whether to make temporary contributions or stay for the long term.[69] On May 23, 1997, ANACOZA dispatched a seven-member delegation to meet with the newly appointed government—which included some of their own members—"to assess the ideas the new government has about democracy and rebuilding the country to see what it can offer."[70] In an effort to unify the diaspora, one member of CongoOnline, an online discussion group, cited Kabila's appointment of ANACOZA's members to cabinet positions—experts who could actually contribute to governing—as a sign that Kabila was "not an enemy of the people."[71]

Following Kabila's inauguration and the installation of several of his ANACOZA colleagues in the government, one ANACOZA activist visited the newly labeled DRC and visited his old friend Mwana Mawapanga Nanga, now the minister of finance, telling him, "By the way we expect something big from you guys because remember our goal was to make sure we develop this society."[72] As recounted, Nanga responded, "Theory, theory! Theory and the practice don't go together!" It was then reported that Nanga purchased two houses in Kentucky—well beyond the means of his formal government salary.[73] By 2003, several members of Kabila's cabinet, including members of ANACOZA (notably Kongolo and Nanga) were named in a UN report as officials suspected of plundering Congo's gold and mineral wealth.[74] Nanga was later vindicated and rejoined a subsequent DRC government as ambassador to Zimbabwe.[75]

Not all of the former ANACOZA members succumbed to the temptations and systems in place in the DRC. Perhaps it is telling that the two members who were appointed to external-relations posts—and therefore not physically immersed in the pressures and access to resources—seem to have maintained their original intentions.

From Transnational to National: Diasporans and Postconflict Government Service

The two examples illustrate complex transnationalism, with the actors influencing both diplomatic and governance processes by invitation of states (or other political elites) and with subsequent reliance of these states on their expertise. Specifically, they illustrate the transnationalism of diaspora political activists and how they can transition from nonstate actors to state actors, becoming government officials. From their bases in the United States, these actors engaged on behalf of their COOs, leveraging resources and relationships in the US and with the international community, with some of them eventually acting directly within the COO to influence government policy and practice. They represent a range of organizational approaches, interacting with diverse political/diplomatic actors (including other transnational actors) and drawing heavily from information technology, when possible, to further their communications, with potentially profound but equally potentially marginal impacts on conflict and peace.

Organization

Both efforts began with a loose affiliation of like-minded diasporans gathering online to exchange ideas about the future of their COOs. From these initial exchanges emerged more formally organized efforts, such as the conferences and eventual nonprofit incorporation of ANACOZA and several organizing attempts in the Chadian diaspora, including GRANIT. Eventually the import of these organizations came to matter less than the individuals who were leading them. Indeed, it is possible that the organizations served only to create a perception of wider legitimacy and representation from the diaspora than these individuals commanded. Such perceptions were likely instrumental in the advocacy stage of these diaspora efforts. They may have paved the way for official meetings with the diplomatic community, for example. This was likely the case for ANACOZA's meetings with the State Department and for the reception of Caring for Kaela's and Adoum's policy recommendations and his participation in the high-level multistakeholder consultation. Ultimately the most significant impacts came not through these organized efforts but through the contributions (both positive and negative) of individual members.

A key finding, then, is that the organizational form of this transnational actor is dynamic and may shift with actors' agendas and their perceived need for the credibility that may come from being part of a larger effort. It is possible that the most potent individuals could have negotiated their positions as state actors in the COO without these organized efforts, depending on their personal networks and connections to COO-based patronage systems. However, international audiences are less credulous when it comes to individual "strongmen," Ahmed Chalabi notwithstanding.[76] Another possibility is that these more ambitious individuals may have become frustrated with or have come to doubt the efficacy of the organized efforts they initiated.

Interaction with Other Actors

The boomerang effect acknowledges diasporans' instrumentality for state elites.[77] However, the tendency is to focus only on diasporans' usefulness for regime change, not for postconflict reconstruction. In the latter sense, diasporan political reformers may be particularly instrumental for the international community in its efforts to rebuild responsive, democratic governments. Both cases illustrate the boomerang effect, though in different ways. Adoum could engage in analytics and dissemination of alternative perspectives that could not be as easily stated and promoted from within Chad, yet they were popular in both Chad and the diaspora. ANACOZA became a boomerang not for government but for a rebel group. The instrumental relationship was not one of state-centricity since the object was to depose the existing state.

The diaspora political reformers combined external and internal status and affiliations.[78] Both Adoum and ANACOZA demonstrate diasporas' use of mediating actors such as host country governments and international bodies.[79] With support from Caring for Kaela, Adoum in particular strategically engaged with a broad range of international policymakers, from US officials to the UN and the EU. In doing so, he called for peace, good governance, and democracy for Chad. Similarly, ANACOZA is credited with securing international support for Kabila. Following Shain's findings, ANACOZA members appealed to US values in meeting with the US State Department, stressing Kabila's responsiveness to the local people as justification for supporting his ascendancy.[80] These diasporans engaged external actors intensively to potentially shift power balances in the COO political regimes.

Beyond their advocacy and diplomatic engagement, diaspora political reformers may also work with other credible actors, some of whom may also be transnational. ANACOZA engaged highly credible governance and development scholars in its conferences, such as Michael Bratton (professor of political science, Michigan State University), as well as representatives of think tanks (for example, the Carnegie Endowment for International Peace) and lobbying firms. Adoum's most important partnership was with Caring for Kaela, an international development NGO.

Communications

These transnational actors utilized the best available technology to further their emergence and impact. Both groups began with blogs, which increasingly welcomed more interactive components. ANACOZA predates Adoum's efforts, with respective communication technologies varying accordingly. ANACOZA relied on a satellite phone to make initial contact with Kabila in the bush and a letter campaign for its lobbying efforts. Some of ANACOZA's online discussion forums are still searchable today. While member-based, they were not protected in the long run from more public viewing, perhaps because they emerged on rudimentary platforms instead of the more formal corporate sources, such as Yahoo. If ANACOZA were active today, it is likely that, as Adoum did during his tenure in Chad, it would organize and disseminate its activities through Facebook or whatever might be the latest popular media forum. Elements of both cases are also reported in online media interviews and diaspora-specific journals and news sources.

Surely much of the most pertinent information is lost due to its temporal and/or individual nature. No doubt a lot of strategizing still occurred face to face (as, for example, a strategic planning meeting I observed between Adoum, members of GRANIT, and Caring for Kaela) and through individual e-mails.

Influence on Conflict/Peace

The illustrations demonstrate diasporan political reformers' potential ingenuity in pursuing political and socioeconomic objectives. However, this ingenuity can be applied for better or for worse outcomes in the COO, and the tendency among policymakers is to exclusively assume one or the other. Objectives may differ among these diaspora political reformers, their ultimate objectives may not always be transparent, and it is possible that they are unknowable to the diasporans themselves. Some may engage in an exploratory way without initially knowing the specifics of what they seek. New opportunities—and temptations—may emerge that cause them to modify these agendas. Certainly Adoum could not have envisioned a weakening of the rebellion that would lead to his joining the Déby government, just as ANACOZA members might not have actually believed Kabila would be effective in overthrowing Mobutu and that they might one day be members of a post-Mobutu government.

Looking at the whole of these experiences to date, we see diasporans' potential to contribute to regime change and possibly government reconstruction or to sustain poor governance, laying the groundwork for failed governance and renewed conflict. Diasporans are potential partners, not necessarily or solely initiators, to those contesting power in the COO and, like members of any international organization, they may be duped by those soliciting their support. They can also be transformed in the process, seduced by the power they gain through their promotion of political reforms. In either of these cases, diasporans' potential to lend their expertise to rebuilding government will be quite limited. ANACOZA provides a cautionary tale for these possibilities.

The Chadian case, on the other hand, suggests diasporas' potential for promoting peace and good governance without resorting to war, though perhaps with reduced challenges to existing power relations in the COO. If Adoum was able to embed good governance in the roots of administration, with vines throughout the country, perhaps he will have a demonstration effect for others in government. And by providing rural populations a stake in stability and hope for the future, perhaps these efforts will deter future rebellions. That said, the likelihood of lasting impact is doubtful; given the patronage politics, the systems he introduced are more likely to revert to the pre-Adoum status quo.

Adoum's example does not negate the existence of conflict-promoting and more explicit power-seeking diaspora agendas as ANACOZA demonstrates. However, encompassing this more complete range of diaspora intentions and actions into our understanding of transnationalism is reasonable and timely.

Implications for Understanding Transnationalism

These diasporan political reformer illustrations at once confirm some aspects of our understanding of transnationalism and challenge us to consider the more nuanced potentialities and dynamism of potentially all transnational actors. First, these nonstate actors hold the potential to contribute constructively to peace or to perpetuate conflict. Sometimes the precise outcomes may be unintentional. This truism likely applies to a much broader array of transnational actors. It is a known aspect of transnationalism generally, yet too often scholars and policymakers may have a tendency to categorize particular actors as either potentially constructive or not. Transnational actors represent particular interests within a system of interest groups. Their perceived intentions, potential for efficacy, and interpretations of their ultimate impacts will vary according to different actors' positions and agendas.

Transnational actors include individual agents, as Ariel Ahram and John Gledhill make clear in their comparative analysis of Ayatollah Ruhollah Khomeini and Osama bin Laden in chapter 5 of this volume. While foreign fighters appear to be less privileged than states and nongovernmental organizations (David Malet, chapter 6), leaders of transnational movements can emerge from among those seeking political change (by force or otherwise) in their countries of origin. Individuals matter, and they may act decisively and independently. While it may seem obvious, the literature seems to privilege organized groups, without sufficiently examining the changing interface between individuals (and the groups that they organize or from which they emerge) and related activist agendas.

Transnational actors are at once agents in their own right and potential instruments of state actors (through the boomerang effect) and of other transnational actors, including international organizations and member states. These diasporan transnational actors both asserted themselves as nonstate diplomats of a sort and were engaged by state (and international) diplomats. Blogs, conferences, and Listservs mobilized actors for transnational advocacy, and these became recognized by actors in target countries who incorporated the emerging ideas into their own political agendas. Transnational actors can also become instruments of other nonstate transnational actors, such as NGOs. Furthermore, the individual-group dynamic suggests that transnational actors can become instruments of members of their own groupings.

Perhaps most important, the transnational phenomenon is a dynamic one and in many different respects. Stated and even intentional agendas are dynamic, shifting with changing circumstances and perceived incentives and opportunities. Transnational actors can move between state and nonstate arenas, sometimes transitioning, themselves, to becoming state actors. This dynamic poses a particular challenge to theorizing about transnationalism. When transnational actors are no longer physically transnational, having returned to and committed primarily to one country, are they still transnational? The psychology of these actors may offer one way for assessing continued transnationalism. Do the actors continue to embody a transnational or hybrid identity? Are they treated or perceived by locals as being outsiders? The illustrations confirm the dynamism of diaspora and transnational engagement, which complicate definitions and make outcomes very difficult to predict.

Finally, this and other chapters in this volume reveal how significant transnational actors have become for state governance. Diaspora political activists, combined with analyses of other transnational actors in this volume, confirm that transnational actors can contribute significantly to the three components of governance. In the examples reviewed here, diaspora political activists provided significant expert advice and subsequent applied expertise to support government effectiveness. David Malet (chapter 6) and Matthew LeRiche (chapter 7) illustrate how political actors, including governments, seek support for security from transnational actors—foreign fighters and private security professionals, respectively. Phil Orchard (chapter 8) reveals a more broadly understood governance contribution of transnational actors: helping states to access legitimacy, a relatively common feature of humanitarian assistance. In reviewing the evolution of transnationalism, this is a significant development. Common perceptions relegate transnational actors largely to nonstate arenas, primarily in advocacy roles. With these examples, we see that transnational actors are beginning to significantly and directly influence and even assume responsibility for core government functions.

Notes

1. For a review of the literature and practice related to diasporans' engagement in peace and conflict, see Jennifer M. Brinkerhoff, *Digital Diasporas: Identity and Transnational Engagement* (New York: Cambridge University Press, 2009).

2. Fiona Adamson and Madeleine Demetriou, "Remapping the Boundaries of 'State' and 'National Identity': Incorporating Diasporas into IR Theorizing," *European Journal of International Relations* 13, no. 4 (2007): 489–526.

3. Margaret Keck and Katherine Sikkink, *Activists beyond Borders: Transnational Advocacy Networks in International Politics* (Ithaca, NY: Cornell University Press, 1998).

4. Douglass C. North, John Joseph Wallis, and Barry R. Weingast, "Violence and the Rise of Open-Access Orders," *Journal of Democracy* 20, no. 1 (January 2009): 55–68.

5. See Markus Perkmann and Andre Spicer, "'Healing the Scars of History': Projects, Skills and Field Strategies in Institutional Entrepreneurship," *Organization Studies* 28, no. 7 (July 2007): 1101–22.

6. For a more extensive discussion of these advantages, see Jennifer M. Brinkerhoff, *Institutional Reform and Diaspora Entrepreneurs: The In-Between Advantage* (New York: Oxford University Press, 2016).

7. Everett Einar Hagen, *On the Theory of Social Change: How Economic Growth Begins* (Homewood, IL: Dorsey Press, 1962); Christos Kalantaridis, *Understanding the Entrepreneur: An Institutionalist Perspective* (Aldershot, UK: Ashgate, 2004), 55.

8. See, for example, Brinkerhoff, *Digital Diasporas*.

9. Yossi Shain, "Multicultural Foreign Policy," *Foreign Policy* 100 (Fall 1995): 69–88; Yossi Shain, *Marketing the American Creed Abroad: Diasporas in the U.S. and Their Homelands* (Cambridge, UK: Cambridge University Press, 1999).

10. Luis Edwardo Guarnizo, Alejandro Portes, and William Haller, "Assimilation and Transnationalism: Determinants of Transnational Political Action among Contemporary Migrants," *American Journal of Sociology* 108, no. 6 (May 2003): 1239.

11. Shain, *Marketing the American Creed*.

12. See, for example, Brinkerhoff, *Digital Diasporas*.

13. Avner Greif, *Institutions and the Path to the Modern Economy: Lessons from Medieval Trade* (New York: Cambridge University Press, 2006).

14. Guarnizo, Portes, and Haller, "Assimilation and Transnationalism."

15. Jennifer M. Brinkerhoff and Derick W. Brinkerhoff, "Governance Reforms and Failed States: Challenges and Implications," *International Review of Administrative Sciences* 68, no. 4 (December 2002): 511–31.

16. Shain, *Marketing the American Creed*.

17. Derick W. Brinkerhoff, "Governance Challenges in Fragile States: Re-Establishing Security, Rebuilding Effectiveness, and Reconstituting Legitimacy," in *Governance in Post-Conflict Societies: Rebuilding Fragile States*, ed. Derick W. Brinkerhoff (Oxford, UK: Routledge, 2007), 185–203.

18. Harry Blair, "Rebuilding and Reforming Civil Services in Post-Conflict Societies," in Brinkerhoff, *Governance in Post-Conflict Societies*, 161.

19. RAND Palestinian State Study Team, *Building a Successful Palestinian State* (Santa Monica, CA: RAND Corp., 2005), 28.

20. See, for example, Sarah Lister and Andrew Wilder, "Subnational Administration and State Building: Lessons from Afghanistan," in Brinkerhoff, *Governance in Post-Conflict Societies*, 241–57.

21. For the Kosovo case, see Jose Luis Herrero, "Building State Institutions," in *Postconflict Development: Meeting New Challenges*, ed. Gerd Junne and Willemijn Verkoren (Boulder, CO: Lynne Reinner Publishers, 2005), 43–58.

22. See, for example, Herrero, "Building State Institutions."

23. This chapter focuses on diaspora return independent from donor sponsorship. Jennifer M. Brinkerhoff, "Exploring the Role of Diasporas in Rebuilding Governance in Post-Conflict Societies," in *Africa's Finances: The Contribution of Remittances*, ed. Raj Bardouille, Muna Ndulo, and Margaret Grieco (Newcastle upon Tyne, UK: Cambridge Scholars Publishing, 2008), 239–62, provides a more extensive review of lessons from internationally supported return programs.

24. Simon Chesterman, Michael Ignatieff, and Ramesh Thakur, *Making States Work: From State Failure to State-Building* (New York: International Peace Academy and United Nations University, July 2004).

25. See, for example, International Organization for Migration, *World Migration 2005: Costs and Benefits of International Migration* (Geneva: Author, 2005).

26. This discussion of the Adoum case draws from Brinkerhoff, *Institutional Reform and Diaspora Entrepreneurs*.

27. Chrysantus Ayangafac, "Resolving the Chadian Political Epilepsy: An Assessment of Intervention Efforts," *Institute for Security Studies Situation Report* (Tshwane [Pretoria], South Africa, June 1, 2009), 10.

28. Gilbert Maoundonodji, remarks on roundtable "Resolving Chad's Political Crisis: A Role for Civil Society?," *Association for the Promotion of Fundamental Liberties in Chad* (Washington, DC: United States Institute of Peace, September 1, 2009).

29. Fund for Peace, *The Failed State Index* (Washington, DC: Fund for Peace, 2012); Transparency International, "Corruption Perceptions Index," Transparency International Web page, http://www.transparency.org/policy_research/surveys_indices/cpi.

30. See Sarah Bessell and Kelly Campbell, "Toward Resolving Chad's Interlocking Conflicts," USIPeace Briefing, United States Institute of Peace, Washington, DC, December 2008.

31. Marc Abdala (senior emergency and rehabilitation coordinator, Food and Agriculture Organization, N'Djamena, Chad), interview by Jennifer M. Brinkerhoff, May 14, 2013.

32. Madeleine Onclin (former adviser and section head for rural development, EU delegation to Chad), interview by Jennifer M. Brinkerhoff, May 16, 2013.

33. Djimé Adoum, interview by Jennifer M. Brinkerhoff, February 25, 2012.

34. Kolyang Palebele (president, National Council for the Rural Producers of Chad), interview by Jennifer M. Brinkerhoff, May 21, 2013.

35. Onclin, interview by Brinkerhoff, May 16, 2013.

36. Abdala, interview by Brinkerhoff, May 14, 2013.

37. Adoum, interview by Jennifer M. Brinkerhoff, May 13, 2013; Onclin, interview by Brinkerhoff, May 16, 2013.

38. Adoum, interview by Brinkerhoff, February 25, 2012.

39. Ibid.

40. Abdala, interview by Brinkerhoff, May 14, 2013.

41. Onclin, interview by Brinkerhoff, May 16, 2013.

42. Adoum, interview by Brinkerhoff, May 13, 2013.

43. Abdala, interview by Brinkerhoff, May 14, 2013.

44. Palebele, interview by Brinkerhoff, May 21, 2013.

45. Adoum, interview by Brinkerhoff, May 13, 2013.

46. Ministers are appointed for three-year terms, though few serve this long.

47. Adoum, interview by Brinkerhoff, May 13, 2013.

48. Adoum, interview by Brinkerhoff, February 24, 2012.

49. Onclin, interview by Brinkerhoff, May 16, 2013.

50. Ibid.

51. Adoum, interview by Brinkerhoff, May 13, 2013.

52. Ibid.

53. Ibid.

54. Palebele, interview by Brinkerhoff, May 21, 2013.

55. Adoum, interview by Brinkerhoff, May 13, 2013.

56. See, for example, Onclin, interview by Brinkerhoff, May 16, 2013.

57. Adoum, interview by Brinkerhoff, May 13, 2013.

58. ANACOZA Articles of Incorporation, Michigan Department of Commerce, East Lansing, October 14, 1996.

59. Emizet Kisangani, discussant remarks for the panel "Diasporas, Business and Post-Conflict Development," Conference on Helping Failed States Recover: The Role of Business in Promoting Stability and Development, University of Kansas Center for International Business Education and Research, Lawrence, KS, April 4–6, 2007.

60. Tatiana Carayannis, "The Complex Wars of the Congo: Towards a New Analytic Approach," *Journal of Asian and African Studies*, 38, nos. 2–3 (2003): 239.

61. Ibid., 240.

62. Quoted in Hugh Dellios and Lisa Anderson, "Front Man for a Strong Man: In Representing the Former Zaire, an Illinois State Professor Crosses the Cultural Boundary between Democracy and Dictatorship," *Chicago Tribune*, June 24, 1998.

63. For example, see Kisangani, discussant remarks for the panel, "Diasporas, Business and Post-Conflict Development."

64. Francois Muyumba, "Politics in the Democratic Republic of Congo," in *The Politics and Policies of Sub-Saharan Africa*, ed. Robert Dibie (Lanham, MD: University Press of America, 2001), 259–306.

65. "ANACOZA Press Release, Report of the Goma Trip, 20 January 1997," quoted in Jean-Claude Willame, *L'odyssée Kabila: Trajectoire pour un Congo nouveau?* (Paris: Karthala Press, 1999).

66. Willame, *L'odyssée*.

67. See New York Times News Service, "Kabila's Success was 30 Years in the Making; Rebel Leader Changes Name of Zaire Back to Congo; Nature of Rule Uncertain," *Baltimore Sun*, May 18, 1997.

68. Gérard Prunier, *Africa's World War: Congo, the Rwandan Genocide, and the Making of a Continental Catastrophe* (New York: Oxford University Press, 2009), 150.

69. Michael O. Allen, "Congo: Come on Back," NYDailyNews.com, May 25, 1997.

70. Jules Kitoy, quoted ibid .

71. Muntuta-Kinyanta, "Toujours pas d'appareil de démocratie," CongoOnline, December 3, 2000, http://www.congonline.com/Forum1/Forum05/Muntuta16.htm.

72. Kisangani, discussant remarks for the panel, "Diasporas, Business and Post-Conflict Development."

73. Ibid.

74. UN Security Council, *Final Report of the Expert Panel of Experts on the Illegal Exploitation of Natural Resources and Other Forms of Wealth of the Democratic Republic of Congo* (S/2003/1207, October 23, 2003).

75. Emizet Francois Kisangani and F. Scott Bobb, *Historical Dictionary of the Democratic Republic of Congo*, 3rd ed. (Lanham, MD: Scarecrow Press, 2010).

76. Self-exiled Iraqi politician Ahmed Chalabi convinced US policymakers that Iraqis would welcome the 2003 US invasion with great enthusiasm and that he enjoyed broad legitimacy from the Iraqi people.

77. Keck and Sikkink, *Activists beyond Borders*.

78. Rainer Bauböck, "Towards a Political Theory of Migrant Transnationalism," *International Migration Review* 37, no. 3 (2003): 700–23.

79. Eva Østergaard-Nielsen, "The Politics of Migrants' Transnational Political Practices," *International Migration Review* 37, no. 3 (2003): 760–86.

80. Shain, *Marketing the American Creed*.

5

Exiles and Political Islam

Contrasting Khomeini's Religious Nationalism with
bin Laden's Violent Globalism

ARIEL I. AHRAM and JOHN GLEDHILL

In June 1989, Iran was wracked by mourning following the death of the country's supreme leader, Ruhollah Khomeini. Hundreds of thousands paid their respects as the ayatollah's body lay in state in the center of Tehran. When funeral proceedings got under way, however, frenzied mourners seized the body in an effort to recover relics. Water cannons turned on the crowd, and helicopters were dispatched to recover the remains. Only hours later was the body finally laid to rest in the presence of the assembled leadership of the Islamic Republic of Iran.[1]

Twenty-two years later, a contrasting exponent of Islamic revolution—Osama bin Laden—died under very different circumstances. The al-Qaeda leader was killed by US special operations forces in a hideout in Pakistan. His body was airlifted out of Pakistan, photographed, then secreted to an aircraft carrier and buried at sea.[2] Although the killing sparked some sporadic street demonstrations around the globe, officials in bin Laden's home country of Saudi Arabia did not protest his death.[3]

Of course, the differences between Khomeini and bin Laden abound; they sought different political goals, employed different means to realize those goals, and met very different fates. The two Islamists did, however, share one key formative experience—both were barred from their homelands for extended periods after denouncing their own governments. Thus, both Khomeini and bin Laden had transnationalism thrust upon them through the condition of exile. This chapter explores and contrasts their exilic experiences.

Exilic political activism is necessarily transnational. Exiles who aim to overthrow the governments that expelled them, for example, try to establish cross-border political networks that link back home, in an effort to mobilize support for political change there. And exiles who dream of global revolution after they are cut off from their homelands seek to foster transnational movements of like-minded globalists, with a view to spreading their messages of resistance to all corners of the globe. Despite the inherent transnationalism of exiles, however, they have received surprisingly little attention from scholars interested in globalization, global politics, or the transnational dynamics of war and peace.[4] By contrasting the experiences of two renowned exiles in this chapter, we aim to partly remedy that oversight.

We focus on Islamic activists in particular due to the distinctive transnational bent in contemporary Islamic politics and the associated challenges that political Islamists face in reconciling transnational and national allegiances.[5] For some Islamic activists, the very idea of the nation-state is a Western artifice that aims to divide the Muslim world. Thus, in lieu of the secular citizenship of nation-statehood, some have offered pan-Islamic unity as a political ideal.[6] Yet, hopes of escaping the nation-state system have often remained largely unfulfilled. For fifteen years in exile (1964–79), Khomeini tried to balance his national aspiration of overthrowing Shah Mohammed Reza Pahlavi on one hand, with a global agenda for worldwide Islamic revolution on the other. Ultimately, the ayatollah privileged the national over the global by leading a popular uprising to unseat the shah. By contrast, bin Laden's response to the challenge of operationalizing a transnational ideology in a state-centric world took a very different form. During his time exiled in Sudan (1991–96), the al-Qaeda leader incrementally globalized his violent political program. Thus, by time he moved on to Afghanistan, bin Laden had come to advocate for global jihad.

To understand and explain these different trajectories, we draw on the contentious politics literature.[7] In so doing, we work from the assumption that the configuration of "opportunity structures" and "organizational resources" that Khomeini and bin Laden each encountered after being cast from their homelands partly shaped their political ideas and activities. In the case of Khomeini, we argue that the experience of exile reinforced his interest in, and ability to, effect political change at home in Iran through civil resistance. For bin Laden, by contrast, the experience of exile in Sudan seems to have triggered a change in his political aspirations. While in Khartoum, the jihadist found himself cut off from the politics of his homeland but connected to a diverse set of militant Islamists who also found exile in Sudan at that time. Bin Laden's interaction with those exiles contributed to a shift away from attacking the supposed apostasy of authorities in his home state of Saudi Arabia toward a much broader commitment to violent global revolution.

In the sections that follow, we develop this argument by first giving a brief overview of contentious political activity at the transnational level and its relevance to the study of exilic politics. We then work our way through short case studies of the exilic experiences of Khomeini and bin Laden. Consistent with the foci of other contributions to this volume, each case study discusses how the respective exiles tried to communicate with their homelands, how they interacted with other exiles while abroad, how their social and political networks were organized during their periods of exile, and how those networks shaped their political goals and activism. We conclude by considering what bin Laden's experience of exile in particular can tell us about the nature—and possible dangers—of transnationalism.

The Transnational, Contentious Politics of Exilic Activism

"Exiles" are actors barred from their homelands for political reasons, typically as a form of punishment for dissent.[8] Once banished, some exiles retreat from political life, hoping to avoid further retribution. Others, however, maintain or even intensify their political activism. Where that is the case, any such activism is necessarily transnational in structure and contentious in form. On the transnational front, politically active exiles cannot help but move across, under, and over borders as they pursue their goals—no matter whether those goals are aimed at effecting change in their home states, shaping outcomes in their host states, or pushing for revolution at the global level. Exilic actors also cannot help but act "contentiously."[9] After all, exiles are barred from engaging in routine political activity in their homelands. Consequently, they are forced to operate outside the realm of formal, institutional politics as they make claims against one or more governments.

Since exilic activism is transnational and contentious, the literature on transnational social movements and advocacy networks can provide us with a useful starting point for understanding the dynamics of exilic politics. While that literature has developed a rich set of causal claims over the past fifteen years or so,[10] we get "back to basics" in the case studies that follow by focusing on two structural influences that shaped the transnational contention of Khomeini and bin Laden, respectively: the political opportunity structures that they encountered after banishment and the organizational resources to which they had access while exiled.

We understand "political opportunity structures" as political, economic, and social arrangements that shape the degree and form of *externally* imposed constraints on contentious political activity.[11] In what remains a largely state-centric world, governments and state security forces tend to dictate those constraints more than any other actor or structure; where governments suppress activism, the opportunity space for contentious politics narrows, and where they do not, opportunity space opens up for contentious activism.[12]

In the context of exilic politics, the very act of sending opposition political figures into exile can be seen as an effort from authorities to close down opportunities for protest. Exiles then face a new set of political conditions abroad, which may constrain or enable their capacities to remain politically active in their homelands from afar. Host-state governments may encourage or discourage efforts from their guests to agitate in their homelands, for example, and various international actors can also constrain or facilitate activism. At the same time, the actions of exiles' home states will continue to matter. Where those states seal their borders and prevent any communication between exiles and their home populations, the opportunity space for exilic activism will be narrow, and where borders remain porous, exiles will have opportunities to continue influencing political audiences in their homelands.

While opportunity structures relate to constraints that are imposed on contentious political groups from the outside, "organizational resources"[13] can be understood as social and material means that boost the *internal* capacity of resistance groups to organize and execute contentious political actions.[14] On the social side of the equation, high levels of within-group trust, commitment, and communication among opposition actors increase the willingness and capacity of those actors to realize a contentious collective action. And on the material side, funds allow resistance groups to sustain themselves and procure the various "tools" that facilitate contentious politics, in practice—ranging from placards to arms.

In the case of political exiles, their access to such resources and the impact of those resources on their contentious political activities are shaped by the sociopolitical contexts into which exiles are banished. After expulsion, some exiles become enmeshed in the social networks of their national diasporas, which provide them with social connections and material resources that facilitate political activism in their homelands—as Khomeini discovered. By contrast, some exiles find themselves banished into cosmopolitan communities, where they develop social networks that connect across the globe, rather than to their homelands. In that case, as bin Laden found, there may be practical reasons to pursue political activism on a global, rather than national, scale.

Khomeini and the Contentious Nationalism of Exile

Khomeini's fifteen years of exile have been largely ignored or, at best, treated as a mere prelude to his climactic return to Iran on February 1, 1979. Yet his time abroad in many ways defined the subsequent trajectory of his political career. It was in exile that Khomeini led the revolution against the shah and in exile that he developed his theory of *vilayet-e faqih* (the rule of jurisprudence), which became the theoretical rubric for the Islamic Republic of Iran. Exile also provided Khomeini with an opportunity to reach beyond Iran and gain networks of supporters in Iraq, Lebanon, the Persian Gulf states, and other Muslim countries—to become, in effect, a pan-Islamic leader. After all, although Shi'ites represented only a small minority within the Muslim world, Shi'a clerical institutions could have provided a ready-made transnational network from which to draw supporters globally.

However, Khomeini ultimately rejected the temptation of transnational pan-Islamism. Instead, he remained oriented toward his national homeland. This was partly a product of his own political ambitions and maneuvering in exile but also a function of the shah's remarkably ineffectual antiexile policy, which allowed Khomeini to have his voice heard in his homeland, even while abroad. Thus, the political opportunity structures that Khomeini encountered while in exile, and the organizational resources that were available to him in Iraq and then Paris, ultimately led him to deepen, rather than abandon, the focus on his homeland.

Khomeini's Journey into Exile

Khomeini entered Iran's clerical establishment at a time of profound political turmoil. Shah Reza Khan's political reforms from the 1920s to 1940s were seen as a challenge to the clergy's supremacy in matters of education, family law, and other facets of social life. Yet Khomeini, like many other junior and mid-ranking clerics, initially avoided politics. Indeed, his only early major political statement was a 1942 response to anticlerical writings in the Iranian press. In the publication, Khomeini actually evinced a marked skepticism toward the nation-state as a political institution and he showed a preference for Islamic cosmopolitanism.[15]

That skepticism began to dissolve, however, after Grand Ayatollah Hossein Borujerdi died in 1960 and a power vacuum emerged at the top of the clerical hierarchy. At the same time, Mohammed Reza Shah (the hereditary successor to Reza Khan) was pursuing his aggressive "White Revolution"—an ambitious program of land reform and societal modernization that went far beyond anything that his father had ever attempted. As changes were rolled out, Khomeini began to denounce Mohammed Reza and his government publicly. Drawing on nationalist rhetoric, he criticized the shah's close relationship with the United States, particularly the decision to grant diplomatic immunity to US military personnel. Khomeini argued that the shah "sold our independence, reduced us to the level of a colony, and made the Muslim nation of Iran appear more backward than savages in the eyes of the world." While emphasizing national sovereignty in that way, Khomeini also invoked a broader pan-Islamic ideal, calling on the *ulama* (Muslim legal scholars) of Najaf and Qom and the "presidents and

Kings of the Muslim peoples! Come to our aid!"[16] One week later, he was arrested and sent into exile—first to Turkey, then Iraq, and finally Paris.

During his period of exile, Khomeini went on to develop a dense network of Shi'a religious institutions and diasporic connections, which allowed him to maintain political ties to his homeland. The political opportunity to realize a broadly nationalist political agenda, meanwhile, came with the incapacity (or perhaps unwillingness) of authorities in Iran to seal their borders and prevent the ayatollah's exiled voice from penetrating the homeland.

The Nationalism of Khomeini's Transnational Network

After a year in Turkey, Khomeini traveled to Najaf, Iraq—one of the most important centers of Shi'a clerical training. Initially the city seemed to invite Khomeini to become politically engaged at the transnational level. Acolytes from across the Islamic world came to Najaf to learn at the feet of senior ayatollahs, who were known as sources of religious and political emulation (*marja' at-taqlid*).[17] But despite Najaf's multinational complexion, Khomeini was arguably disappointed by the city's provincialism and quietism. Students tended to cluster according to national and regional origins. Senior clerics exhibited little notion of Shi'ism as a global venture and were politically withdrawn. Khomeini, for his part, was forced to play a delicate game during his time in Najaf—especially after the rise of Saddam Hussein and the Ba'th Party in 1968. When Ba'th officials approached him about denouncing Iran's claims to the Shatt al-Arab, for example, the ayatollah declined and pointed out privately that the Iraqi regime had behaved no better.[18] At the same time, when the Ba'th Party expelled a number of seminary students of Iranian origins, Khomeini did not protest.

Given the provincialism that he encountered in Iraq, Khomeini's political thinking and rhetoric remained largely fixed on his homeland during this period, despite occasional nods toward transnationalism. His vocal support for the Palestinian cause, for instance, can be understood as a deliberate effort to draw attention to the shah's pro-Israel stance. Also, he praised the Qom clergy as a font of political resistance, while ridiculing Najaf as apathetic to the plight of believers in Iran.[19]

Further reflecting a nationalist bent, Khomeini's seminal political treatise during his time in exile, *Hukumat-e Islami*, gestured toward transnational Islam but ultimately remained anchored in Iran. Derived from lectures delivered in Najaf in 1970, *Hukumat-e Islami* ostensibly provided a blueprint for the reunification of the Islamic world. However, a closer look at the document suggests little real commitment to realizing that goal in practice. For example, Khomeini offered no clear guidelines for overcoming ethnic, sectarian, and national cleavages within the Muslim world. He also paid no attention to the fact that Shi'ites represented just a small minority within Islam and would, as such, have struggled to be the driving force behind transnational Islam.[20] Not only did these positions give short shrift to pan-Islam, but the text's core concept—*vilayet-e faqih*—seemed customized to suit Iran alone. The idea itself derived from a strictly Shi'a understanding of clerics as custodians who interpret and execute divine law. Since the Sunni tradition has no analogous idea, implementation of *vilayet-e faqih* was only feasible where Shi'ites held a demographic preponderance and the clergy enjoyed a long history of autonomy. Iran alone met these criteria.[21] In that way, *vilayet-e faqih* can be seen as a political idea designed uniquely for Khomeini and addressed specifically to his homeland.

Khomeini cultivated a diasporic social network to communicate his ideas back to the Iranian public sphere. Iranian seminarians in Iraq were the most obvious medium; they smuggled copies of Khomeini's writings and cassette recordings of his lectures back into Iran. He also built ties to Iranian university students across the globe, who lobbied Western governments to roll back support for the shah.[22] When the shah began a tentative process of liberalization in the fall of 1977, opportunities arose for Khomeini to use those networks as a basis for mobilizing support for popular protest in Iran. Although he initially seemed hesitant to exploit those opportunities, the death of his eldest son under mysterious circumstances in Najaf in October 1977 proved a catalyst. Shortly thereafter, Khomeini began urging his followers to avail of the connections that he had established between Iranians inside and outside of the homeland to foment change at home: "Inform the world. You can't reach the world from inside Iran; send [letters] outside the country for them to publish, or send them here somehow, and we'll get them published."[23]

In response to these pleas, Khomeini's supporters managed to activate clandestine clerical associations within Iran itself, and in short time mobilization began to have an effect. Whereas Iranians had previously tried to avoid government recriminations by referring to Khomeini only by his first initial or calling him the "*Seyyad* [holy man] who is far from his homeland," now they began to chant, "Hail to Khomeini."[24] By late 1978, the mobilization effort led from abroad had developed so much momentum that revolutionaries flooded onto the streets of Tehran. As they did, the shah sought Khomeini's deportation from Iraq, and so the exile chose to move to France. As media swarmed to his rented house in the Paris suburbs, Khomeini assembled a staff of spokesmen and advisers, who facilitated his effort to assert political control over the growing revolutionary movement.[25] When the shah fled in early 1979, the way was opened for Khomeini's assumption of power.

The End of Exile and a Nation Regained

Khomeini's adoption of a kind of "transnationalist nationalism" had a significant impact on the founding of the Islamic Republic of Iran, and it continues to shape Iran today. The constitution, for instance, avows that "all Muslims form a single nation," and it commits the government to cultivate friendship and unity within the Islamic world.[26] Yet the subsequent passages are thoroughly national in orientation: Persian is defined as the national language, while Arabic is relegated to a second language (Article 15); rather than offering all Muslims citizenship, nationality is based on residence or patrilineal descendants (Article 155); and dual citizenship is highly restricted (Articles 41 and 42). Most important, the move to establish the political position of *vilayat-e faqih* as a constitutionally endowed ruler of the Islamic Republic runs directly contrary to the idea that a cleric might serve as the source of emulation for the entire transnational Shi'a world.

Through his charisma, Khomeini may have been able to play the role of a "transnational nationalist." Yet there was no way to institutionalize and bequeath this role to his successor.[27] The appointment of Ali Khamenei as supreme leader after Khomeini's death illustrates the problem. Although Khamenei enjoyed political backing within the Iranian elite, he was initially seen by some critics to lack the clerical stature necessary to become a source of emulation for the wider Shi'a world. Over time, he has attracted followers abroad, yet other senior ayatollahs, such as the Najaf-based Ayatollah Ali Sistani, remain alternative religious leaders and alternate sources of authority. Consequently, the sociopolitical institutions of *vilayat-e faqih* that Khomeini developed while in exile retain unique relevance to Iran but are deeply at odds with the transnational elements of Shi'ism.[28]

Bin Laden and the Violent Globalism of Exile

While studies of Osama bin Laden and al-Qaeda abound, relatively little attention is given to how his experience of exile in Sudan shaped his radical, and violent, political agenda. This section explores that period of his life and political development.

We argue that bin Laden's political interests after he fled Saudi Arabia initially remained focused on his homeland and, specifically, on overthrowing the Saudi government. After some time abroad, however, Osama found that Saudi authorities were able to block him from projecting his political voice into the kingdom from afar. He had no real opportunity from exile to challenge his "near enemy"—the government of his homeland.[29] Isolated in that way, bin Laden began to reconsider his political goals and activities. Drawing on the social networks that were available to him in Khartoum—including those of Arab veterans of the Afghan wars and other Islamic activists who found refuge in Sudan— bin Laden began to envisage building a truly global, rather than primarily national, jihad.

From Traveler to Exile

Bin Laden's political career began with his first trip to Afghanistan shortly after the Soviet invasion of 1979.[30] The son of one of the richest construction magnates in Saudi Arabia, he had already gravitated toward the activism of the Muslim Brotherhood while attending King Abdulaziz University in Jeddah.[31] Over the years that followed, he shuttled between Saudi Arabia, Pakistan, and Afghanistan, trying to raise funds for the mujahideen's resistance of the Soviets.[32] In Afghanistan, bin Laden was reportedly an efficient administrator—organizing and coordinating the diverse Arab fighters who came to join the mujahideen. Indeed, it was a desire for efficiency that saw him establish al-Qaeda ("the Base") in 1988 as a kind of bookkeeping office for these foreign fighters.[33] Following the withdrawal of Soviet forces, however, the various mujahideen factions started to turn on each other, and so bin Laden returned to Saudi Arabia to work in the family business.[34]

Upon his return home, bin Laden tried to find ways to put his so-called Afghan Arabs into the national service of the Saudi kingdom. He offered to lead a campaign against South Yemen, for example, which the Saudis had long-viewed as an outpost of communist radicalism on their flank.[35] And when Iraq invaded Kuwait in 1990 and threatened Saudi Arabia, bin Laden offered to recruit an army from among the Afghan veterans.[36] But the Saudi authorities were wary of empowering bin Laden by allowing him to lead a private army. Ignoring bin Laden's offer, they turned to the United States, their longstanding ally, for military assistance.[37] Dismayed by Saudi willingness to allow foreign troops on sacred soil to wage war against a fellow Muslim country, however, bin Laden broke with the monarchy.[38] Saudi officials responded by putting him under house arrest, which triggered him to flee into exile in 1991—initially in Pakistan, then elsewhere.[39]

Bin Laden the Abortive Nationalist

Bin Laden quickly found his way to Sudan, where he and his family were received by the Islamist-oriented government of President Omar al-Bashir and Prime Minister Hassan al-Turabi, the leader of the governing National Islamic Front (NIF).[40] As an honored guest, bin Laden initially found a measure of safety and comfort in Khartoum. He lived in a wealthy neighborhood, spent time with his children, and reportedly taught them the intricacies of gardening.[41] He also launched a dizzying array of business ventures, including a construction company, an import-export firm, a bakery, orchards, and a stake in an Islamic bank.[42]

Though his economic activities focused on projects in Sudan, his political attention lay elsewhere. Specifically, alongside several failed efforts to establish an al-Qaeda presence across eastern Africa,[43] the exiled bin Laden initially focused on denouncing the government in his homeland of Saudi Arabia. To that end, Osama penned a barrage of communiqués and démarches in 1994 and 1995 attacking the Saud dynasty and its allies for supposedly corrupting the "land of the two Great Mosques."[44] In an open letter to King Fahd, bin Laden accused the Saudi ruler of introducing blasphemous laws, bowing to the will of the United States, mismanaging the wealth and resources of "our nation," and supporting secular authorities in conflicts with Muslim parties abroad.[45] This last point was emblematic of pan-Islamist language that ran through many of his complaints. However, even when purporting to defend the global Islamic community in that way, bin Laden initially turned the blame toward authorities in his home state, whom he accused of waging "war against Islam."[46] Osama focused his ire on the Saudi religious establishment as well. Specifically, he complained about religious scholars supposedly "befriending bad leaders,"[47] and, in a letter to the wider community of clerics across the Gulf, he drew attention to the Saudi government's supposed desecration of the holy land.[48]

While the safety of exile meant that bin Laden was free to voice his complaints against authorities in his home state, the distance of exile also meant that he faced barriers to having that voice heard and acted upon in Saudi Arabia. In large part, those barriers were put in place by Saudi authorities, who actively shut down opportunities for bin Laden to penetrate the country's public sphere. To that end, officials froze his vast material assets,[49] stripped him of his citizenship,[50] and pressured his family to silence their prodigal son. That pressure was seemingly effective, since the bin Laden family publicly denounced Osama in 1994 and cut off the stipend that they had previously provided him from the family's trust.[51]

Over time, bin Laden found it increasingly difficult to maintain the kinds of organizational networks that could have facilitated diffusion of his political message inside Saudi Arabia. When he had first fled to Sudan, he had been relatively well connected to the small but closely knit community of Saudi dissidents—some of whom were associated with the Islamic Awakening / Muslim Brotherhood movement and shared bin Laden's antipathy for the Saudi regime (albeit quietly).[52] Yet bin Laden struggled to maintain contact with them from abroad—particularly after Saudi authorities began to crack down on dissenters who remained in the country in 1993 and 1994.[53] For example, the Committee for the Defense of Legitimate Rights, which may have served as a medium for articulating bin Laden's political complaints in Riyadh, was shut down after just one week of operations.[54]

Not only were bin Laden's networks in Saudi Arabia dissolving, but the al-Qaeda leader also found it hard to establish new networks of sympathetic Saudis in his adopted home of Sudan. Khartoum teemed with political Islamists, to be sure, but only a small number in bin Laden's entourage were Saudi nationals.[55] In an apparent effort to remedy that shortcoming, Osama brought his fellow Saudi, Khalid al-Fawwaz, to East Africa.[56] Al-Fawwaz became bin Laden's major intermediary in efforts to project his political voice back home. Perhaps due to the scarcity of the Saudi network in Sudan, however, bin Laden chose to run those efforts through the United Kingdom, where laws regarding freedom of speech were manipulated to disseminate anti-Saudi propaganda.[57] From London, al-Fawwaz established the Advice and Reformation Committee as a transnational mouthpiece for publishing bin Laden's denunciation of the Saudi regime.[58] Still, given the paucity of Osama's connections to his homeland at that time, it is unclear how loudly that mouthpiece was heard at home, if at all.[59]

By the mid-1990s, it must have been clear to bin Laden that he had little chance of fomenting revolution in Saudi Arabia from his place of exile. He faced a home government that was actively closing down his personal access points to the Saudi public sphere, he had a diminishing network of contacts in his homeland, and he had no real organizational network of Saudi dissidents on the ground in his state of asylum. His career as a nationalist exile, therefore, was bleak. Thus, he began to look for other possibilities.

Globalizing Jihad

While bin Laden faced increasing challenges in his effort to remain politically connected to Saudi Arabia, he initially had an opportunity to lay down roots and assimilate in Sudan. Prime Minister al-Turabi actively courted and welcomed the wealthy Saudi expatriate. By way of thanks, bin Laden reportedly donated vast sums to al-Turabi's NIF party,[60] underwrote Sudan's wheat imports,[61] and backed a state-owned munitions company.[62] His firms also handled major construction contracts for the Sudanese government, including completion of the al-Rusayris Dam,[63] an airport,[64] and several highway projects.[65] Beyond these civilian development projects, bin Laden and the NIF-led government also seem to have shared political and military ties; bin Laden was allegedly allowed to maintain active training camps for mujahideen,[66] and NIF militias are said to have trained at some of these camps.[67] Some of bin Laden's jihadists are also alleged to have offered assistance to the government in its efforts to repress rebel movements in the country's south.[68]

Although he flirted with Sudanese politics, bin Laden never fully committed himself to an active role in Sudanese public life. Rather, his relationship with Khartoum was always built on mutual advantage, rather than loyalty. Sudan offered bin Laden asylum, while bin Laden offered the Sudanese government economic and political assistance. When international pressure began to mount on Sudan to cut off ties with suspected terrorists, however, some in Khartoum began to reconsider the government's relationship with bin Laden (and the other extremist groups that had based themselves in Sudan under al-Turabi's stewardship). That international pressure was first applied in 1993, when the United States declared Sudan a state sponsor of terrorism and imposed sanctions.[69] It then intensified in 1995, when Egypt threatened to invade after Egyptian militants exiled in Sudan tried to assassinate President Hosni Mubarak, with the apparent knowledge of Sudanese authorities.[70]

As Sudanese officials came to see bin Laden as a liability, the opportunity for any kind of political activism in Sudan ended for the Saudi exile. Even before then, however, the door to the global political sphere had begun to open up for bin Laden through his engagement with the transnational network of Islamic extremists who were based in Khartoum at that time. The core of that network was built around the one or two thousand al-Qaeda foot soldiers who moved to Sudan with bin Laden after 1991,[71] each of whom had political contacts in their respective homelands and in countries where they had previously lived and fought. This gave bin Laden access to a global address book. He then added names through connections that he made after al-Turabi established the Popular Arab Islamic Congress (PAIC) as a vehicle for connecting Islamist "anti-imperialist" groups from around the world.[72] The PAIC ran annual summits in Sudan and created a standing membership that quickly included extremists from across the Muslim world.[73] To be sure, many PAIC member organizations remained based in their homelands. However, a number of militant groups (PAIC members and others) reportedly spent time in Sudan—including the Libyan Islamic Fighting Group, the Algerian Armed Islamic Group, and various other organizations from across the Middle East and South Asia.[74] Although most militants were focused on attacking the governments of their home states from the safety of Sudan, their congregation in Khartoum provided bin Laden with an organizational platform for violent global activism.

Bin Laden's contact with the exiled leader of the (Egyptian) Islamic Jihad, Ayman al-Zawahiri, seems to have been particularly important in allowing the al-Qaeda leader to expand his network.[75] Like bin Laden, al-Zawahiri had wandered the globe for several years before alighting in Sudan. Al-Zawahiri also initially focused his efforts on overturning the incumbent government of his home state (Egypt).[76] And, in a final reflection of bin Laden, al-Zawahiri had found it difficult to remain politically active in his homeland while living in exile because Egyptian authorities had begun to crack down on militants abroad during the early-to-mid-1990s—even reportedly trying to assassinate al-Zawahiri.[77] That crackdown, which was mirrored by governments across the Arab world, narrowed the opportunity space for al-Zawahiri, bin Laden, and other militant exiles to use violence in an attempt to shape politics in their home states.

Given pressures at home and abroad, the diverse exiled extremists based in Khartoum found themselves sitting in perilous limbo by the mid-1990s. Hopes of triumphant returns to their homelands were growing distant, and their day-to-day lives were dictated by developments in Sudan rather than in their distant countries of origin. Their Sudanese hosts, meanwhile, were only welcoming to a point. Given the self-interest that seems to have underwritten Sudan's relationship with the exiled extremists, there was always a risk that those who had been granted asylum could run afoul of the local authorities and be banished again. That tenuous connection to their host state, combined with ongoing disconnection from their homelands, meant that the extremist exiles—including bin Laden—started to look outside the state system for political inspiration. They seem to have viewed *global* jihad, in particular, as an ideological refuge because it held out promise of a transnational intellectual and operational framework that transcended problematic questions of national borders and parochial political allegiances. Such a transnational ideology also mapped neatly onto the transnational organizational network of exiled extremists that had taken shape in Khartoum.

As the personnel networks available to bin Laden became increasingly global in nature, al-Qaeda shifted from being an organization with a state-centric focus to one that held transnational—even global—aspirations. To that end, al-Qaeda may have lent support to Mohammed Farah Aidid in the Somali warlord's confrontation with US-led peacekeeping efforts in Mogadishu in 1993.[78] Anarchic conditions in Somalia made sustaining operations there impossible, however, and so al-Qaeda agents then turned their attention to Kenya,[79] where they laid groundwork for what would be the 1998 double bombings of the US embassies in Kenya and Tanzania.[80] It was during the planning of these regional operations that bin Laden developed his idea of global jihad, which culminated in the infamous "Declaration of War against the Americans Occupying the Land of the Two Holy Places" (released in August 1996).[81] No longer would bin Laden primarily concern himself with the supposedly apostate regimes of Saudi Arabia or Afghanistan. Rather, he and his supporters would also wage war against the "far enemy"—the West and, more specifically, the United States.

While it seems that bin Laden had planned to release the missive while he was still based in Khartoum, Sudan expelled bin Laden in mid-1996 following intense international pressure, including United Nations Security Council sanctions.[82] Thus, his declaration of war was only issued once the Saudi expatriate had moved on and taken up another offer of exile—this time in Afghanistan, where he was welcomed by a Taliban movement that was still trying to consolidate its power.[83] Given the evolution of his political objectives while in Sudan, it was bin Laden's return to Afghanistan that marked the real beginning of his global war.

Conclusion: Implications for the Study of Transnationalism

We opened this chapter by suggesting that political exiles are, in many ways, paradigmatic transnational actors. Having now detailed the diverse experiences and political trajectories taken by two of the most renowned exiles of recent times, it is worthwhile reflecting on what our study of exilic actors tells us about transnationalism broadly.

A paradoxical implication of transnational exilic politics is that the state remains the dominant political institution. The very condition of exile begins when state authorities compel an opposition figure to flee and authorities in a second state offer asylum to the fleeing actor. Once asylum is established, an exile's ability to remain politically relevant in his or her homeland depends on whether the home state has the will and capacity to block efforts from the exile to transmit his or her political voice back into the homeland. In the case of bin Laden, Saudi authorities succeeded in blocking his ability to communicate and organize within the kingdom, essentially cutting him off. Consequently, his calls for national revolution went largely unheard at home. By contrast, Iranian authorities were unable to stop Khomeini from establishing channels of communication and connecting with networks of supporters within Iran. By maintaining a cross-thatched, internal/external organizational structure, Khomeini was able to ensure that his call for popular uprising in Iran was widely heard at home during his many years in exile.

Although states undoubtedly influence the impact of exiles on the domestic politics of their homelands (or lack thereof), our study also suggests that state authority diminishes when it comes to the *transnational* political activities of exiles. Saudi authorities were able to shut down bin Laden's activism within the kingdom, for example, but they had little influence over the political opportunities and resources that Osama encountered in Sudan (or, later, in Afghanistan). Thus, in exile, bin Laden was able to develop a political network that connected to all corners of the globe rather than to his homeland. As he was presented with the possibility of accessing a global audience, bin Laden increasingly crafted his political message in a way that would resonate with such an audience. Thus, his shift from denouncing the near enemy to declaring war on the far enemy can be seen as an instrumental step taken in response to the opportunity structures and organizational resources that he encountered under conditions of exile in Sudan.

Given the exclusivist and violent nature of the global ideology that bin Laden developed while in Sudan, it is worth concluding by reflecting on the kinds of ideas that circulate in the transnational public sphere. This borderless civic space is sometimes celebrated as a venue in which cross-cultural deliberations can give rise to inclusive political ideologies and forms of global governance.[84] Seen that way, there is a clear normative case to be made for the merits of transnational deliberation and global civil society.[85] Indeed, in this volume, Jennifer M. Brinkerhoff's analysis of the role of Chadian and Zairean diasporas in postconflict resolution and reconstruction provides evidence that the transnational "boomerang effect" can deliver positive results. However, as David Malet cautions in his chapter on foreign fighters in Syria, transnational actors can also contribute to violence.[86] Our analysis echoes Malet's work in some ways, since the example of bin Laden and al-Qaeda illustrates how globalist ideas forged through transnational networking are not necessarily democratic and constructive. Rather like its domestic counterpart, a "global" civil society can be a space for manipulation and abuse.[87] This sobering realization does not negate the merit of transnational deliberation. It does, however, warn that the transnational arm of the boomerang effect may be dictatorial and destructive.

Notes

1. Patrick Tyler, "Khomeini Buried in Chaotic Scene; First Attempt Fails When Anguished Mourners Seize Corpse," *Washington Post*, June 7, 1989.

2. See Nicholas Schmidle, "Getting Bin Laden," *New Yorker*, August 8, 2011.

3. Ned Parker, "Saudi Arabia: Muted Response to Osama bin Laden's Death," *Babylon and Beyond* (blog), *Los Angeles Times*, May 2, 2011.

4. In fact, exiles have received little scholarly attention altogether. The work of Yossi Shain is a notable exception. See, for example, his *The Frontier of Loyalty: Political Exiles in the Age of the Nation-State* (Ann Arbor: University of Michigan Press, 2005), and "Who Is a Political Exile? Defining a Field of Study for Political Science," *International Migration* 26, no. 4 (1988): 387–400.

5. Anoushiravan Ehteshami, "Islam as a Political Force in International Politics," in *Islam in World Politics*, ed. Nelly Lahoud and Anthony Johns (Abingdon, UK: Routledge, 2005), 33.

6. See Peter G. Mandaville, *Transnational Muslim Politics: Reimagining the Umma* (London: Routledge, 2001); Fred Halliday, "The Politics of the Umma: States and Community in Islamic Movements," *Mediterranean Politics* 7, no. 3 (2002): 20–41; and James Piscatori, "Imagining Pan-Islam: Religious Activism and Political Utopias," *Proceedings of the British Academy* (New York: Oxford University Press, 2005): 421–42.

7. See, for example, Doug McAdam, Sidney Tarrow, and Charles Tilly, *Dynamics of Contention* (Cambridge, UK: Cambridge University Press, 2001), and Doug McAdam, John D. McCarthy, and Mayer N. Zald, eds., *Comparative Perspectives on Social Movements: Political Opportunities, Mobilizing Structures, and Cultural Framings* (Cambridge, UK: Cambridge University Press, 1996).

8. See the discussion in Sara Forsdyke, *Exile, Ostracism, and Democracy: The Politics of Expulsion in Ancient Greece* (Princeton, NJ: Princeton University Press, 2005), 9. This is also reflected in several common dictionary definitions.

9. See the discussion of the concept of "contentious politics" in Sidney Tarrow, "Silence and Voice in the Study of Contentious Politics: Introduction" in Ronald R. Aminzade et al., *Silence and Voice in the Study of Contentious Politics* (Cambridge, UK: Cambridge University Press, 2001), 7.

10. See, in particular, works that have built upon Margaret E. Keck and Kathryn Sikkink, *Activists beyond Borders: Advocacy Networks in International Politics* (Ithaca, NY: Cornell University Press, 1998).

11. This understanding is based on the definitions given by Peter Eisinger (1973) in Karl-Dieter Opp, *Theories of Political Protest and Social Movements: A Multidisciplinary Introduction, Critique, and Synthesis* (London: Routledge, 2009), 161–62; Sidney Tarrow, "States and Opportunities" in McAdam, McCarthy, and Zald, *Comparative Perspectives on Social Movements*, 54; and Sidney Tarrow, *Power in Movement: Social Movements and Contentious Politics* (New York: Cambridge University Press, 1998), 20.

12. Tarrow, *Power in Movement*, ch. 5.

13. See writings on "resource mobilization," including John D. McCarthy and Mayer N. Zald, "Resource Mobilization and Social Movements: A Partial Theory," *American Journal of Sociology*, 82, no. 6 (1977): 1212–41, and J. Craig Jenkins, "Resource Mobilization Theory and the Study of Social Movements," *Annual Review of Sociology* 9 (1983): 527–53.

14. This external/internal distinction builds on Tarrow, *Power in Movement*, and Charles Tilly, *From Mobilization to Revolution* (New York: McGraw-Hill, 1978).

15. R. K. Ramazani, "Khumayni's Islam in Iran's Foreign Policy," in *Islam in Foreign Policy*, ed. Adeed Dawisha (New York: Cambridge University Press, 1983), 16–17.

16. Cited in Baqer Moin, *Khomeini: Life of the Ayatollah* (New York: I. B. Tauris, 1999), 123, 125.

17. Abbas Amanat, "From Ijtihad to Wilayat-i Faqih: The Evolving of the Shi'ite Legal Authority to Political Power," *Logos* 2, no. 3 (2003): 1–13.

18. Moin, *Khomeini*, 145.

19. Devin Stewart, "The Portrayal of an Academic Rivalry," in *The Most Learned of the Shia: The Institution of the Marja Taqlid*, ed. Linda Walbridge (New York: Oxford University Press, 2001), 216–30; Mohammad Samiei, "Najaf and Iranian Politics: Analysing the Way the Hawzah of Najaf Influenced Iranian Politics between Two Revolutions," *Journal of Shi'a Islamic Studies* 5, no. 3 (2012): 277–94.

20. David Menashri, "Khomeini's Vision: Nationalism or World Order?" in *The Iranian Revolution and the Muslim World*, ed. David Menashri (Boulder, CO: Westview, 1990), 48.

21. Chibli Mallat, "Religious Militancy in Contemporary Iraq: Muhammad Baqer as-Sadr and the Sunni-Shia Paradigm," *Third World Quarterly* 10, no. 2 (1988): 699–729; Hamid Mavani, "Analysis of Khomeini's Proof for al-Wilaya al-Mutlaqa (Comprehensive Authority) of the Jurist," in Walbridge, *Most Learned of the Shia*, 183–204.

22. On student activism, see Afshin Matin-asgari, *Iranian Student Opposition to the Shah* (Costa Mesa, CA: Mazda, 2002), and Luca Trenta, "The Champion of Human Rights Meets the King of Kings: Jimmy Carter, the Shah, and Iranian Illusions and Rage," *Diplomacy and Statecraft* 24, no. 3 (2013): 482.

23. Charles Kurzman, *The Unthinkable Revolution in Iran* (Cambridge, MA: Harvard University Press, 2004), 22.

24. Ibid., 27.

25. Moin, *Khomeini*, ch. 10; Kurzman, *Unthinkable Revolution*, 3, 79.

26. Article 11 of Constitution of the Islamic Republic of Iran, http://iranonline.com/iran/iran-info/Government/constitution.html.

27. Daniel Brumberg, *Reinventing Khomeini: The Struggle for Reform in Iran* (Chicago: University of Chicago Press, 2001); Mehdi Mozaffari, "Changes in the Iranian Political System after Khomeini's Death," *Political Studies* 41, no. 4 (1993): 611–17.

28. Abbas Djavadi, "The Difference between a Marja and a Supreme Leader," Radio Free Europe / Radio Liberty, February 25, 2010, http://www.rferl.org/content/The_Difference_Between_A_Marja_And_A_Supreme_Leader/1968177.html; Laurence Louër, *Transnational Shia Politics: Religious and Political Networks in the Gulf* (New York: Columbia University Press, 2008); Frederic M. Wehrey, *Sectarian Politics in the Gulf: From the Iraq War to the Arab Uprisings* (New York: Columbia University Press, 2013), 53–55, 113–15.

29. For discussion of this term, see Fawaz A. Gerges, *The Far Enemy: Why Jihad Went Global* (Cambridge, UK: Cambridge University Press, 2009).

30. Michael Scheuer, *Osama bin Laden* (New York: Oxford University Press, Kindle ed., 2011), 49.

31. For an overview of bin Laden's early years, see Steve Coll, *The Bin Ladens: An Arabian Family in the American Century* (New York: Penguin, 2008), 137–52.

32. Peter L. Bergen, *Holy War, Inc.: Inside the Secret World of Osama bin Laden* (New York: Free Press, 2001): 50.

33. Camille Tawil, *Brothers in Arms: The Story of al-Qa'ida and the Arab Jihadists*, trans. Robin Bray (London: Saqi, Kindle ed., 2011), 25. On the founding and early evolution of al-Qaeda, see Peter Bergen and Paul Cruickshank "Revisiting the Early Al Qaeda: An

Updated Account of Its Formative Years," *Studies in Conflict and Terrorism*, 35, no. 1 (2012): 1–36.

34. Bruce Riedel, *The Search for al Qaeda: Its Leadership, Ideology, and Future* (Washington DC: Brookings Institution Press, Kindle ed., 2010), 46.

35. Ibid., 47; Michael Scheuer, *Through Our Enemies' Eyes: Osama bin Laden, Radical Islam, and the Future of America* (Washington, DC: Potomac Books, Kindle ed., 2006), 122.

36. 9/11 Commission, *The 9/11 Commission Report* (Washington DC: National Commission on Terrorist Attacks upon the United States, 2004), 57, http://govinfo.library.unt.edu/911/report/911Report.pdf.

37. Riedel, *Search for al Qaeda*, 46, 48–49.

38. Bergen, *Holy War, Inc.*, 77–78.

39. Scheuer, *Osama bin Laden*, 83, 218.

40. 9/11 Commission, *9/11 Commission Report*, 57; Scheuer, *Osama bin Laden*, 102; Lawrence Wright, *The Looming Tower: Al-Qaeda and the Road to 9/11* (New York: Alfred A. Knopf, 2006), ch.8.

41. Jean P. Sasson, Najwa bin Laden, and Omar bin Laden, *Growing Up bin Laden: Osama's Wife and Son Take Us Inside Their Secret World* (Oxford, UK: Oneworld, Kindle ed., 2011), 118.

42. Bergen, *Holy War, Inc.*, 80; Scheuer, *Through Our Enemies' Eyes*, 132.

43. Bin Laden and al-Qaeda operatives became active in the Horn of Africa shortly after he arrived in Sudan. However, those efforts seem to have been relatively unfocused at the outset, and they failed. See the discussion in Clint Watts, Jacob Shapiro, and Vahid Brown, *Al-Qaida's (Mis)Adventures in the Horn of Africa* (West Point, NY: Harmony Project, Combatting Terrorism Center, 2007), https://www.ctc.usma.edu/posts/al-qaidas-misadventures-in-the-horn-of-africa.

44. "Letter from Osama bin Laden to King Fahd Regarding a Recent Cabinet Reshuffle, Board of Advice and Reformation," ca. July 11, 1995, Record Number AQ-MCOP-D-000-918, Conflict Records Research Center Archives, Washington DC. For an overview of these letters, see Scheuer, *Osama Bin Laden*, 93–98.

45. "Letter from Osama bin Laden to King Fahd."

46. "Saudi Arabia Unveils Its War against Islam and Its Scholars," September 12, 1994, Record Number AQ-MCOP-D-000-919, in a document that collates "Various Statements of Osama bin Laden, Committee for Advice and Reform," Conflict Records Research Center Archives, Washington DC.

47. "To Shaykh Abd al-Aziz bin Baz . . . ," January 29, 1995, Record Number AQ-MCOP-D-000–919, in a document that collates "Various Statements of Osama bin Laden, Committee for Advice and Reform," Conflict Records Research Center Archives, Washington DC.

48. Osama bin Laden, *Messages to the World: The Statements of Osama bin Laden*, ed. Bruce Lawrence, trans. James Howarth (London: Verso, 2005), 16–19.

49. Sasson, bin Laden, and bin Laden, *Growing Up bin Laden*, 158.

50. Bergen, *Holy War, Inc.*, 89.

51. Riedel, *Search for Al Qaeda*, 54.

52. Stéphane Lacroix, "Osama bin Laden and the Saudi Muslim Brotherhood," *Foreign Policy Online*, October 3, 2012, http://foreignpolicy.com/2012/10/03/osama-bin-laden-and-the-saudi-muslim-brotherhood/; Scheuer, *Osama bin Laden*, 80.

53. See Scheuer, *Osama bin Laden*, 93.

54. J. Millard Burr and Robert O. Collins, *Revolutionary Sudan: Hasan al-Turabi and the Islamist State, 1989–2000* (Leiden: Brill, 2003), 148.

55. Thomas Hegghammer, "Islamist Violence and Regime Stability in Saudi Arabia," *International Affairs* 84, no. 4 (2008): 707.

56. Scheuer, *Through Our Enemies' Eyes*, 139.

57. See the discussion in John Kampfner, "Why the French Call Us Londonistan," *New Statesman*, December 9, 2002, http://www.newstatesman.com/node/156771.

58. Bergan and Cruickshank, "Revisiting the Early Al Qaeda," 25.

59. Lawrence Wright suggests that the dispatches caused a "sensation" in Saudi Arabia, although he does not give details. Wright, *Looming Tower*, 195.

60. Scheuer, *Osama bin Laden*, 102.

61. Ann M. Lesch, "Osama bin Laden's 'Business' in Sudan," *Current History* 101, no. 655 (2002): 204.

62. Scheuer, *Through Our Enemies' Eyes*, 133–34.

63. Lesch, "Osama bin Laden's 'Business,'" 204.

64. Burr and Collins, *Revolutionary Sudan*, 70.

65. Lesch, "Osama bin Laden's 'Business,'" 204; 9/11 Commission, *9/11 Commission Report*, 57.

66. Wright, *Looming Tower*, 187.

67. Scheuer, *Through Our Enemies' Eyes*, 137–38.

68. Ibid.

69. US Department of State, "State Sponsors of Terrorism," https://www.state.gov/j/ct/list/c14151.htm.

70. Burr and Collins, *Revolutionary Sudan*, 189–95. On allegations of Sudanese involvement, see Lesch in "Osama bin Laden's 'Business,'" 207–8.

71. Bergen, *Holy War, Inc.*, 83.

72. Burr and Collins, *Revolutionary Sudan*, 56–57; Lesch, "Osama bin Laden's 'Business,'" 203.

73. Burr and Collins, *Revolutionary Sudan*, 62, 137–38.

74. Ibid., 62; Tawil, *Brothers in Arms*, 93–95.

75. For a treatment of al-Zawahiri in Sudan, see Wright, *Looming Tower*, ch. 9.

76. Gerges, *Far Enemy*, 12.

77. Tawil, *Brothers in Arms*, 99–100.

78. Scheuer, *Osama bin Laden*, 89–90; Lesch, "Osama bin Laden's 'Business,'" 205.

79. See Watts et al., *Al-Qa'ida's (Mis)Adventures*.

80. Bergen and Cruickshank, "Revisiting the Early Al Qaeda," 21–23.

81. "Declaration of War by Osama bin Laden, 1996," Council on Foreign Relations, http://www.cfr.org/terrorist-leaders/declaration-war-osama-bin-laden-1996/p13174; Osama bin Laden, "Declaration of *Jihad*, August 23 1996," in bin Laden, *Messages to the World*, 23–30.

82. Riedel, *Search for al Qaeda*, 55–56; 9/11 Commission, *9/11 Commission Report*, 62–63.

83. See Daniel Byman, *Deadly Connections: States That Sponsor Terrorism* (Cambridge, UK: Cambridge University Press, 2005), ch. 7.

84. See discussions in Margaret E. Keck and Kathryn Sikkink, "Transnational Advocacy Networks in International and Regional Politics," *International Social Science Journal* 51, no. 159 (1999): 89–101; Helmut Anheier, Marlies Glasius, and Mary Kaldor, "Introducing Global Civil Society," in *Global Civil Society 2001*, ed. Helmut Anheier et al. (Oxford, UK: Oxford University Press, 2001); and Timothy J. Sinclair, *Global Governance* (Cambridge: Polity, 2012), ch. 4.

85. Amartya Sen, "Elements of a Theory of Human Rights," *Philosophy and Public Affairs* 32, no. 4 (2004): 315–56.

86. This finding is echoed in multiple studies in the field of conflict studies. See, for example, Erik-Lars Cederman, Luc Girardin, and Kristian Skrede Gleditsch, "Ethnonationalist Triads: Assessing the Influence of Kin Groups on Civil Wars," *World Politics* 61, no. 3 (2009): 403–37, and David Malet, *Foreign Fighters: Transnational Identity in Civil Conflicts* (Oxford, UK: Oxford University Press, 2013).

87. Sheri Berman, "Civil Society and the Collapse of the Weimar Republic," *World Politics* 49, no. 3 (1997): 401–29.

6

Foreign Fighters in the Syrian Civil War

DAVID MALET

This chapter surveys the major transnational groups that brought foreign fighters to Syria during the period 2011 to 2016, including the arrival of the first foreign volunteers and the declaration of the transnational caliphate of the Islamic State straddling the Iraq-Syria border. It examines decentralizing patterns in communications between transnational organizations and their constituents as social media have become new loci of mobilization. Finally, it addresses what these developments mean for our understanding of transnational militants and transnational politics broadly.

Foreign fighters are in the category of transnational violent actors (TVAs), who seek to coerce states or repudiate them entirely through their actions. Unlike the transnational corporations (TNCs) or transnational advocacy networks (TANs) examined in other chapters in this book, TVAs are generally not afforded any legitimacy by states, although they may act as "state sponsors" and provide them with clandestine logistical support against other states or their proxy forces. Foreign fighters, which include armed militants as well as those who provide them logistical and service support, violate both national and international laws to travel to civil war zones from other countries. As part of the insurgent, nonstate forces in conflicts (as opposed to foreign citizens serving in a country's regular military or foreign legion), they enjoy no legal rights as combatants or citizens, as their frequent fates in the era of Guantanamo Bay and drone warfare attest.

As described in the introduction to this volume, the Syrian Civil War became a center of complex transnationalism, with a variety of nonstate entities interacting and TVAs using extreme violence displayed across global communications. Initially, however, there was no reason to assume that this would occur. When the Arab Spring began in early 2011 with a series of civil protests against authoritarian regimes, it appeared to herald a victory for transnational civil society. Broad swaths of the publics in various countries across the Middle East and North Africa were able to communicate with each other, to organize and mobilize like-minded citizens using the global tools of the Internet and social media, and to obtain support and encouragement from other individuals and groups around the world. They inspired similar protests regionally and internationally, setting the zeitgeist for the transnational Occupy movement, effecting people-powered regime change in Tunisia and Egypt, and leading to armed uprisings that toppled dictatorships in Yemen and in Libya.

But as the movement spread across the Arabian Peninsula, it crossed out of the Sunni Muslim states where it had begun and into the so-called Shi'a Crescent. And there it encountered not only the postmodern politics of the Internet age but also premodern transnational sectarian identities underlying the colonial division of the region into modern states during the twentieth century. The prospect of the ouster of the ruling family of Bahrain, members of the national minority Sunni population, caused their coconfessionalists in Saudi Arabia to send military assistance to crush the Shi'a protestors, whom they feared would install a pro-Iran regime. The state in this instance chose to demolish its internationally identifiable national monument, the Pearl Roundabout, rather than have it continue to serve as a rallying point for protests. This deliberate sacrifice of modern national identity to preserve a premodern transnational community is emblematic of the choice confronting states whose aspirations to sovereign Westphalian status must still be weighed against transnational identity cleavages.

But the crushing of the Arab Spring in Bahrain through foreign intervention on sectarian grounds was only prologue to how these same dynamics would shape what would become an outright civil war in Syria, one that by its fifth anniversary would see over four hundred thousand dead[1] and more than thirteen million displaced.[2] But these refugees and the aid organizations that attempted to tend to them were only some of the transnational actors involved in the Syrian conflict.

Foreign fighters, including both armed belligerents and supporters who provided them with material assistance, had arrived in Syria from other countries before the first anniversary of the war. Although their precise number is difficult to confirm, intelligence agency estimates were that by 2016 as many as thirty-five thousand Sunni foreign fighters affiliated with the jihadi movement had traveled to the Syrian theater, most of them under the black banner of the Islamic State of Iraq and Syria (ISIS).[3] They were opposed by an unknown number of Shi'a volunteers who joined Iraqi and Afghan militias, the Syrian army, or units sent by the transnational terrorist organization Hezbollah, with reports ranging from ten thousand total to twenty thousand just from Afghanistan.[4] Additionally, several hundred mostly Christian Westerners had become foreign fighters for Kurdish or other ethnic militias that were fighting against Islamist foreign fighters.[5]

By 2014, this mobilization of foreign Islamist fighters was the largest recorded, surpassing decades of volunteers in Afghanistan since the 1980s and reaching numbers double that of the Iraq War in the 2000s in less than half as much time.[6] However, it was below the benchmarks set by communist foreign fighters in twentieth-century conflicts, such as the more than fifty thousand foreign fighters during the less than three years of the 1936–39 Spanish Civil War.[7]

How Were the Foreign Fighters in Syria Organized?

Nonstate groups have recruited their own combatants through transnational outreach efforts across international history. They have followed this strategy when they are at a material disadvantage in an internal conflict and want to change the balance of forces but cannot get sufficient assistance through a state-led military intervention. They therefore turn to private individuals, usually already members of transnational organizations that identify with their cause, and persuade them that their shared identity group faces an existential threat requiring their personal involvement in the name of communal duty and self-preservation.

This has been the approach of the groups regardless of whether their identity is ideological, national, or religious; communists, ethnic diasporas, and sectarian orders from Catholic to Sunni have honed these practices over decades. Globalization and a refusal by their home states to provide amnesty to jihadi Arab volunteers has also produced a steady cohort, replenished with new members over time, of transnational Islamists who are now a regular presence in civil wars with Muslim populations.[8]

This emergent professional class of foreign fighter may be changing the dynamic of transnational mobilization. For instance, because the narrative of the urgency for jihadi collective action has been applied without interruption to numerous conflicts for decades, it is now one that target audiences have grown up with, and framing may be less important to recruitment efforts. Likewise, because movement leaders now have entrenched global networks with decades of experience, their strategies and procedures have become institutionalized and are exported to every new conflict. Thus, the local dynamics of the conflicts are irrelevant to this professionalized peripatetic transnational cohort.

In Syria, the transnational combatants arrived subsequent to and against the resistance of local rebels. Foreign fighters did not have a significant visible role in the conflict until nearly a year after it began and played no role whatsoever in the uprisings in other Arab states in 2011 despite the shared antipathy of the jihadi groups toward the secular Arab regimes targeted by the civil protestors.[9] The Syrian uprising began as a response to the arrest in February of a number of children for antigovernment graffiti in the wake of the revolutions in the Maghreb and to the unflinching response by Bashir al-Assad's regime to demonstrations for their release.[10] The use of deadly force by the regime produced domestic groups that coordinated with exiled opposition leaders and with foreign governments, which shipped them arms and supplies, as well as a few nationalist Lebanese volunteers who crossed the border in the hopes of prying Lebanon from Damascus's grasp.[11]

But President al-Assad and his Ba'th Party would prove to be intractable because they were willing to take any measures, including the use of chemical weapons, against the opposition and its civilian supporters. More crucially, like Bahrain and unlike Libya, Syria enjoyed significant state support—in this case from Russia and Iran—who viewed al-Assad's survival as a strategic interest and reinforced him rather than isolating him. The conflict ground to sectarian stalemate, with al-Assad's regime dominated by Alawites (a Shi'a sect) and supported by Christians who feared the consequences of Sunni majority rule. The rising civilian suffering provoked the entry of transnational "armed humanitarians"[12] seeking to alter the status quo.

Overall, the foreign fighters constituted a small percentage of the actual rebels, with estimates during the second year of the war of a little under 10 percent of the opposition forces, or approximately six thousand out of sixty thousand, although other estimates put the number of foreign insurgents as high as ten thousand.[13] Still, they had an outsized influence on the conflict because they tended to use more violent tactics such as suicide bombings and because of their access to the material and propaganda support of other jihadists.

Arab Spring Foreign Fighters

However, the first wave of transnational volunteers in Syria were veterans of the recently concluded conflict in Libya who shared multiple identities with the local resistance opposition but were not a part of the transnational jihadi movement. The Libyan volunteers fought "on behalf" of the local rebels but did not integrate into their command structures. They did, however, operate their own training bases for units locals could join, while importing their own "specialists in communications, logistics, humanitarian issues and heavy weapons." Although in most ways their organization, the Umma Brigade (Liwwa al-Umma), is a national rather than a transnational group, its name, which refers to "the global community of the faithful," is a direct invocation of the transnational community that is also typically invoked by the Salafi jihadists fighting to overturn Westphalian order and establish a theocratically governed space. However, the Umma Brigade's leaders expressly stated that they did not wish to be perceived to be linked to al-Qaeda. Instead, they reported having arrived on their own volition because Libyans wished to continue the fight against tyranny that they had won with the support of an international military intervention that the Syrians lacked.[14]

Sunni Foreign Fighters ("Jihadists")

By the first anniversary of the war, the national aspirations of the local rebels and supporting parties that at least purported to share their ambitions were forced to contend with a new faction with an explicitly transnational agenda. On the insurgent side, a variety of organizations linked to the global jihadi movement descended upon Syria, ostensibly to protect Sunni civilians from the Alawite regime that was now engaging in overt human rights violations to break support for the rebels. Regionally active armed groups, including Lebanon's Fatah al-Islam, established operations in Syria, but the course of the conflict was soon shaped by al-Qaeda affiliates.[15] The two most prominent were ISIS, which had operated under several names in the previous decade (including al-Qaeda in Iraq), and the Support Front for the People of the Levant (Jabat al-Nusra), a previously unknown al-Qaeda affiliate that announced its existence in early 2012 with a series of suicide car bombings in Damascus.[16] The Sunni foreign fighter groups soon developed a reputation for extensive use of roadside bombs, which their members had learned to manufacture in Iraq.[17]

The al-Qaeda affiliates and other groups in the wider transnational jihadi movement operated in accordance with a long-established narrative that framed every local conflict involving Sunni Muslims as an attempt to crush the *umma* by apostate or secular local tyrants who are puppets of the interests of hegemonic infidel powers.[18]

Some volunteers who undertook the fight in what they initially understood to be defensive terms were radicalized during their time on the battlefield and came away with the jihadi core ideological conviction that winning this struggle meant shifting to offensive missions. The more ambitious among them viewed the conflict as paving the way for a proper emirate to be established in the heart of the Arab Middle East and on the front line against Israel, a more consequential and attractive opportunity than fighting in hinterlands such as Afghanistan.[19] The groups also enjoyed "indirect encouragement from some regional governments, which seek to topple the Assad regime and view the struggle as a proxy for a broader conflict with Iran."[20]

However, previously Arab governments had largely eschewed supporting foreign fighters since the 1980s because they suspected them of training to return home to continue their jihad. Among the Sunni volunteers in Syria, Libyans and Tunisians were some of the largest national groups because of greater liberty to recruit and organize after 2011, with the Ansar al-Shariah group facilitating travel and glorifying the martyrdom of volunteers. There had not been large Tunisian cohorts recorded in other recent conflicts, so this "real surprise"[21] contradicted pre–Arab Spring analyses that contended that volunteers from Arab states become foreign fighters principally because they were so effectively shut out of political processes at home that they sought alternative venues in weak or failed states.[22]

In addition to volunteers from Arab states, there were a significant number of Chechen fighters and a small but growing contingent of Southeast Asians. Additionally, "the Pakistani Taliban announced . . . that it had established a presence in Syria. Among those killed in recent battles was a Moroccan commander who had spent years as a prisoner of the U.S. government at Guantanamo Bay, Cuba, and was eulogized in one of the many videos prepared by the foreign volunteers to advertise their presence."[23] Many of the over sixty-five hundred recruits from Western countries would be used for propaganda value in highly touted campaigns on social media that alternately depicted intense cruelty against prisoners in an attempt to demonstrate that ISIS was formidable against its enemies but in other messages attempted to portray normal family life with the creature comforts of the West.[24]

Shi'a Foreign Fighters

The relatively recent body of literature on foreign fighters typically restricts the definition to nonstate groups.[25] And while many Shi'a foreign forces in Syria were there under the command of Iran, including the nonstate terrorist organization Hezbollah, the private volunteers from around the world who entered Syria on the side of the regime bear examination. Iran's government relied on the al-Assad regime to find common cause with the main non-Sunni Muslim power in the region and to provide access, via Syria and Lebanon, for Iran's influence in the region, in particular, its proxy force Hezbollah. Iran therefore sent regular forces to assist the Syrian military and police, Hezbollah to the battlefields to match the zeal of the Sunni groups, and its Revolutionary Guard to train to individual volunteers and militia units.[26]

Like the profascist foreign fighters who joined pro-Franco militias in 1937 Spain, foreign Shi'a fighters benefited from greater centralization and effective integration with existing military forces than did their otherwise more prominent adversaries.[27] Aaron Zelin estimated that the total number of foreign Shi'a fighters in Syria as of 2014 was as high as ten thousand, including three thousand to five thousand Hezbollah fighters who rotated in and out on a monthly basis.[28]

Iraqi Shiites joined the conflict despite an antipathy for al-Assad over his Ba'th Party affiliation, shared with Saddam Hussein, and their belief that al-Assad had tacitly encouraged the destabilization of the post-Hussein Shi'a bloc government by permitting Sunni foreign fighters to transit through Syria. However, as the uprising became an armed rebellion that began to attract Sunni extremists, many Shiites came to see the war in existential terms. Devout Shiites in Iraq often described the jihadi presence in the Syrian conflict as the beginning of the fulfillment of the prophecy of a diabolical army arising in Syria and conquering them in the end of days.[29]

In a March 2013 interview, Abu Ajib, secretary-general of the al-Abbas Brigade, said that his militia had formed to defend the Damascus shrine of Sayyida Zaynab, a pivotal figure in Shia Islam, from Salafi-jihadi attacks. The brigade was a transnational contingent of fighters, "including Iraqis, Syrians, Lebanese, Iraqi refugees in Syria, other Arabs, and Afghans." It had purportedly been armed by the Syrian government and trained in Iran:

> In the media operations of the al-Abbas Brigade and its supporters, Shi'a militiamen fighting in Syria are portrayed as "Zaynab's guardians" (*hurras Zaynab*) who are defending her shrine and, in turn, her honor, through self-sacrifice (*fida'*) from Salafist/Wahhabi hordes, which is how Syrian rebels are described in the discourse of the militias and their supporters. . . . Salafist creedal beliefs are virulently anti-Shi'a, and thus there is a long history of polemics between the two groups. By portraying all Syrian rebels as Salafists, the Shi'a militias and their supporters are essentially arguing that dialogue is hopeless.[30]

Sources of Transnational Recruitment

By 2014, individuals from at least seventy-four countries were fighting in Syria. Nearly 80 percent were from Arab and European countries, but Australia, North America, Southeast Asia, and Sub-Saharan Africa were also represented.[31] Documents captured from Jabat al-Nusra provided, much like the Sinjar Records of the Iraq War during the previous decade, detailed demographic profiles of the recruits, or at least some proportion of the Sunnis.[32] Present were "a mix of fighters from Tunisia, Bahrain, Turkey, Iraq, and Syria, with a variety of specialties from baking, car bombs, nursing, Sharia law, and media expertise. About a quarter of the men are married, and the majority appear to have 'bad' finances."[33]

Still, and while some projihad groups raised funds to support foreign fighter travel, most recruits apparently found the means to self-fund their journeys. Indeed, prospective Australian volunteers declared that they sold their furniture to help cover the costs of travel to Syria.[34]

In other instances, they faced the active opposition of their families, as in Tunisia where relatives of foreign fighters organized demonstrations demanding that the government intervene to bring their sons home. To avoid these pressures, recruits from across the Maghreb convened in isolated camps "in the desert triangle between Libya, Tunisia and Algeria" and were subsequently taken to Turkey for infiltration into Syria. According to one Tunisian newspaper, their rushed and inadequate training only "facilitate[d] their death or capture."[35] Similar methods have been employed in other foreign fighter cases, including indoctrination in remote training camps established, in part, to prevent their families from dragging them home.[36]

Among the foreign fighters around the city of Aleppo in 2013, local coordinators reported that "Saudis, Egyptians and Moroccans make up the largest number of Arab fighters, whereas many of the European fighters are of Moroccan origins. Moreover, there [was] a small percentage of fighters from former Soviet countries, especially Chechnya and Kyrgyzstan." Local rebel groups referred to non-Syrians fighting against the regime as "immigrants." While they were generally distributed across fighting units, Jabat al-Nusra kept them organizationally distinct, allocating them to immigrant brigades, "assigning them to support operations and giving them their own headquarters in northern Aleppo."[37] In this regard, al-Nusra demonstrated its al-Qaeda roots in following the model for Arab volunteers initiated by Osama bin Laden in 1980s Afghanistan.[38] Once across the Turkish border, Sunni recruits were received by Syrian training camp staff organized around several fighting units: "Some are fresh-faced idealists driven by a romantic notion of revolution or a hatred for the Assads. Others are jihadi veterans of Iraq, Yemen and Afghanistan. The different nationalities come to the war with disparate skill levels and quality of equipment and uniforms evident." Chechens in particular "carried their weapons with confidence and distanced themselves from the rest, moving around in a tight-knit unit-within-a-unit. . . . Each team was assigned an Arabic speaker and given 10 days' basic training, the point of which was not to learn how to shoot but to learn to communicate and work together." The fighters were then dispersed among the different jihadi organizations, with some exceptions, such as the Chechen contingent, allowed to remain in units based on nationality.[39]

Interactions with Transnational and International Actors

Beyond their parallel cross-border mobilization structures, the various foreign fighter groups in Syria have been both enabled and constrained by each other's presences. While insurgencies tend to operate transnationally to obtain havens and to resupply,[40] the rebellion in Syria has been uniquely impacted by the presence of multiple transnational groups that operate variously in conjunction with established branches in war zones in neighboring states, with direct state assistance or with state material support.

The decade-long conflict in Iraq meant that there was already a deep pool of battle-hardened militants organized along sectarian lines ready to deploy into the new war zone. By October 2012, two hundred proregime Iraqi recruits serving in Shi'a militias had traveled to Syria, most of them with groups affiliated with cleric Moqtada al-Sadr and his Mahdi Army and "Iranian-supported militias originally formed to fight U.S. and coalition military forces in Iraq."[41]

The Shi'a militias also enjoyed the protection of the al-Assad regime's air force. In this regard, they shared something in common with the Sunni Libyan forces whose prior success had been attributable to the North Atlantic Treaty Organization (NATO) establishing first a no-fly zone and then conducting air strikes in their country in 2011. In the past, other foreign fighters have been victorious with air dominance, such as the Israeli MACHAL and the Kosovo Liberation Army, whereas those that did not have it, such as the International Brigades in 1930s Spain, were ultimately defeated. The Sunni foreign fighters in Syria were never out of reach of the government's airpower.[42]

The Sunni side, lacking the primary organizational conduit enjoyed by the Tehran-backed Shi'a groups, remained fragmented. When ISIS leader Abu Bakr al-Baghdadi announced a merger between the two groups in March 2013, it was publicly rebuffed not only by Jabat al-Nusra but also by al-Qaeda leader Ayman al-Zawahiri.[43] By 2014, the two groups were actively targeting each other,[44] as well as local secular rebel groups such as the Free Syrian Army, in a bid to control rebel-held regions and to emerge as the preeminent anti-al-Assad faction in the competition for international recognition and funding.[45]

Divisions over strategy concerning how to best gain international support were evident among the jihadists. For example, in one Salafi instance, a fighter with the Farouq Brigade pleaded for the black jihadi flag at his camp to be lowered because it would alarm NATO and thus threaten to disrupt supplies coming in from Turkey. However, his compatriots disagreed: "They told me they were here to stop NATO."[46]

The al-Assad regime labeled the rebels "Gulf-Turkish forces," accusing the Sunni-led Arab Gulf states and Turkey of arming, funding, and leading them.[47] Indeed, there were a number of regional sources of financial support behind both the indigenous and imported rebels, including wealthy Syrian traders, Syria's Turkish-backed branch of the Muslim Brotherhood, and wealthy individuals in the Gulf states.[48]

While Saudi citizens had been among the largest national contingents found in studies of foreign fighters in Iraq,[49] the kingdom sponsored religious decrees barring fighting in Syria and backed them up with prison time for offenders.[50] By contrast, other reports claimed that "Qatar is funneling money to Tunisian NGOs [nongovernmental organizations] to recruit jihadists and dispatch them to Syria. From Qatar, these networks obtain 'a pledge of $3,000 in exchange for every Tunisian youth who enlists.'"[51]

Finger-pointing is perhaps inevitable in the global governance of transnational security challenges. The collective-action problems inherent to stopping foreign fighters from reaching Syria—as well as from returning to their countries of origin or to another state—led to an international coordinated response using the tools available to state actors. United Nations (UN) Security Council Resolution 2178 on "foreign terrorist fighters," promulgated by the United States and passed in 2014 three months after the declaration of the ISIS caliphate, required all governments to harmonize law enforcement and information-sharing to aid in the prosecution of would-be foreign fighters and those who provide them with material support. All participants in the foreign fighter recruitment and transit chain, even those based purely domestically, would subsequently be treated as transnational actors responsible for events in distant conflict zones.[52] The elevation of the issue to the Security Council is similar to the series of resolutions referenced by Miriam J. Anderson (chapter 9) in that in both cases the Security Council sought to compel states to take a particular course of action in their dealings with transnational actors.

Ironically, even the Syrian government itself was accused of facilitating the flow of Sunni rebels into the country. Syria had been a conduit for jihadi foreign fighters into Iraq in the prior decade, and early in the war there was at least the rumor that al-Assad hoped to reactivate these networks to bring jihadists into the country "to discredit the revolutionaries, deter international support for the opposition and create conditions under which the harsh crackdown by authorities will appear justified."[53]

If the regime was indeed involved in such a machination, it would mark a novel response by a state to transnational insurgents in using their generally illegitimate presence in international politics to bolster its own legitimacy and claims of the necessity of its sovereign authority. On the other hand, states have permitted transnational groups to operate within their borders in areas related to military security, as Luke Flanagan describes the American and Canadian Knights of Columbus in Great Britain in chapter 1. Kate Macdonald, in chapter 10, evaluates how some regimes cooperate with transnational organizations because they calculate that doing so confers legitimacy upon their policy courses in contentious politics. The Syrian government, by contrast, sought to portray itself as a Westphalian bulwark against jihadism, exercising unpalatable but necessary violence against transnational actors who wielded illegitimate force and threatened the state-based order.

Communications Strategies and the Growing Importance of Cyberspace

Regardless of these machinations, there was no shortage of volunteers. Indeed, "so alluring is Syria that jihadist groups in Chechnya and al-Qaeda in the Islamic

Maghreb [to retain fighters had to urge] people to stay put and fight the local fight, rather than doing battle on the streets of Aleppo."[54] Propaganda and recruitment messaging also emanated from a variety of other sources and with less centralized control than foreign fighter insurgencies enjoyed in the past.

Initially, the jihadi movement took to the Internet to circumvent physical and legal restrictions on recruitment efforts. Although the direct recruitment of members was the ultimate objective, the dissemination of propaganda still had a valuable strategic purpose because it provided legitimacy by demonstrating that effective action was possible.[55] The term "jihad" was by then so familiar in accepted connotation that it was held as self-explanatory online and used by would-be volunteers as a search filter to take them to appropriate enabling websites.[56]

Different monitoring groups gave wildly different estimates of how many terrorist websites were online in the post-9/11 period. During the height of foreign fighter intervention in Iraq during 2007–8, estimates ranged from eight thousand to fifty thousand. Regardless of how effective any individual website or social media account might have been, their collective weight had the added propaganda value of feeding the perception of a large global movement capable of radicalizing individuals ubiquitously.[57]

Prior to the Syrian Civil War, there had been a number of known instances of individuals who had been drawn into TVAs through online contact, including American Adam Gadahn, who became involved in the jihadi movement and spent seventeen years with al-Qaeda in Pakistan as a propagandist before dying in a drone strike. Online jihadi communication channels have proven impossible to fully shut down because blocked accounts immediately reemerged with slightly different addresses or handles.[58] Conversely, some counterterrorism agencies have argued that transnational media corporations should not shut down jihadi social media accounts because they provide open sources of intelligence.[59]

In the case of ISIS, brigades of keyboard warriors were deployed to use social media to build a brand of effective fighting against the entrenched world order—a broader appeal than al-Qaeda's declaration of war against United States political hegemony—that made jihad cool. Ironically, social media platforms operated by American corporations provided a no-cost means of transnational organization that permitted ISIS to pursue a far more effective Internet outreach strategy than trawling chat rooms for disaffected individuals.[60]

As evidenced by the public display of tensions between Jabat al-Nusra, ISIS, and the central leadership of the transnational al-Qaeda network, a variety of different voices spoke for the jihadi foreign fighters in and around Syria. Part of the reason for this fragmentation was the result of the spread of personal communication devices that had been unavailable to previous fighters. With every smart phone now a printing press with global reach, a cohort of fighters who came of age in the Internet era recognized that they could blog or give interviews from the conflict and record their personal narratives, shaping the discourse about jihad. However, their individual narratives weakened efforts to exert centralized leadership.[61]

Initially, although the secular, nationalist Free Syrian Army stated explicitly in 2011 that foreign jihadists were neither required nor welcome, in early 2012 "al-Qaeda leader Ayman al-Zawahiri called on 'mujahedin' to head to Syria in support of the rebels."[62] In keeping with the framing used since the recruitment of Arabs to Afghanistan in the 1980s, recruiters told potential foreign fighters that overcoming local resistance to their doctrines was just part of the necessary struggle:

> For a Mujahid it is very important to be tolerant towards others, for in this Jihad you will be meeting people from different nations, with different habits and cultures. Furthermore you are in a completely different country, far away from life as you knew it. You have to adapt to the situation and the variety of people you will deal with. If you do not have an open heart and are impatient then you will probably not persevere this Jihad. It is during Jihad that you will truly get to know your comrades; it is here your true friends will be revealed.
>
> One may believe the only thing you will deal with in Jihad are bullets and shelling. A Mujahid however must also stand hunger, pain, insomnia. He must be patient with the people he meets and has to adapt to a whole new situation. Sometimes you will have to stay put for weeks, enduring hunger, cold, rain. . . . This asks for endurance and patience.[63]

The formal recruitment messaging emphasized the necessity of shared sacrifice and spiritual benefit rather than individual glory or the opportunity for material gain. Presumably recruits coming through the intake camps were provided some form of media relations information in addition to their other training. In practice, the ability to post online and evident latitude given to speak to foreign journalists meant that the central groups appeared to either have less control over how they were presented to the world or engaged in a decentralized social media strategy of permitting fighters to personalize the conflict for a global audience.

Foreign fighter groups used social media as "a constant avenue for communication and an open path to share critical information, solicit contributions, and recruit fighters. Each day on Facebook, new names and photos of deceased foreign fighters [were] posted by rebel supporters who hope[d] that their willingness to sacrifice will inspire others to follow in their footsteps."[64]

Video trailers promising suicide bombings in America posted to YouTube, and Twitter warnings to residents of Baghdad to prepare for the arrival of ISIS, were simply the logical adaptation of the media strategies of effective terrorist groups.[65] Published manifestos gave way in the 1970s to hostage-taking on live international satellite broadcasts, and later social media provided a relevant and expedient means to reach a global audience through intimidation and, the militants hoped, inspiration.

A study of 190 jihadists with social media presences examined not only their Facebook and Twitter accounts but also whom they followed, including spiritual leaders who had been "liked" by more than 10 percent of foreign fighters who had social media accounts. Of these, two of the three most popular were Western-based, English-speaking preachers: an American and an Australian convert.[66] Thus, the flow of ideas from Syria-based transnational insurgencies to the West was ultimately either circular or completely deterritorialized.

ISIS in particular employed an aggressive social media strategy, using retweets to amplify its presence and make its numbers appear greater and to achieve prominence in search results. It even developed an app to direct-stream relevant jihadi tweets outside of the user's normal Twitter feed to avoid observations and reduce the potential costs of supporting the organization.[67] In early days, its supporters in Western countries promoted content on YouTube and added logos to their own Twitter and Facebook accounts.[68] The central leadership subsequently employed the terrorist strategy of propaganda by deed when it used online videos, also shared globally through social media, of decapitations and other cruel executions of prisoners. The doctrine was based on the recommendations of theoretician Abu Bakr Naji, who argued in *The Management of Savagery* that a polarizing approach would attract the most committed volunteers.[69]

And such joiners in turn became the means for the group to expand its membership still further. Official group Twitter accounts were less important to effective communications than disseminator accounts. Disseminators had no formal ties to the group and were therefore not as readily locked out by service provider TNCs. They translated material from Arabic to other languages for global consumption, and because they were outside of the war zone they had access to more sources of news and could provide commentary for a wider readership. Unlike fighters, they were able to interact with readers and generate more interest.[70]

Outreach in Western nations followed a social-media-based strategy, as evidenced by one twenty-three-year-old Briton who sent ten thousand tweets to three thousand followers in under two years before being killed in Syria. Common tropes appeared in the messages disseminated by the jihadi blogging brigades: All wrote zealously about defending fellow Muslims and saving women and children, although all "regard[ed] Assad's Alawite regime—if not all Shias—as evil."[71]

Western recruits were a part of the jihadi groups' strategy to connect with Western audiences via social media, which had also been the approach of al-Shabaab in Somalia.[72] One American convert posted a video of himself engaged in target practice and in battles, as well as of his wedding to a woman from Sweden who had also traveled to aid the jihad. A Canadian recruit spoke freely to a reporter, noting of his mother: "'She said: 'Make sure you're not at the back. Go to the front.' Laughing, he adds: 'I don't think my mother loves me that much. No, I'm joking. She must love me for her to say that. Hamdullah [thank God], she understands.'"[73]

Westerners, particularly converts to Islam, are frequently brought into jihadi social networks by individual acquaintances at the local level.[74] However, the importance of bricks-and-mortar meeting places may be diminishing as cyber-space enables connections and organization of the like-minded unimpeded by geographic distances. An example outside the confines of the transnational jihadi movement is a group of eight Syrian American university students who met on Facebook and organized via Skype a two-week trip to work with refugees, although at least one chose to become involved in combat, engaging in a shoot-out with a government sniper. Since returning to his studies, he noticed that "his friendships at home have faded as the number of his 'revolution friends' grew."[75]

In 2013, not long before departing for Syria with his wife, American-born Australian convert Yusuf Ali posted a series of messages on his Facebook wall, among the last of which was the following:

> This life will not last forever! Your family, your friends, your wealth, your busi-ness, the good times and the bad times, everything will come to an end. The life time you spent acquiring these things will not benefit you in the least but only your belief along with your record of deeds. How can one enjoy this world when he knows one day he will have to face his lord! May God give us under-standing and the reality of life and death.

After the couple was killed during an attack in January 2014, Ali's wife's sister posted a congratulatory message—which also attacked the secular local rebels—on social media, and other enthusiasts posted directly on Ali's page in terms that honored him as a noble combatant.[76] While these posts may have been sincere in their affect, there is also the possibility that at least some of them were attempts to spin the deaths of the Alis, framing them as heroes so that the traffic of visitors driven by media coverage to his page would view them as examples to be emulated. Some took a more direct approach on social media, exploiting the visible networks of second-order acquaintances and reaching out to potential recruits whom they had not met before, in messages and friend requests.[77]

Shi'a groups were responsive rather than innovative in cyberspace in the virtual battle, developing slogans that were retorts to the anti-al-Assad Face-book campaigns of the jihadists. Shi'a communication materials tended to depict martyrs and information about their units but also slain rebels and com-manders from the Sunni groups, to demonstrate that they were effective in combating them.[78]

Overall, the foreign fighters in Syria used the infrastructure of globalization—essentially free, fully transnational communication platforms—to inspire self-starters to join their cause rather than devoting resources to maintaining extensive recruitment networks through traditional institutions such as mosques. But while these various actors were rhetorically cohesive, it begs the question of the impact upon esprit de corps when fighter groups are collections of self-starters rather than webs of acquaintances recruited via their collective ties to communal institutions.

The Influence of Syria's Foreign Fighters on Conflict and Peace

The divisions between the locally based resistance movement that originated in early 2011 and the transnational insurgents that had arrived by the end of the year ensured that Syria's foreign fighters had an immediate and significant impact on the early course of the Syrian conflict. The divergent interests of the transnational jihadists in Syria and the local population that initially rose against the regime transformed the dynamic of the Syrian uprising from one of rebels against the regime to one of multiple armed groups battling for pockets of territory under a sectarian dynamic that polarized Muslims worldwide.

Local insurgents such as the Free Syrian Army made it expressly clear that they did not want jihadists arriving and attempting to restructure Syrian society to conform to their views of sharia. The earliest fighting between rebel groups appears to have been local rebels attempting to drive away foreign jihadists, whom they warned to stay out of their communities.[79] As one Free Syrian Army commander put it, "I will not allow the spread of Takfiri. . . . The Islam we had during the regime was disfigured Islam and what they are bringing us is also disfigured."[80] By contrast, the initial foreign fighters were obliged to "try to connect with a small number of homegrown Syrian groups in the country who at least partly share their ideology."[81]

While there is evidence that some local fighters shifted their allegiances to what they viewed as more effective opposition groups,[82] reports of such realignments were not widespread.[83] Instead of being a contest for hearts and minds, the rival armed factions began in 2014 to attack each other directly, enabling the regime to reconsolidate its hold on most of the country. Even the two al-Qaeda-linked groups became bitter rivals, with ISIS executing dozens of Jabat al-Nusra fighters after battles for key towns, and the homegrown rebels largely melting away because they saw no advantage to fighting the transnational jihadists.[84] This pattern is consistent with previous cases of foreign fighters, in which doctrinaire transnationals have embraced combat shunned by locals who had more pragmatic concerns for the preservation of their family and property.[85] Within two months of the open internecine fighting between transnational jihadists, more than three thousand people had been killed, and Jabat al-Nusra threatened that ISIS must accept external mediation from the global jihadi movement or it would remove it from the region.[86]

However, ISIS soon eclipsed the more traditional al-Qaeda affiliate in Syria and contested with its franchises elsewhere in the Muslim world. In particular, the savvy ISIS media strategy in foregrounding Western foreign fighters and encouraging supporters in Western states to carry out lone attacks made it at least appear to be the group that was the natural home for transnational militants.[87]

Sectarian violence also flowed on to the home countries of the volunteers. In Australia, home to one of the largest groups of foreign fighters relative to population, tensions between Sunni and Shi'a Muslims over the war led to street attacks and intimidation campaigns in major cities, with the firebombing of mosques and community centers and the storming of the Syrian embassy by a group of forty men.[88]

Of even greater concern to foreign governments was the prospect that foreign fighters in Syria would return to their home countries better trained and more implacable in their views on political Islam than when they left. They might also distinguish themselves for transnational support from fellow jihadists and become key connectors of terrorist activity.[89] While historically foreign fighters have reintegrated into civilian life with little noticeable impact upon their society of origin,[90] by some estimates as many as 10 percent of returned foreign fighters since the origins of the al-Qaeda network in 1980s Afghanistan have become involved in domestic terrorism and been responsible for particularly successful and lethal attacks.[91]

The specter of returnees from Syria becoming as significant a security threat as the Arab Afghans became twenty years earlier prompted a number of governments to take what were in a historical context unusually aggressive steps in tackling transnational mobilization. These included the United States selectively arresting individuals in transit to or from Syria and the United Kingdom preemptively seizing passports of individuals determined likely to go to Syria.[92]

By 2014, the UN secretary-general had come to identify transnational insurgency as one of the six factors of the Syrian Civil War that threatened the stability of the international community: "Foreign fighters are in action on both sides, increasing the level of violence and exacerbating sectarian hatreds. While we should not blindly accept the Syrian Government demonization of all the opposition as terrorists, neither should we be blinded to the real threat of terrorists in Syria. The world must come together to eliminate funding and other support for Jabat al-Nusra and the Islamic State of Iraq and al-Sham."[93]

The Syrian conflict was therefore instrumental in alarming states into reasserting their Westphalian privileges against the threat of boomeranging transnational violence.

What Foreign Fighters in Syria Tell Us about Transnationalism

Aside from fears of terrorist blowback, the foreign fighters in Syria generated international approbation for violating standards of armed conflict. For example, the UN Human Rights Council voted by a wide margin to condemn the Syrian government for employing foreign fighters who operated in accountable militias prone to attacking civilians. One of the dissenting states was Syria's ally Russia, despite that country's past experience with foreign fighters in Afghanistan and its shoot-on-sight policy in Chechnya.[94] Russia also apparently began to target Jabat al-Nusra fighters in air strikes as a means of eliminating an alternative force to the al-Assad regime.[95] This approach indicates that states are more likely to value national interests and pursue them using "illegitimate" transnational forces than they are to worry about weakening Westphalian norms of monopolies on violence.

The reaction of both Arab and Western states to the growth of transnational insurgencies in Syria may be largely explained by their broader concerns over the lingering threat of the jihadi movement and their strategic preferences for who controls a pivotal area of the Middle East. However, they also illustrate the weak position of transnational movements—normatively, materially, and legally—compared to the position of states and intergovernmental organizations.

The experiences of the families of foreign fighters also highlighted difficulties in balancing competing loyalties between family, civil society communities, and national citizenship. Despite the fact that some relatives were evidently proud that their children were serving as foreign fighters, in Syria, as in past instances, many times volunteers sneaked away without letting their families know where they were going.[96] In some cases, and perhaps because they were afraid of the reactions of their governments, families turned to civil society groups for assistance. For example, "the families of these jihadists are also demanding that humanitarian organizations lend their weight to the cause of bringing their sons home. [However,] an official in the Tunisian League for Human Rights [stated] that 'quite frankly, getting them back would be a very difficult process.'"[97] Interaction between armed transnational groups and more cosmopolitan transnational civil society remains understudied and might be substantially different from how such groups interact with states.

The experience of both the Sunni and Shi'a foreign fighters also provided evidence that transnational identities are as contested as any others. While the groups battled each other and the local rebels, they regularly faced divisions along national and other parochial lines. Christopher Anzalone noted that "localism [was] also often a factor in militant recruitment and the formulation of strategic goals and ideological positions."[98] The use of particular foreign fighters in propaganda material to recruit their countrymen, such as Americans in videos pitched to potential recruits in the United States, is also evidence that transnational identities are not exclusive of other interests.[99]

Foreign fighters are strategic communicators, crafting emotional appeals designed to reframe contentious politics.[100] Like TANs, they aim to create a boomerang effect upon their home societies by virtue of their enhanced capacities.[101] As with some peaceful activist groups, the nonstate actors involve states in collaboration to achieve "transnational collective action."[102]

Although religious communities are among the oldest forms of transnational civil society,[103] both Sunni and Shi'a foreign fighter movements found their organizational prowess in the Syrian conflict based to a large extent on building social capital through online virtual communities.[104] In so doing, they employed the same approaches used by militant groups tied to the Congolese diaspora twenty years earlier (as described by Jennifer M. Brinkerhoff in chapter 4). And, as with other forms of collective action, the rise of social media appears to have created movements that are less easily directed but potentially more resilient and, in relation to the speed of the buildup in this particular conflict, more pervasive and ubiquitous. Ariel I. Ahram and John Gledhill (chapter 5) note that even by the late twentieth century, states had proven incapable of blocking communication by transnational extremist networks seeking to radicalize citizens within their borders.

Social media platforms appear to be accelerating this trend and perhaps account for increased transnational participation in armed conflicts by involving more parties in the discourse. Before 2011, the conventional wisdom was that jihadists went elsewhere to fight because the odds were stacked against them in their repressive home states. Yet, while neither democracy nor Islamist rule had consolidated power in Tunisia or Libya in the years after the Arab Spring, citizens of those states went to fight in Syria rather than take the opportunity to reshape their own countries at a critical historical juncture. Because they had the opportunity to make a difference at home after the Arab Spring, it remains necessary to explain why they went to Syria instead. Although they evidenced characteristics shared with other transnational actors, Syria's foreign fighters challenged established patterns of foreign fighter behavior and demonstrated the need for continued examination of evolving patterns of transnational organizations.

Notes

1. "Syria Death Toll: UN Envoy Estimates 400,000 Killed," Al Jazeera, April 24, 2016, http://www.aljazeera.com/news/2016/04/staffan-de-mistura-400000-killed-syria-civil-war-160423055735629.html.

2. "Syrian Arab Republic: Key Figures," United Nations Office for the Coordination of Humanitarian Affairs, http://www.unocha.org/syria.

3. Reuters, "Is the Number of Foreign Fighters Joining ISIS Really Plummeting?," *Newsweek*, April 28, 2016, http://www.newsweek.com/isis-foreign-fighters-90-percent-iraq-syria-decreasing-general-claim-453741.

4. Daniel Byman, "Syria's Other Foreign Fighters," *Lawfare*, January 12, 2014; Hashmatallah Moslih, "Iran 'Foreign Legion' Leans on Afghan Shia in Syria Civil War," Al Jazeera, January 23, 2016, http://www.aljazeera.com/news/2016/01/iran-foreign-legion-leans-afghan-shia-syria-war-160122130355206.html.

5. Nathan Patin, "Syria's Other Foreign Fighters," Bellingcat, August 26, 2015, https://www.bellingcat.com/news/mena/2015/08/26/the-other-foreign-fighters/.

6. Aaron Y. Zelin, Evan F. Kohlmann, and Laith al-Khouri, *Convoy of Martyrs in the Levant: A Joint Study Charting the Evolving Role of Sunni Foreign Fighters in the Armed Uprising against the Assad Regime in Syria* (Washington, DC: Flashpoint Global Partners, 2013), 2.

7. David Malet, *Foreign Fighters: Transnational Identity in Civil Conflicts* (New York: Oxford University Press, 2013).

8. Ibid.

9. Ibid.

10. Joe Sterling, "Daraa: The Spark That Lit the Syrian Flame," CNN, March 1, 2012, http://edition.cnn.com/2012/03/01/world/meast/syria-crisis-beginnings/.

11. Zelin, Kohlmann, and al-Khouri, *Convoy of Martyrs*.

12. Evan F. Kohlmann, *Al-Qaida's Jihad in Europe: The Afghan-Bosnian Network* (New York: Berg, 2004).

13. Mohammad Gharibo, "Foreign Fighters in Syria . . . between Religious Duty and the Islamic Political Project," Middle East Monitor, May 22, 2013, http://www.middleeastmonitor.com/articles/middle-east/6092-foreign-fighters-in-syria-between-religious-duty-and-the-islamic-political-project.

14. Reuters, "Libyan Freedom Fighters Join with Syrian Rebels," *Times Live* (Johannesburg), August 17, 2012, http://www.timeslive.co.za/world/2012/08/17/libyan-freedom-fighters-join-with-syrian-rebels.

15. Martin Chulov, "Syria's Rebels Fear Foreign Jihadis in Their Midst," *Guardian*, November 1, 2012.

16. "Islamist Group Claims Syria Bombs 'To Avenge Sunnis,'" AFP, March 21, 2012.

17. "Uzbek Jihadis Join Syrian Guerilla Fighters," CA *News*, republished by Stratrisks, August 22, 2012.

18. Olivier Roy, *Globalized Islam: The Search for a New Ummah* (New York: Columbia University Press, 2004); Mohammed M. Hafez, *Suicide Bombers in Iraq: The Strategy and Ideology of Martyrdom* (Washington, DC: United States Institute of Peace, 2007); Thomas Hegghammer, "The Rise of Muslim Foreign Fighters," *International Security* 35, no. 3 (Winter 2010–11): 53–94.

19. Chulov, "Syria's Rebels Fear."

20. Byman, "Syria's Other Foreign Fighters."

21. Zelin, Kohlmann, and al-Khouri, *Convoy of Martyrs*, 4.

22. Graham E. Fuller, "The Future of Political Islam," *Foreign Affairs* 81, no. 2 (2002): 48–60; Roy, *Globalized Islam*.

23. Liz Sly, "Foreign Extremists Dominate Syria Fight," *Washington Post*, October 1, 2013.

24. Brendan I. Koerner, "Why ISIS Is Winning the Social Media War," *Wired*, April 2016.

25. Hegghammer, "Muslim Foreign Fighters"; Malet, *Foreign Fighters*.

26. Byman, "Syria's Other Foreign Fighters"; Reuters, "Libyan Freedom Fighters."

27. Malet, *Foreign Fighters*.

28. Byman, "Syria's Other Foreign Fighters."

29. Yasir Ghazi and Tim Arango, "Iraqi Sects Join Battle in Syria on Both Sides," *New York Times*, October 27, 2012.

30. Christopher Anzalone, "Zaynab's Guardians: The Emergence of Shi'a Militias in Syria," *CTC Sentinel*, July 23, 2013.

31. Zelin, Kohlmann, and al-Khouri, *Convoy of Martyrs*.

32. Joseph Felter and Brian Fishman, *Al Qaida's Foreign Fighters in Iraq: A First Look at the Sinjar Records* (West Point, NY: Combating Terrorism Center, 2007).

33. Eliot Higgins, "Captured Jabat Al-Nusra Administrative Documents Show Details of Arms, Foreign Fighters," November 17, 2013, http://brown-moses.blogspot.co.uk/2013/11/captured-Jabat-al-nusra-administrative.html.

34. Ian Lloyd Neubauer, "G'Day Damascus: Australians Are Joining Syria's Rebels in Surprising Numbers," *Time*, July 16, 2013.

35. Nesrine Hamedi, "Tunisian Jihadists Fighting in Syria,"*Assafir*, March 18, 2013, translation in *al-Monitor*, March 24, 2013.

36. Malet, *Foreign Fighters*, 144, 173, 231; David Malet, Bryan Priest, and Sarah Staggs, "Involving Foreign Fighters in Somalia," in *Globalizing Somalia*, ed. Emma Leonard and Gilbert Ramsay (London: Bloomsbury, 2013), 94, 100.

37. Gharibo, "Foreign Fighters in Syria."

38. Malet, *Foreign Fighters*, 177.

39. Ghaith Abdul-Ahad, "Syria: The Foreign Fighters Joining the War against Bashar al-Assad," *Guardian*, September 23, 2012.

40. Idean Salehyan, *Rebels without Borders: Transnational Insurgencies in World Politics* (Ithaca, NY: Cornell University Press, 2009).

41. Anzalone, "Zaynab's Guardians."

42. Reuters, "Libyan Freedom Fighters."

43. "Iraqi al-Qaeda Chief Rejects Zawahiri Orders," Al Jazeera, June 15, 2013.

44. Kevin Sullivan, "Jail for Saudis Who Join Foreign Conflicts," Al Jazeera, February 9, 2014.

45. "UN Human Rights Body Condemns Foreign Fighters in Syria," BBC News, May 29, 2013.

46. Abdul-Ahad, *Syria*.

47. Reuters, "Libyan Freedom Fighters."

48. Chulov, "Syria's Rebels Fear."

49. Felter and Fishman, *Al Qaida's Foreign Fighters*.

50. Kevin Sullivan, "Saudis Line Up against Syria's Assad," *Washington Post*, October 8, 2012; Sullivan, "Jail for Saudis."

51. Hamedi, "Tunisian Jihadists."

52. "Security Council Unanimously Adopts Resolution Condemning Violent Extremism, Underscoring Need to Prevent Travel, Support for Foreign Terrorist Fighters," UN Security Council, September 24, 2014.

53. Sly, "Foreign Extremists."

54. "Will They Come Home to Roost?," *Economist*, May 4, 2013.

55. Hafez, *Suicide Bombers*, 169–70.

56. Gilbert Ramsay, *Jihadi Culture on the World Wide Web* (London: Bloomsbury, 2013).

57. Ibid., 11, 16.

58. Natalie O'Brien and Leila Abdallah, "Iraq Conflict Spills onto Australian Social Media," *The Age*, June 21, 2014.

59. Ramsay, *Jihadi Culture*, 2.

60. J. M. Berger and Jonathon Morgan, *The ISIS Twitter Census* (Washington, DC: Brookings Institution Press 2014).

61. Clinton Watts, remarks at "Foreign Fighters in Syria and Beyond," roundtable, Foreign Policy Research Institute, Washington DC, 2013, https://www.youtube.com/watch?v=zm4t04f3I80.

62. Sly, "Foreign Extremists."

63. Aaron Y. Zelin, "Dutch Foreign Fighters: Some Testimonials from the Syrian Front #2; The Story of 28 Year Old Chokri Massali–Abu Walae," Jihadology.net, October 17, 2013, http://jihadology.net/2013/10/17/guest-post-dutch-foreign-fighters-some-testimonials-from-the-syrian-front-2-the-story-of-28-year-old-chokri-massali-abu-walae/.

64. Zelin, Kohlmann, and al-Khouri, *Convoy of Martyrs*, 2.

65. Michael Schmidt, "Syria Suicide Bombing Puts U.S. Face on Jihad Video," *New York Times*, June 14, 2014.

66. Joseph A. Carter, Shiraz Maher, and Peter R. Neumann, *#Greenbirds: Measuring Importance and Influence in Syrian Foreign Fighter Networks* (London: International Centre for the Study of Radicalisation and Political Violence, 2014), 18.

67. Berger and Morgan, *The ISIS Twitter Census*.

68. O'Brien and Abdallah, "Iraq Conflict Spills."

69. Abu Bakr Naji, *The Management of Savagery*, trans. William McCants (Washington, DC: Brookings Institution, 2006).

70. Carter, Maher, and Neumann, *#Greenbirds*, 15–17.

71. Sam Jones, "Jihad by Social Media," *Financial Times*, March 28, 2014.

72. Malet, Priest, and Staggs, "Involving Foreign Fighters in Somalia."

73. Barney Henderson and Chris Irvine, "Syria: US to Arm Rebels—Latest," *Telegraph*, June 14, 2013.

74. Andrew Katz, "The Belgian Teen Who Went to Fight in Syria: The Brian De Mulder Story," *Time*, May 22, 2013.

75. Jenna Johnson, "After Uniting on Facebook, Syrian Americans Travel to War's Edge," February 4, 2013.

76. Suzanne Dredge and Matt Wordsworth, "Yusuf Ali, Australian Man Killed in Syria, Had Links to Al Qaeda, Court Documents Allege," ABC News, January 17, 2014.

77. Mark Schliebs, "Next Generation of Jihadi Family Joins Syrian War," *Australian*, January 28, 2014.

78. Anzalone, "Zayanb's Guardians."

79. Sly, "Foreign Extremists."

80. Abdul-Ahad, *Syria*.

81. Martin Chulov, "Syria: Foreign Jihadists Could Join Battle for Aleppo," *Guardian*, August 22, 2012.

82. Loveday Morris, Joby Warrick, and Souad Mekhennet, "Rival al-Qaeda-Linked Groups Fortifying in Syria with Mix of Pragmatism and Militancy," *Washington Post*, October 14, 2013.

83. Sly, "Foreign Extremists."

84. "Jail for Saudis."

85. Malet, *Foreign Fighters*.

86. Associated Press, "ISIL Says It Faces War with Nusra in Syria," Al Jazeera, March 8, 2014.

87. Jonah Goldberg, "How ISIS Came to Eclipse al Qaeda," *New York Post*, June 14, 2015.

88. Neubauer, "G' Day Damascus."

89. "Will They Come Home to Roost?"

90. Malet, *Foreign Fighters*.

91. Hegghammer, "Muslim Foreign Fighters."

92. Mark Hosenball, "U.S. Steps Up Scrutiny of American Fighters in Syria," Reuters, May 22, 2014; David Barrett, "New Powers to Strip Passports from British Terror Suspects," *Telegraph*, April 25, 2013.

93. Ban Ki-moon, "Crisis in Syria: Civil War, Global Threat." *Huffington Post, June 25, 2014.

94. "UN Human Rights Body Condemns"; Malet, *Foreign Fighters*.

95. Laura Rozen, "Will US, Russia Start Coordinating against Jabhat al-Nusra in Syria?" Al-Monitor, July 5, 2016, http://www.al-monitor.com/pulse/originals/2016/07/syria-russia -discussion-target-jabhat-nusra-restore-truce.html#ixzz4FQMNpqfn.

96. Malet, *Foreign Fighters*.

97. Hamedi, "Tunisian Jihadists."

98. Anzalone, "Zaynab's Guardians."

99. Henderson and Irvine "Syria: Us to Arm Rebels."

100. Martha Finnemore and Kathryn Sikkink, "International Norm Dynamics and Political Change," *International Organization* 52 (1998): 887–917.

101. Margaret E. Keck and Kathryn Sikkink, *Activists beyond Borders: Advocacy Networks in International Politics* (Ithaca, NY: Cornell University Press, 1998).

102. Donatella della Porta and Sidney Tarrow, eds., *Transnational Protest and Global Activism* (Lanham, MD: Rowman & Littlefield, 2005); Clifford Bob, *The Global Right Wing and the Clash of World Politics* (New York: Cambridge University Press, 2012).

103. Ann M. Florini, *The Third Force: The Rise of Transnational Society* (Washington, DC: The Carnegie Endowment for International Peace, 2000).

104. Jennifer M. Brinkerhoff, *Digital Diasporas: Identity and Transnational Engagement* (New York: Cambridge University Press, 2009).

7

Mercenaries Gone Legit

Private Security Professionals and Private Military Security Companies as Transnational Actors

MATTHEW LERICHE

Since the idea of transnational actors developed approximately one hundred years ago, there has been major technological and social change. Both globalization and privatization form the backdrop for my discussion of the evolution of a classic transnational actor—the mercenary or mercenary company gone legitimate as a private military security company (PMSC), within a community of private security professionals (PSPs).[1] Within the context of complex transnationalism set out in this work, and functioning in ways similar to other transnational actors examined, PMSC/PSPs have become significant players influencing security and development policy.

Despite efforts by international organizations, governments, and civil society to legislate them out of existence, mercenaries continue to exist. Their role in fostering insecurity has been a particular problem in Africa, where the majority of antimercenaryism has been focused.[2] There were, for instance, the mercenaries hired, despite international intervention, by former Libyan leader Muammar al-Ghaddafi and the foreign military pilots the Sudanese government hired to fly some of its military aircraft, among a myriad of similar examples.[3] However, the most significant change regarding the private provision of arms has been the increasing role of PMSCs in security and intelligence. Evolved from the merce-naries of the mid-twentieth century, today's professional security actors provide a major component of policing, intelligence, facilities security/protection, risk management, training, and direct support to state militaries and security services. They are credible and effective, have wealth and influence, and have become largely legitimate in the eyes of governments and wider society; they are merce-naries gone legit.

Connected to the processes described by Virginia Haufler in chapter 3 regarding mechanisms of transnational business governance, the PMSCs/PSPs have developed self-regulating mechanisms and effectively garnered legitimate and credible recognition by state actors. The evolution of PMSCs/PSPs is also connected to the discussion on transnational natural resource firms, as much of the industry has been driven in direct relation with the mining and oil sectors, and some now have formal partnerships with such firms. Features of other transnational actors discussed in the book are reflected by, or relate to, PMSC/PSPs. The use of transnational PMSCs/PSPs has become increasingly signifi-cant in parallel with the increase in violent nonstate/transnational actors such as terrorist networks (chapter 5) and foreign fighters (chapter 6). PMSCs/PSPs now play a major role in influencing humanitarian organizations (chapter 8) to take on roles as security experts. PMSCs/PSPs also play controversial roles in corporate-community relations (chapter 10), with much controversy sur-rounding the conduct of personnel, particularly in high-profile cases of civilian killings.

Maintaining a monopoly on the legitimate use of violence is fundamental to what constitutes a sovereign state. The roles associated with that use are con-ventionally considered the purview of legitimate governments. Yet the private security/military sector has grown from providing the "mall cop" to managing entire prisons, from supporting police domestically to providing protection for diplomats abroad, to military logistics, and to actual military and intelligence services internationally. Increasingly, the use of violence is privatized, and gov-ernments contract it. Such privatization has been theorized to "indicate the state [is] losing its monopoly over coercive military power to private security."[4] An alternative argument contends that contracting states transfer their legiti-mate agency as user of force to those contracted. This debate continues. The core services offered by PMSCs include but are not limited to:

- Business intelligence
- Close protection of VIPs
- Facilities security and protection
- Confidential investigations
- Corporate advisory services

- Fraud prevention
- Risk analysis—political and security
- Kidnapping, extortion, and ransom mitigation/response
- Safeguarding intellectual property
- Cyber/IT security
- Security-sector reform
- Military and police training
- Intelligence training
- Corporate restructuring services
- Travel security
- Hostile environment training and assistance (typically for journalists, humanitarians, and development workers)[5]

In *Corporate Warriors*, his seminal contribution to the discourse surrounding privatized security and military, P. W. Singer describes the PMSC as an important new global actor and shows that "the new industry ha[s] entered global politics."[6] Most discussions of private security actors have focused on their legitimacy and regulation; a smaller body of material has considered their impact on security governance or their role in setting agendas and framing politics.[7] I seek to establish that they are important transnational actors that not only play in the global political space but also help shape it. In a very short time, these relatively new transnational actors have come to influence policy and practice and to frame understanding of international security/insecurity. They are involved in the height of politics, deliberating and setting the rules of the game.

Private Security Transnational?

PMSCs and PSPs operate across the globe anywhere there is a high-risk environment. With most operations occurring outside their country of incorporation and often outside the borders and jurisdiction of the contracting state, PMSCs are truly transnational. This "complex and transnational nature of the PMSC industry is a dynamic variable that itself hinders the creation of effective regulation."[8] The majority of the work on PMSCs and their transnational nature focuses on how (little) they are regulated.

Scholarship on international policing has argued that "concentrating upon the role of these security professionals provides new insights into previously neglected aspects of transnational security governance."[9] Key actors in the neoliberal global political economy, PSPs and PMSCs represent the depoliticization and marketization of security.[10] As Rita Abrahamsen and Michael Williams claim, "the effect of the commodification of security is to de-link it from local issues of justice and politics, making it a commodity that can be bought and sold on the free market and a technique that is universally acceptable everywhere."[11]

The mercenaries of past eras have legitimized themselves as an industry and become key business lines for major multinational corporations.[12] Most are now organized into firms referred to as PMSCs, which vary in size.[13] Some are subsidiary or constituent parts of much larger firms engaged in a wide set of services—everything from peacebuilding to sanitation, from intelligence support and information technology to management advisory services. Often known as "Beltway bandits," they provide consultancy and advisory services primarily to the US government.[14] AECOM, PAE (part of Lockheed Martin), DynCorp, G4S, L-3 Communications, and Securitas—to name a few—span the gamut of contracting, from road construction and facilities management to training security services and other states' militaries. They are part of the widening of the military-industrial complex. G4S, at the time of writing the world's largest private security actor, is one of the one hundred largest companies on the London Stock Exchange. What Walter Adams, in discussing the consequences of the emergence of massive defense contractors in the United States, described in 1968 as a shift from economic capitalism to political capitalism is an apt characterization for the addition of private security services to these same corporate behemoths.[15]

Smaller, more specialized firms, such as Control Risks and Aegis, focus on risk management, training, or protection services. Smaller still, but more numerous, are firms that focus on specific services such as direct training. Finally, there are individual consultants with risk-management expertise who work for private firms, intergovernmental organizations (IGOs), government, and so forth. Many are now part of professional groups and self-regulation associations.

The industry grew rapidly with the wars in Iraq and Afghanistan and has continued to grow. In 2008, the private security sector was worth an estimated $100 billion to $120 billion annually.[16] In Japan the industry has grown beyond the $30 billion mark. PSPs outnumber police in the United Kingdom approximately two to one. In the United States the ratio is three to one.

Indeed, worldwide most states' private security sectors outnumber official police. In Russia there were more than 850,000 private security personnel by 2009. The story is similar in India, with more than five million private security personnel. In Latin America, particularly Brazil, the market has ballooned; in 2001, there were reportedly more than 330,000 private security guards. In Africa, all major urban centers have become markets for private security: Nairobi, Cairo, Cape Town, and Lagos are all major, growing markets. South Africa has the largest private security market as a percentage of GDP in the world.[17]

While these figures reflect all private security actors, it is worth considering the domestic component. I contend that the private security/military profession is central for transnational actors and that domestic and international PMSCs businesses are linked. Many employed in a domestic capacity as security advisers or managers also take contracts in foreign countries—managing the security of Massport, the port authority in Boston, one day and the next a group of security advisers and trainers in Basra, Iraq, for example. Historically localized and domestic security businesses have grown into the globalized private security market, exemplified by the massive and rapid growth of firms such as G4S and GardaWorld.

Growing international security concerns and operational needs of international corporations and nongovernmental organizations (NGOs) have created a demand for support alternatives with fewer transaction and political costs. Human security discourse and securitization has drawn many international policy areas issues into the security sphere, rendering much foreign policy programming the remit of former military or associated security/risk professionals. Since the end of the Cold War and especially since the 9/11 terrorist attacks, increasingly complicated military operations have challenged conventional state-security actors. PMSCs have become central in international development and global security efforts, even in United Nations (UN) operations. Some have even proposed that PMSCs provide an objective, high-quality, standby peace-keeping force.[18] This is especially ironic since "for years, the U.N.'s top peace-keepers have been among the world's staunchest critics of private security contractors, often portraying them as unaccountable mercenaries. Now they are clients."[19] The UN security official overseeing this major reorientation of the organization's position is Gregory Star, former head of security for the US State Department.

The private security sector has benefited from this increased focus on peace-keeping, peace support, and economic development by major Western governments. Increasingly there are even indications that China is moving toward engaging the private security sector in its international business interests; particularly interesting is the emerging relationship between American private security mogul Erik Prince and China.[20] The private security sector influence now extends to the conduct and policy of humanitarian organizations, the UN, and other IGOs, as well as the direct bilateral programs of development agencies such as the US Agency for International Development / US State Department and the UK Department for International Development. Even states less associated with these actions, such as Norway, rely heavily on PSPs/PMSCs for implementing their foreign policy.[21] This is connected to the evolution and growth of international humanitarian agendas and the complex of international action discussed by Phil Orchard in chapter 8. Of all of these factors, the most significant is the drive from leaders in the West to privatize security as a part of wider privatization of government services. This was largely spearheaded by the United States, under the leadership of Vice President Dick Cheney, President George W. Bush, and Defense Secretary Donald Rumsfeld; interestingly both Cheney and President George H. W. Bush are major players in the PSMC world.

The controversy that surrounds PSMCs and their conduct is to some extent the result of their increasing influence. High-profile cases of killings and detentions in countries where they operate drive the deeper debate about the ramifications of privatizing security and the use of violence: Should war and security be entrusted to those with a profit motive, rather than an ethos of loyalty and responsibility to the state and its people? The privatization of security poses an enormous challenge for democratic institutions and accountability. What kinds of democracy will emerge when shaped by the rising prominence of private security actors, engaged in rebuilding, training, and supporting emerging national institutions, if those actors are driven by profit and loyalty to their client rather than to the public?

The following sections engage directly with the five key points of comparison discussed in the book's introduction: (1) organization of the actor, (2) how the actor interacts with other transnational actors, (3) how the actor communicates, (4) how the actor influences conflict/peace, and (5) how PMSCs/PSPs (the actor) reflect developments in transnationalism.

From Soldiers of Fortune to Private Military Contractors: Making the PSP/PMSC Transnational Actor

During the Cold War, Western governments faced not only perceived security threats from the Soviet Union but also economic competition for scarce resources. Supporting the private sector, particularly extractive industries, required strong security and risk management. Chapter 3 of this volume by Virginia Haufler engages in more detail on natural resource firms and the regulating bodies of the wider extractive industry, framing them as transnational actors. Considering the centrality this industry has had in the emergence of the PSMCs/PSPs, it follows that the two entities would evolve in similar ways. While governments were uncomfortable engaging in direct security activity, they were content supporting private security actors in aid of operations because those involved in the firms were former members of official/uniformed services. Most continued to support PMSCs, and PSPs quietly cleared their contracts and projects with authorities in the security services of their home states.

The industry's growth continued with the end of the Cold War and increased competition over emerging markets. While in the past multinational firms used mercenaries to take advantage of insecurity, now there was a growing demand for legitimate support to secure business activity worldwide. Risk management, negotiating hostage releases, and training became the core of the PSPs/PMSCs by the 1990s; employing mercenaries might be taboo, but employing PSPs/PMSCs was not.

Having sidestepped the mercenary taboo, governments, particularly that of the United States, could become crucial customers for PSPs/PMSCs with much less controversy attached. The end of the Cold War also brought an increase in operations such as peacekeeping and peace-enforcement in the Balkans, Africa, and Southeast Asia. Where once formal bilateral arrangements between governments would have supported training of other states' militaries, shrinking post–Cold War defense budgets and the entrenchment of liberal privatization increased demand for the purportedly cheaper subcontracting option.

As the primary client for PMSCs, the US government has shifted its demand over the past ten years. The need for contractors has moved from the Middle East and Afghanistan to Africa, as evidenced in the State Department's decision to increase its program AFRICAP (African Contingency Operations Training and Assistance), in which a small number of vetted companies compete for task orders, training African militaries purportedly for peacekeeping or the goals of peace and security. The mandate is broader than peacekeeping proper: Any purpose that reinforces peace or supports peace, such as bolstering a national force, could be construed as peace support or peacebuilding.

Spending approximately $100 million a year since 2005, PMSCs have trained approximately 77,000 African soldiers under AFRICAP.[22] While the quality and/or consequence of this training is debatable, it is regardless no small feat. Also, AFRICOM, the US military's command for operations in the African theater, increasingly engages in subcontracting. For example, it has hired teams from DynCorp to support the capture of Joseph Kony, the leader of the Lord's Resistance Army (LRA) in the Democratic Republic of the Congo, the Central African Republic, and South Sudan.[23] A testament to the acceptance of subcontracting practice, activists were supportive of American efforts to bolster anti-LRA efforts—so much so that a large network, including the controversial conservative Christian activist group Invisible Children, successfully campaigned to have anti-LRA legislation passed by the US Congress unanimously.[24]

Concurrently, the World Bank framed an approach to security focused on socioeconomic development with good governance at the center and saw governments increase programs meant to bring poor and fragile states into the global economy.[25] Soon development agencies, humanitarian actors, and IGOs were increasing "security"-oriented programs and capacity building of security services as a precursor to economic development. They required only the justification (linking development and the need for security) and budget to subcontract the rest.

The changing global political situation also created a supply of well-trained soldiers, intelligence agents, and officers. Many became involved in consulting work or started their own firms. Building on credibility gained from official service, senior officers linked up with wealthy backers and political figures to transform the formerly questionable industry into a reputable one. Several firms went public, and government contracts took off as the leaderships of the new PSMCs were deeply connected to the established decision makers in Washington, London, and other capitals.

While the supply-driven argument for the rise of private security is an important part of the political economy of PMSCs, it is also "to a large extent the story of neo-liberalism and post-Fordist, or post-Keynesian, trajectories." Set forth by Abrahamsen and Williams, this narrative describes the growth of private security as having its roots in "the 'fiscal crisis' of the Keynesian state that gathered force in the late 1970s."[26] As government contracted from welfare-state activity, the private sector expanded to fill the gaps. For example, the US government's move to cut costs and minimize government service provision during the 2000s saw the greatest growth in private security, focused around the wars in Iraq and Afghanistan after 9/11. The issue was not government spending per se but a distinct interest in privatization by the American elite for political, economic, and personal reasons, reflecting broader neoliberal trends toward transnational corporate outsourcing throughout the developed world.

An ideal example of the transformation from mercenary to PSP/PMSC legitimacy is Tim Spicer,[27] the former British Army officer who has leveraged his scandal-ridden mercenary activities in Papua New Guinea and Sierra Leone into Aegis Defense, one of the world's most successful PMSCs and risk-management firms.[28] The most recent incarnation of Spicer's private security activities is Aegis, launched in 2002 and based in London, with a US subsidiary in Virginia launched in 2006. Aegis was recently purchased by Canada's Garda despite a scandal about Aegis's use of former child soldiers to cut costs.[29] The company has a backbone of highly reputable executives and an impressive contract list, including the State Department's largest contract for protection services in Iraq.[30] Its chairman, former Conservative member of Parliament Nicholas Soames, presides over a group of executives that includes lawyers, oil and gas executives, former senior British generals, and a former head of several UN missions.[31] Having escaped the scandals of its founding chief executive officer's past, the company is extremely careful of the legality of its dealings. It has even established the charitable Aegis Foundation to engage in charitable endeavors.[32]

The story of Aegis is illustrative of the contemporary emergence and legitimization of such firms from the scandal-ridden past of mercenary firms, especially those operating in Africa. With connections in government and the security services of most major powers, members of this industry now frame political issues as security experts and act as major financial contributors; they are thus an important new epistemic community. The largest and most influential PMSCs are connected to the major corporations that form part of the US military-industrial complex.[33] Recognizing the potential for operating in risky environments, firms such as Lockheed Martin, General Dynamics, BAE Systems, Halliburton, and the Carlisle Group have all formed divisions focused on private security and military tasks. For example, Detica, a firm hired by the UN to help design its peacekeeping procedures and train peacekeepers, is a subsidiary of

BAE Systems, one of the world's largest defense contractors and arms producers, providing services to most Western governments.[34] When a firm of this size and scope is involved, the potential for influence and the ability to deflect controversy is substantial. Thus, we can see that the American military-industrial complex has expanded into a global private security–industrial complex, similar to what Abrahamsen and Williams describe as a "global security assemblage."[35]

The concerns of then outgoing president Dwight Eisenhower regarding the emerging military-industrial complex's potential power can be echoed at a global level in the contemporary setting: "We must guard against the acquisition of unwarranted influence, whether sought or unsought, by the military industrial complex. The potential for the disastrous rise of misplaced power exists and will persist."[36] As the global socioeconomic reality grows increasingly neoliberal, the privatization of core government roles will continue, most acutely in the realm of security. It follows that private security professionals will become increasingly important in global security and governance. Correspondingly, as privatization is increasingly accepted within the neoliberal frame, the increasing privatization and globalization of security will be acceptable. This raises major questions about whose security is in the interest of these new transnational actors.

Structure, Organization, and Network of PSPs: Corporations and Consultants

There are three kinds of PMSCs, plus the lone consultants working for various organizations on short contracts, moving from firm to firm, theater to theater. Quite similar is the rota at the upper levels of PMSCs: Executives and senior managers bounce from firm to firm fluidly; personalities in the industry can be volatile, and clashes are not uncommon. Experience as a senior military officer or executive at any major firm secures opportunities at others; experience remains highly prized because most contracts are won or lost based on the CVs of the key personnel involved in the contract at competition.

Companies such as PAE; KBR (formerly Kellogg Brown & Root), a subsidiary of Halliburton (of which Cheney was chief executive officer from 1995 to 1999); Booz Allen Hamilton; L-3 (owners of Military Professional Resources Incorporated [MPRI]); and the Carlisle Group (owners of Vinnell—one of the first PMSCs; this firm's executives and owners include former president George H. W. Bush and his secretary of state, James Baker) have broad service lines and products, offer logistics, construction, and other support services, and provide such highly skilled personnel as intelligence analysts or engineers. These large firms, whose parent companies are often publicly traded, directly influence government policy. Mergers create major companies that lend the industry credibility and influence. Research conducted by the International Consortium of Investigative Journalists in 2002 showed that, from 1994 to 2002, the Department of Defense entered into 3,061 contracts, worth over $300 billion, with PMSCs; 2,700 of the contracts went to KBR or Booz Allen Hamilton. The number of contracts has grown rapidly since 2002, and the diversity of firms winning contracts from the US government has increased, yet the major firms continue to receive the bulk of contracts.[37]

The second type of PMSCs, middle-sized firms, stands alone from major parents and focuses on specific security, intelligence, risk-management, or military fields. Large enough to be seen as reliable brands, firms such as Control Risks Group have carved a special niche for themselves and tend to be key players in training. Major conglomerates or capital investors purchased many firms like this to bolster government contractors' service lines as the market for private security services grew in the 1990s.

The third type is much smaller businesses; turning over several million US dollars a year, they tend to operate with a small group, frequently radiating around a single dynamic figure. They are often composed of people who operated together while in formal service and tend to take bigger risks than larger firms in terms of contracts. They willingly operate on the fringes of regulation and are often used to test new opportunities. Also, larger firms frequently use them in "teaming arrangements," whereby the smaller firms take on discrete tasks, such as compliance oversight. The sharp edge of the PSP/PMSC industry, they typically arrive on scene first in a new environment. According to US contracting rules, small businesses have to be included in the consortiums that bid for major contracts—part of the American philosophy that small business drives national wealth.[38]

For the most part, PMSCs do not maintain many permanent staff. Drawing on networks of former colleagues and associates, these firms hire specifically for each contract. In practice, the private security world is a group of corporations that pull from a fluid pool of personnel. Executives and owners draw on the "old boys" network of retired and semiretired service personnel. This can be good for the individual consultants as it tends to mean higher fees; competition can be stiff and favors individuals who enjoy credibility and recognition by a particular prime contractor or client.

From the "the Circuit" to Professional Associations

A popular book by former British SAS soldier Bob Shepherd, *The Circuit*, described in illustrative detail the life of a private security operative in the war on terrorism, including the conflicts in Iraq and Afghanistan. The image of PSPs circulating from one contract to the next, earning upward of $15,000 a month, comes vividly to life. While Shepherd explains "the Circuit" in his preface as "shorthand for the international commercial security circuit, an industry which caters to government, military, commercial and individual clients,"[39] the PSP/PMSC industry has evolved into a mixture of professional associations.

Although still in their infancy, the various private security industry associations have produced codes of conduct and provide opportunities to further the interests of the industry's firms and individuals. One of the more prominent associations is the International Stability Operations Association (ISOA), which includes a large number of PMSCs as well as other contractors involved in postconflict reconstruction.

In Europe, the Confederation of European Security Services oversees and supports monitoring and self-regulation of the industry. It feeds directly into the large, global International Code of Conduct for Private Security Providers' Association, known as the ICoCA. Facilitated by the Swiss government, the ICRC, and the Centre for the Democratic Control of Armed Forces, the ICoCA has collated international law and principles to bring self-regulation to the private security industry. In early 2014, six governments, thirteen civil society organizations, and 126 PMSCs were members of the ICoCA.[40] By the end of 2013, 698 PMSCs were signatories to its voluntary standards, having agreed to be regulated in terms of those principles. In affiliation with these efforts, the University of Denver has collaborated with the facilitating bodies to establish the Private Security Monitor, which reports on the industry's conduct. This independent research project recognizes the large private security businesses in domestic environments but focuses on "services that have a transnational dimension."[41]

The United States and the United Kingdom, as do most states, have their own regulatory regimes based on national legislation. Most working in the industry retain a loyalty to—often a formal relationship with—their governments and former services, as Shepherd comments: "The vast majority of advisers work on contracts servicing their own governments, governments closely allied to their own or industries regulated by their home countries, allies or international law. Many security advisers have served in the military or supported their communities as police officers. They regard their employment on The Circuit as a continuation of their public service, not an end to it."[42] Many retain security clearances or remain bound by security provisions after leaving employment with their national governments. Thus, the regulatory framework of PSPs/PMSCs has an underlying ethos of service and responsibility to national authorities.

As in any profession, work for PMSCs has aspects where certification of skill and standards of practice exist, yet it is also similar to older apprentice-modeled professions. Within the Circuit, references, typically from former officers, are most important. Rarely do all those involved in a particular project meet for the first time at its outset. Teams often stick together, especially in the case of protection and other harder roles. This is less often the case on the intelligence and risk-management side of the profession, where certifications and education are the standard but being vouched for by someone respected by a new employer or client is essential. Thus, groups of PSPs commonly remain loyal to a small network of leaders and associates.

Establishing and maintaining a professional construct is crucial for the industry's legitimacy. The trust imparted, given the nature of the profession, has been an important part of drawing PSPs and PMSCs close to authorities and has allowed them to speak as "experts" on security—which lies at the heart of their significance as transnational actors. Unlike those serving in a national military or security service, PSPs and PMSCs can speak authoritatively to multiple governments, multiple industries, and the IGO world, as well as humanitarians, the news media, and even to some extent academia. Further, the general public, at least in the West, has come to regard PSPs as authority figures on all things security, which today includes most critical areas of social life.

Interaction and Relationships of PSPs: Regulation, Corruption, and Gentlemen's Agreements

The private security industry is largely self-regulating via its professional associations. While existing international humanitarian law and laws of many states have a bearing on the operation of PMSCs, a wide operating space has been left for them, compared to such industries as telecommunications and even banking.

Government relations with PSPs/PMSCs often seem too close for comfort: The "revolving door" between government departments and industry main players raises public observers' suspicion and ire.[43] The industry definitely would not be as large or as lucrative without government contracts for services historically associated with national security and military services. PMSCs offer better pay than governments; thus, for many government workers a close relationship with the industry affords options to move into higher-paying work later. This fact poses a major risk for corruption. Movement between government and private firms by senior officials, as well as mid-level managers, has created an "increasingly difficult distinction between public and private service in the security sphere."[44]

The sensitive nature of their work helps governments and the contractors deflect corruption concerns. Because national or corporate security concerns purportedly require a unique form of trust, special competition arrangements are established. Groups of vetted and cleared firms are organized; only firms cleared may compete for contracts. Often there is very little competition, or, due to security concerns, single organizations are approached by a particular department, ministry, or company through the connections between senior government managers and executives in the PMSCs. This is why personalities become critical; the more former and publicly legitimate figures associated with the firm, the more likely it will benefit from these semiclosed competitions and contracting arrangements.

Between themselves, PSPs and PMSCs often operate by "gentlemen's agreements"—they share contracts and divide labor in an operational theater. It is typically the case, such as with major US government contracts, that an exclusive group of vetted firms are given a special right to compete for "task orders" so that the large funds for security contracts are spread within the industry.[45] Although competition can be intense for very lucrative contracts, the fact that the mid and upper levels of most major firms circulate between them means good relations with competitors must be maintained in case there is a need later on to move positions.[46]

Finally, the relationship between contractors and recipient states, in cases where a donor government has contracted security-sector reform or similar assistance to be delivered to the third party, is significant. It generates concerns similar to those surrounding the relationship between humanitarian and development actors, their recipient/beneficiary, and the donor funding programming. How responsive are contractors to the beneficiary when financial and business accountability rests with the contracting government or organization?

For instance, the United States was assisting the development of the Nigerian army via MPRI. Although senior Nigerian officers were critical, stating that MPRI's work was out of touch with local realities and poorly implemented, the US government judged MPRI's project successful.[47] A similar case existed in South Sudan, where locals criticized US and UK assistance to the army and other security services; the situation did not change until assistance was pulled out as South Sudan descended into civil war, in part due to the collapse of the security services and military-reform programs. The relationship of primary importance was between the contractor and the paying government, not the government or organization receiving the service, thus ignorance of existing doctrine and practice, an inability to garner understanding of how they are perceived by locals, and a corresponding inability to internalize criticisms and adapt resulted. As Eeben Barlow, a founding director of Executive Outcomes and well-known PMSC figure, has commented: "A number of PMCs/PSCs are sponsored by Western governments who have motives that are not always obvious. These PMCs become their favoured companies to use—and they act on behalf of the sponsoring government's foreign policy and also act as intelligence fronts. They are not there to help clients but rather to advance their government's agendas—usually to the detriment of the client-government."[48]

In their development, security-sector reform, and peace-support roles, PSPs/PMSCs struggle; they focus on technical delivery of services but are caught up in very political processes. In the midst of social and cultural change, they apply conventional military or security training with a very technical approach. Workshops, drills, and classroom sessions like those implemented in a Western state's security service or military are run with a view of the problems requiring a technical solution. In actual fact, social, cultural, and political forces are very much at play, and the PSP/PMSC actors' apolitical approach leaves them struggling to engage.

How PSPs and PMSCs Communicate: Public Relations, Escaping Being a "Mercenary," Elite Networks, and Credibility

Avoiding being seen as "mercenary" occupies a great deal of PSPs' and PMSCs' energy. The term is considered deeply offensive. Unfortunately, it contains an element of accuracy. Squarely for profit, the industry is arguably not primarily focused on the public good. Its trades include the management of security and risk, which may mean using deadly force when necessary. And even senior executives of the major firms, such as Erik Prince of Blackwater (now known as Academi) and Tim Spicer of Aegis, cultivate images of themselves as adventurers, warriors, or rogues, beyond the controls of the state.

To escape this conceptualization, PMSCs have engaged various public relations strategies. Much of their efforts focus on high-level, elite communication with governments and executives, based on the assumption that "the imagery and romantic notions of the mercenary and soldier of fortune are already engrained in the public."[49]

Building on this idea of expertise, the industry grew from being the functionaries of close protection and security assessments to managers of risk and intelligence providers. By providing expert knowledge, often as contributors on media networks favorable to the community, the PSPs and PMSCs remade their image. Key members of the industry increasingly became contributors to major think tanks and arms-length intellectual institutions of the armed forces in the United States and the United Kingdom. The industry also drew in a broad range of intellectuals, including academics and technical analysts, further boosting credibility and opening up new, potentially lucrative business lines.[50]

A key factor bringing the industry into greater repute was the perceived increase in risk to humanitarian workers. Whether missionaries or relief workers, internationals of the well-meaning, often volunteer organizations have always, rightly or wrongly, held an aura of inviolable moral authority.[51] They have long espoused a view that their role as providers of social goods lacking in the insecure parts of the world would protect them. Divorced from politics and focused on providing impartial aid, they would not be targeted. However, with the documented increase in the targeting of humanitarians and in risk more generally, some kind of security became necessary.[52]

As it professionalized, the humanitarian industry became increasingly comfortable with the PSPs' and PMSCs' for-profit motive. Claiming legitimacy as professional relief workers, they responded to corresponding professionalism in security service; facing greater insecurity, they turned to the professional security providers. Fearful of the direct politics of working with government militaries, the second-best (or less bad / lesser-evil) option was the private security profes-sional. Some organizations hired one or two onto their own staffs; others con-tracted firms. Regardless of which option they chose, the humanitarians were drawn into the Circuit. By 2007, according to the Overseas Development Insti-tute, approximately 60 percent of NGOs and 50 percent of UN agencies employed PMSCs in one fashion or another. (The involvement with the UN increased drastically after the attack on UN offices in Iraq in 2003 in which UN diplomat Sérgio Vieira de Mello was killed, along with fourteen others.[53]) With the UN, Oxfam, the United Nations Children Fund, Save the Children, and others on the list of clients, PSMCs and PSPs gained significant credibility.[54] While the role of PMSCs in the humanitarian world remains one of the more controversial debates associated with the industry,[55] many organizations employ private security in the face of increased risk to personnel and operations.[56]

The final element in this public relations effort was the creation of associ-ated foundations with humanitarian and charitable activity mentioned above. Aegis in the United Kingdom has the Aegis Foundation, and ICI from Oregon has the ICI Foundation, which, for example, ran a medical training program in Sudan.[57] There are many others that, like churches in the past, operate in the elite charity/philanthropy circuit, helping brand the PSMCs and the PSPs as good global citizens.

Influencing War and Peace

According to Anna Leander, "To show that the re-emergence of PMCs has sig-nificance it is necessary to demonstrate that they have gained 'power.'"[58] It is not their mere presence that is of greatest consequence—it is in the setting of agendas and defining of concepts and understanding that their new power lies. The imme-diate impact on battles, the outcome and cost of wars, and the corresponding likelihood of engaging in them all become important when considering PMSCs' power. Understanding their actions from a constructivist angle allows a view that might not be recognized simply by assessing their specific actions or the industry's scale. Yes, the industry has become large, but with regard to the PSPs' and PMSCs' influence on war and peace what does that matter?

First and foremost, their influence comes from their growing roles in the provision of security services. They can be used to fight war or support fighting, as was the case in Iraq and Afghanistan. Increasingly important is their role in information provision, as well as their capacity-building role in many nations' emerging security services and militaries. This has become a centerpiece of Western peacebuilding efforts in Africa.

The PSPs'/PMSCs' immediate interaction with war and peace is via their roles as hard-security actors. They provide physical protection in conflict set-tings. Particularly important is their provision of support services to formal militaries, especially the US armed forces. Once the task of the military proper, fighting war now relies on private security for manufacturing the implements of war and the support of logistics and information provided by the private sector.

In their training, capacity-building, and institutional-development roles in postconflict / developing country aid, PMSCs affect the emerging structure of many states' security services. How official actors conduct themselves and their understanding of security is largely framed by private security actors who influence the implementation of global governance under the guise of offering limited technical assistance. By courting key elites and supporting their positions in the security establishments of fragile states, private security actors influence agendas and policy. Whether PMSCs have made the national military more or less effective has major consequences for security. A weak military is more susceptible to security threats, which in much of the developing world are real and acute. However, an empowered army may be less likely to follow democratic designs and more likely to overthrow a government. Such dynamics, determined by local contexts, are deeply political, even though private security actors are purportedly only carrying out technical restructuring or capacity-building tasks.

PSPs/PMSCs have a deeper and more pervasive influence on war and peace than their immediate action in war and postconflict/insecure environments. The growing process of securitization means that these global security actors influence the programs of diplomats, development agencies, UN officers, and even humanitarians. A UN antimalaria program, for example, has to be designed with the input of the UN Department of Safety and Security and in some cases the private company providing that office's security in-country.

Mark Duffield best captures the international humanitarian and development world's changing behavior in what he calls "bunkering."[59] This is about physical security but has ramifications for how people interact and the way a situation is understood. Policy is therefore informed, and a kind of detached governance by the protected over the unprotected results. Duffield draws parallels to the colonial and imperial approaches to governance of the past, arguing that the prominence of security as a consideration has influenced approaches to global governance.

PSPs and PMSCs respond to the risk-adverse nature of governments and major corporations and work to limit staffs' exposure to risk, but this can undermine genuine understanding and human relations. It may potentially affect the understanding of political and social reality, and correspondingly programs, thereby entrenching the need for PSPs/PMSCs. They, in turn, are increasingly relied upon as experts on security as others seek knowledge about interaction with "the locals" in purportedly insecure environments. The analysts in this case begin defining the human terrain they set out to describe and understand.

Securitization (particularly as manifested through concepts such as "human security," which draws in food, health, and most social spheres) means that experts in security gain a very wide remit. In assessing a country's food security situation today, it is common for someone working with a PMSC to support the World Food Programme's or Food and Agriculture Organization's efforts. Risk mapping and the use of geographic information systems tools further focus expertise on a narrow technical community, which the PSPs/PMSCs capture well. All areas of public policy are now open to a security conceptualization, thus granting the PSPs/PMSCs major transnational influence.

As our understanding of how poverty and underdevelopment drive conflict increases, and the PSPs continue to expand their expertise in security-relevant issues, their defining of the problem and correspondingly the solution to conflict will increase. For example, in the peace process in South Sudan led by the Inter-Governmental Authority on Development, PSPs that are part of PMSCs are monitoring the cease-fire agreement. Similar processes took place when the Comprehensive Peace Agreement of 2005 in Sudan / South Sudan was being negotiated. As then, current information on the security situation is fed to mediators who subsequently influence the peace process.

A result of the increasingly neoliberal tendency toward the privatization of public services and thus the public good, PMSCs are remaking the relationship between democratic publics and their security providers/guarantors. This is the case both domestically and internationally: Largely the same set of private actors, such as G4S, frames and defines security. Even national security is increasingly the purview of the private sector. As security becomes less a political and social consequence and increasingly a set of technical solutions to be delivered by professionals, the PSPs/PMSCs will only grow in importance and authority. Governments intent on cheaper solutions with minimal political consequences internationally will also continue to turn to private security actors. It remains unclear whether this approach to security governance and implementation will prove more effective; however, PSPs/PMSCs are likely here to stay.

One problem with the privatization of security is that by setting the agenda and framing the understanding of security, the PSPs/PMSCs effectively establish the demand for more security services. By producing information that insecurity is on the rise or more acute in location "A" versus location "B," they create demand for their security products. More significantly, the PMSCs as a group are involved in shaping how we think about risk, vulnerability, and threat. By defining how these key variables are understood by powerful actors in government and business, as well as the general public via the news media, PSPs/PMSCs define the criteria by which the demand for their services is determined.

Even more concerning, they influence how decision makers and publics understand war and peace, making them ideally positioned to offer technical apolitical solutions to the security problems. Technical knowledge is asserted by the private sector, and the major multinationals effectively lay claim: It is difficult to refute the technical prowess of corporate entities such as Northrop Grumman,

Lockheed Martin, and L3. They avoid the conceptual issues arising from the very political process of privatizing security, which has serious consequences for the modern state, particularly democracies.

The private sector has become increasingly dominant engaging on international public goods. And correspondingly large corporations with private security business lines are most significant when talking about the impact on war and peace. An illustration of the scale is how the Bill and Melinda Gates Foundation, an outgrowth of Microsoft, spends more on medical assistance than the Australian government does on foreign aid.[60]

Conclusions: What PSPs and PMSCs Tell Us about Transnationalism

Transnational actors such as PSPs/PMSCs have grown out of neoliberal privatization and globalization. As they grow in size and prominence, their roles challenge conventional understanding of security and the exclusivity of legitimate force wielded by the state. The combination of their global reach and the substance of their expertise mean PSPs and PMSCs are emerging as supranational, not just transnational, actors.

The private security industry tells us how neoliberal, capitalist market forces drive international development. Such transnationalism is defined by privatization and the way it shapes groups or transnational actors, whether civil society groups, NGOs, or for-profit commercial actors such as PMSCs.

As transnational actors, PMSCs and PSPs reveal the extent to which American thinking pervades global institutions and even local notions of security, the state, and governance. They are entrenching a major American national project—the development of free markets and the faith that they will bring better democracy, security, and peace.

Notes

1. The idea of the private profession of arms being a profession is based upon Samuel Huntington's idea of soldier as profession. S. P. Huntington, *The soldier and the state: The theory and politics of civil-military relations* (Harvard: Harvard University Press, 1957): 7, 8, and 222.

2. A. F. Musah, K. Fayemi, and J. K. Fayemi, *Mercenaries: an African security dilemma* (London: Pluto Press, 2000).

3. There was considerable reporting on this matter during 2010–11; see, for example, Ofeibea Quist-Arcton, "Libya's Gadhafi Accused of Using Foreign Mercenaries," NPR, February 23, 2011, http://www.npr.org/2011/02/23/133981329/who-are-foreign-mercenaries-fighting-for-gadhafi. Others contended no such thing occurred: Wayne Madsenm, "Gaddaffi's African 'Mercenary' Story Is a Disinformation Ploy by the CIA," Global Research, April 4, 2011, http://www.globalresearch.ca/gaddaffi-s-african-mercenary-story-is-a-disinformation-ploy-by-the-cia/24129.

4. Christopher Kinsey, "Problematising the Role of Private Security Companies in Small Wars," *Small Wars and Insurgencies* 18.4 (2007): 585.

5. Drawn from various PMSC websites, as well as Conor O'Reilly, "The Transnational Security Consultancy Industry: A Case of State-Corporate Symbiosis," *Theoretical Criminology* 14, no. 2 (2010): 185. See also John Gainer, "The Business of War: A Content Analysis of Private Military Companies' Websites," Paper 337, Applied Research Projects, Texas State University–San Marcos, 2010, http://ecommons.txstate.edu/arp/337.

6. P. W. Singer, *Corporate Warriors: The Rise of the Privatized Military Industry* (Ithaca, NY: Cornell University Press 2004), 230.

7. Examples include: Østensen, Å. G., *The political agency of private military and security companies: Governors in the making* (Doctoral Dissertation, University of Bergen, 2013); Østensen, Å. G., "In the business of peace: the political influence of private military and security companies on UN Peacekeeping" *International Peacekeeping*, 20, no. 1 (2013): 33–47; Abrahamsen, R., & Williams, M. C., *Security beyond the state: Private security in international politics.* (Cambridge: Cambridge University Press, 2010); Abrahamsen, R., & Williams, M. C., "Public/private, global/local: the changing contours of Africa's security governance" *Review of African Political Economy*, 35, no. 118 (2008): 539–553; Abrahamsen, R., & Williams, M, Beyond the Privatised Military. *Human Security Bulletin*, 6, no. 3 (2008): 24–6; Aning, K., Jaye, T., & Atuobi, S. "The role of private military companies in US-Africa policy" *Review of African political economy*, 35 no. 118, (2008): 613–628; McFate, S., "Outsourcing the making of militaries: DynCorp international as sovereign agent," *Review of African Political Economy*, 35 no. 118, (2008): 645–654.

8. Stephanie Brown, "Bottom-Up Law Making and the Regulation of Private Military and Security Companies," *Cuadernos de Derecho Transnacional* 2, no. 1 (March 2010): 51.

9. O'Reilly, "Transnational Security Consultancy Industry," 184.

10. This thinking is based on ideas presented in James Ferguson, *The Anti-Politics Machine: "Development," Depoliticization, and Bureaucratic Power in Lesotho* (Minneapolis: University of Minnesota Press 1990).

11. Rita Abrahamsen and Michael Williams, "Public/Private, Global/Local: The Changing Contours of Africa's Security Governance," *Review of African Political Economy* 118 (2008): 552.

12. Some argue that private security personnel should be considered professionals, as are their official service counterparts. Most are former service members and/or often maintain affiliation with official security/military services. See Gary Schaub and Volker Franke, "Contractors as Military Professionals," *Parameters* (Winter 2009–10): 88–104.

13. The appropriate terminology is debated; some prefer "private military companies" (PMCs) for those with more discretely military focus and "private security companies" (PSCs) for those with more general security, risk-management roles. Some private security actors prefer PSC as a relatively neutral term. In the UK academic lexicon, the tendency is to conflate the two, as many firms are involved in both security and military roles. I use the broader "PMSC."

14. This term is in reference to their tendency to operate along Washington, DC's ring road. Security and defense contractors are housed along the Beltway's Virginia section nearer to the Pentagon and Central Intelligence Agency (CIA) headquarters, while more civilian firms are typically based along its Maryland section. This proximity to the US government is essential, as it is the primary source of revenue for most PSPs/PMSCs.

15. Walter Adams, "The Military-Industrial Complex and the New Industrial State," *American Economic Review* 58, no. 2 (May 1968): 653.

16. José L. Gómez del Prado, "Impact on Human Rights of Private Military and Security Companies' Activities," Global Research, October 11, 2008, www.globalresearch.ca.

17. Jenny Irish, "Monograph 39: Policing for Profit: The Future of South Africa's Private Security Industry," Institute for Security Studies, August 1, 1999, http://www.issafrica.org/publications/monographs/monograph-39-policing-for-profit-the-future-of-south-africas-private-security-industry-by-jenny-irish.

18. Traci Huckill, "Firm Seeks to Sell UN on Privatized Peacekeeping," *National Journal*, May 17, 2004, available on Global Policy Forum, https://www.globalpolicy.org/nations-a-states/private-military-a-security-companies/pmscs-and-the-un/51063-firms-seek-to-sell-un-on-privatized-peacekeeping.html. See also Ase Gilje Ostensen, "In the Business of Peace: The Political Influence of Private Military and Security Companies on UN Peacekeeping," *International Peacekeeping* 20, no. 1 (February 2013): 1–15.

19. Colum Lynch, "UN Embraces Private Military Contractors" in *Foreign Policy*, January 17, 2010, http://blog.foreignpolicy.com/posts/2010/01/17/un_embraces_private_military_contractors.

20. "Erik Prince, Beijing's Jack-of-All-Trades in Africa," Intelligence Online, no. 749, December, 16 2015, https://www.intelligenceonline.com/corporate-intelligence/2015/12/16/erik-prince-beijing-s-jack-of-all-trades-in-africa,108117227-EVE.

21. Ase Gilje Ostensen, "Norway Keeping Up Appearances," in *Commercializing Security in Europe: Political Consequences for Peace and Reconciliation Efforts*, ed. Anna Leander (London: Routledge 2013).

22. David Isenberg, "Africa: The Mother of All PMC," *Huffington Post*, March 22, 2010, http://www.huffingtonpost.com/david-isenberg/africa-the-mother-of-all_b_509111.html.

23. PMSC executive, author interview, Juba, South Sudan, June 26, 2009.

24. "Senate Unanimously Passes Kony 2012 Legislation," Invisible Children, http://invisiblechildren.com/blog/2012/08/03/senate-unanimously-passes-kony-2012-resolution/.

25. Most prominently this poverty- and development-focused approach to security is embodied by the World Bank's 2011 *World Development Report: Conflict, Security and Development*.

26. Abrahamsen and Williams, "Public/Private, Global/Local," 544.

27. For a more dynamic account of Spicer and the rise of Aegis in Iraq, see Robert Baer, "Iraq's Mercenary King," *Vanity Fair*, April 2007, http://www.vanityfair.com/politics/features/2007/04/spicer200704.

28. Charles Dokubo, "'An Army for Rent': Private Military Corporations and Civil Conflicts in Africa; The Case of Sierra Leone," *Civil Wars* 3, no. 2 (2000): 51–64; Tim Spicer, *An Unorthodox Soldier: Peace and War and the Sandline Affair; An Autobiography* (Edinburgh, UK: Mainstream, 1999); Alan Axelrod, *Mercenaries: A Guide to Private Armies and Private Military Companies* (Washington, DC: CQ Press, 2013), ch. 4.

29. "Garda Struggles to Integrate Aegis," Intelligence Online, no. 746 (April 11, 2015), http://www.intelligenceonline.com/corporate-intelligence/2015/11/04/garda-struggles-to-integrate-aegis,108109769-BRE.

30. See "Company Overview of Aegis Defense Services LLC," Bloomberg, http://www.bloomberg.com/research/stocks/private/snapshot.asp?privcapId=133890790. See also "US State Department's Five Year $10B WPS Security Contract," *Defense Industry Daily*, http://www.defenseindustrydaily.com/US-State-Departments-5-Year-100B-WPS-Security-Contract-06594/.

31. See Aegis World's website at http://www.aegisworld.com/who-we-are/key-personalities/. See also Source Watch entry on Aegis World, http://www.sourcewatch.org/index.php/Aegis_Defence_Services.

32. See "Foundation" on Aegis World's website, http://www.aegisworld.com/foundation/.

33. Gin Armstrong, "Mapping the Shadow Government: Booz Allen Hamilton," Little Sis News, August 29, 2013, http://littlesis.org/news/2013/08/29/mapping-the-shadow-government -booz-allen-hamilton/.

34. Ostensen, "In the Business of Peace," 40.

35. See Rita Abrahamsen and Michael Williams, "Security beyond the State: Global Security Assemblages in International Politics," *International Political Sociology* 3 (2009): 3.

36. Dwight D. Eisenhower, "Military-Industrial Complex Speech," Public Papers of the Presidents, Dwight D. Eisenhower, 1960, 1035–40, http://coursesa.matrix.msu.edu/~hst306/documents/indust.html.

37. See *Making a Killing*, a project of the International Consortium of Investigative Journalists, https://www.icij.org/projects/makingkilling. In particular, see Laura Peterson, "Privatizing Combat the New World Order," October 28, 2002, https://www.icij.org/project/making-killing/privatizing-combat-new-world-order, and Phillip Van Niekerk, "The Business of War," October 28, 2002, https://www.icij.org/project/making-killing/business-war. See also Marfruza Khan, "Business on the Battlefield: The Role of Private Military Companies" Corporate Research project, December 30, 2002, http://www.corp-research.org/e-letter/business -battlefield.

38. On this see the Office of Small and Disadvantaged Business Utilization, http://www.state.gov/s/dmr/sdbu/.

39. Bob Shepherd, *The Circuit: An Ex-SAS Soldier's True Account of One of the Most Powerful and Secretive Industries Spawned by the War on Terror* (London: Macmillan 2008), i.

40. http://psm.du.edu/index.html

41. Ibid.

42. Shepherd, *Circuit*, i.

43. O'Reilly, "Transnational Security Consultancy Industry," 190.

44. This quote was discussing the "criss-crossing for the state and corporate security sectors" by William H. Webster, former director of the CIA and of the Federal Bureau of Investigation, chairman of the Homeland Security Advisory Council, and a member of the American PMSC Diligence. The Diligence senior advisory council also includes senior UK figures such as the Rt. Honorable Michael Howard, QC, MP. See O'Reilly, "Transnational Security Consultancy Industry," 185.

45. For details, see the US government's contracting site (FedBizzOps.gov) for the major State Department Protective Services contract in 2010, at https://www.fbo.gov/index ?s=opportunity&mode=form&tab=core&id=4847a60695ff81fec0ccf77771bd942b& _cview=0.

46. PMSC officials, interview with author, London, June, 2014.

47. Kwesi Aning, Thomas Jaye, and Samuel Atuobi, "The Role of Private Military Companies in US-Africa Policy," *Review of African Political Economy* 35, no. 118 (2008): 613–28; Human Rights Watch, *World Report 2002: Events of 2001* (New York: Human Rights Watch, 2002), 73, 74. See also David Leatherwood, *The Hazards of Strange Bedfellows. The United States, Nigeria, and Peacekeeping in West Africa* (Washington, DC: National War College, 2001), 24, 25.

48. Quoted in Isenberg, "Africa."

49. David Jones, PMSC executive based in London, interview with author, June 26, 2014.

50. Major debates grow out of the use of social scientists supporting military operations, largely hired by PMSCs. See "The End of Debates about the Human Terrain System," Zero Anthropology, http://zeroanthropology.net/2013/02/17/the-end-of-debates-about-the-human -terrain-system/.

51. Alexander De Waal has been a leading critic of humanitarian organizations, and his body of work has exemplified revelations of the false altar behind which many organizations have taken refuge. For example, see *Famine Crimes: Politics and the Disaster Relief Industry in Africa* (Bloomington: Indiana University Press, 1997). Other key texts in this vein include David Rieff, *A Bed for the Night: Humanitarianism in Crisis* (New York: Simon & Schuster, 2003), and Tony Vaux and Anthony Vaux, *The Selfish Altruist: Relief Work in Famine and War* (Sterling, VA: Earthscan, 2013).

52. A 2006 Overseas Development Institute study indicated a rise (nearly double) in violent incidents between 1995 and 2005. And from 2006 to 2009, incidents rose a further 89 percent. See Birthe Anders, "Tree-Huggers and Baby Killers: The Relationship between NGOs and PMSCs and Its Impact on Coordinating Actors in Complex Emergencies," *Small Wars and Insurgencies* 24, no. 2 (2013): 282.

53. "Top UN Envoy Sergio Vieira de Mello Killed in Terrorist Blast in Baghdad," UN News Centre, August 19, 2003, http://www.un.org/apps/news/story.asp?NewsID=8023#.U8GL R6jPpT0.

54. Anders, "Tree-Huggers," 282.

55. For a discussion of key debates, see Benjamin Perrin, "Humanitarian Assistance and the Private Security Debate," On the Edges of Conflict, Liu Institute for Global Studies.

56. Anders, "Tree-Huggers," 282.

57. Gary Schaub Jr. and Ryan Kelty, eds., *Private Military and Security Contractors: Controlling the Corporate Warrior* (Lanham, MD: Rowman & Littlefield, 2016), 10, 23. See also Alan Axelrod, *Mercenaries: A Guide to Private Armies and Private Military Companies* (Washington, DC: CQ Press, 2013), ch. 12/9.

58. Anna Leander, "The Power to Construct International Security: On the Significance of Private Military Companies," *Millennium Journal of International Studies* 33 (2005): 806.

59. Mark Duffield, "Risk Management and the Bunkering of the Aid Industry," *Development Dialogue*, April 2012, www.globalstudies.gu.se/digitalAssets/.../1430096_riskmanagement1.pdf.

60. Alison Stranger, *One Nation under Contract: The Outsourcing of American Power and the Future of Foreign Policy* (New Haven, CT: Yale University Press, 2009), 53.

8

Transnational Humanitarian Action and Regime Complexity

The Case of Syria

PHIL ORCHARD

Since the outbreak of civil war in Syria in 2011, the international community has faced an unprecedented humanitarian emergency. Beyond the estimated 400,000 dead, the civil war has created 5 million refugees, 6.5 million internally displaced persons (IDPs), and over 4 million besieged people. The United Nations (UN) estimates that 13.5 million—more than half of the Syrian population of 21.4 million—require humanitarian assistance.[1] The transnational humanitarian community—which includes nongovernmental organizations (NGOs), international organizations, and state bureaucracies—has sought to mobilize a global response to this crisis.[2] The UN appealed for $3.18 billion for assistance within Syria for 2016 alone.[3]

In focusing on this community, rather than an individual actor, I follow Virginia Haufler's discussion in chapter 3 of transnational actors who have adopted a common frame, in my case to provide humanitarian assistance during conflicts. These actors, while diverse, are bound together by the core belief that, as Fiona Terry notes, they have an "obligation to provide humanitarian action wherever it is needed and is predicated on the right to receive, and to offer, humanitarian aid."[4] This assistance is guided by four key principles, designed to create a humanitarian space that is detached from the conflict. These principles include that of humanity, a general commitment to prevent and alleviate suffering; impartiality, that assistance should be based solely on need; neutrality, that organizations providing such assistance have a duty to not take part in hostilities; and independence, that these organizations should be free from political, religious, and other extraneous influences. As David Malet and Miriam J. Anderson proposed in the introduction, transnational actors are entities that work through cross-border, nonstate mobilizing structures, that are perceived to be beyond the state, and that self-identify as transnational. Within the humanitarian community, actors regularly interact, exchange information, and rely on specialized knowledge. They "understand themselves to be part of a common enterprise."[5]

On the one hand, the transnational humanitarian community is immense. Estimates suggest there are some 4,400 NGOs worldwide undertaking humanitarian action on an ongoing basis. Its core actors are UN humanitarian agencies, the International Committee of the Red Cross (ICRC), and the International Federation of the Red Cross and Red Crescent Societies (IFRC), and large international NGOs, including Médecins Sans Frontières (MSF), Catholic Relief Services (CRS), Oxfam International, the International Save the Children Alliance, and World Vision International.[6] It is also a multibillion-dollar industry, with significant state support. A total of $17.9 billion was provided for humanitarian assistance in 2012—$12.9 billion from governments and $5 billion through private voluntary contributions.[7]

At the same time, this community is circumscribed in a number of ways. It is, after all, primarily a nonstate phenomenon, one that is increasingly reliant on states for financial support. Further, the activities of this community are also limited by the issue of state consent. The core humanitarian principles have been institutionalized in the UN, based around UN General Assembly Resolution 46/182,[8] the Office for the Coordination of Humanitarian Affairs (OCHA) within the UN Secretariat, and the Emergency Relief Coordinator. And yet Resolution 46/182 introduces a significant limitation to these efforts: While assistance "must be provided in accordance with the principles of humanity, neutrality, and impartiality," it should also "be provided with the consent of the affected country" and that "the affected State has the primary role in the initiation, organization, coordination, and implementation of humanitarian assistance within its territory." In effect, the actions of the transnational humanitarian community are limited by the principles of sovereignty and noninterference enshrined within the UN Charter. Thus, not surprisingly, the aid effort within Syria looks considerably different from the effort outside of its borders.

Further, while the core principles of humanitarian action are widely entrenched and frequently referred to as forming an "international humanitarian regime" (IHR), this regime is a complex one, with assistance to civilians balanced against assistance to and protection of other identified groups with specific statuses as defined in hard and soft law, including refugees and IDPs. Thus, while the UN High Commissioner for Refugees (UNHCR) provides significant assistance to IDPs within the UN's cluster approach, it also has a legal mandate to provide protection to refugees. As such, and as discussed below, the transnational humanitarian community functions with a humanitarian regime complex, with the principles of humanitarian action nested in or interacting with a number of other distinct international regimes.

At the same time, the humanitarian community has become much more overt in communicating its core principles externally and in so doing directly affecting its involvement in conflict and postconflict situations. Thus, in the case of Syria, it has successfully linked these humanitarian principles to the Responsibility to Protect (R2P) doctrine in a way that uses other international institutions—notably the UN Security Council—to circumvent strong limitations on its ability to fulfill its primary goals.

This chapter begins at a theoretical level by examining the three core regimes within the regime complex: the IHR, the international refugee regime, and the IDP protection regime. It then highlights the regime interactions that occur. These interactions help to constitute and define the space in which these actors operate and their capacities to do so. To illustrate the dynamics this creates, it ends by focusing on the relationship between the IHR and sovereignty to illustrate how this alters aid delivery to refugees and to civilians and IDPs, using the case of Syria to work through the dilemmas this relationship creates.

The Foundations of the IHR Complex

The transnational humanitarian community operates within an IHR complex. The basis of this complex lies in three distinct regimes, each led by its own transnational actors and with its own foundations in international law and in sovereignty: the IHR, the international refugee regime, and the developing IDP protection regime.

The international humanitarian and refugee regimes emerged as separate regimes, while the IDP protection regime, a more recent development, draws significantly on both of these prior regimes. This occurs even as growing intersections and changes in practice link together these discrete regimes as well as forge links with other regimes.

What do I mean by "regime"? Historically, regimes were composed of four discrete components: "implicit or explicit principles, norms, rules, and decision-making procedures." These components were seen as critical, as around them "actors' expectations converge in a given area of international relations."[9] This view has been criticized both for its complexity and for the difficulty in distinguishing between these different components.[10] Equally important, the idea that actors' expectations converge suggests, per Robert O. Keohane and Joseph S.

Nye, that they "define their own self-interest in directions that conform to the rules of the regimes" and that "the principles and norms of the regime may be internalized by important groups and thus become part of the belief systems which filter information."[11] Through participation in regimes, consequently, "iterated acts of cooperation can lead to an internalized commitment to the social practice of cooperation itself."[12]

Because of this, regimes can be thought of as social institutions, ones that have suasion by both providing "benefits to participants, but also through the shared understandings and international norms they embody."[13] Hence, regimes provide a "web of meaning" in which individual issue-specific norms can interact and become linked, thereby providing a behavior guide for states and other actors.[14]

The origins of the IHR lie in the nineteenth century, as the ICRC initially sought to provide protection for wounded soldiers and then the wider community of war-affected civilians.[15] Thus, the ICRC predates but reflects similar activities as both the Knights of Columbus, as discussed in chapter 1, and the growth of the Women's International League for Peace and Freedom, as discussed in chapter 2. And yet, through the codification of international humanitarian law, culminating in the 1949 Geneva Conventions and their additional protocols, the ICRC has played an almost unique role as a legal custodian of the regime, even as it has sought to broaden its scope to include issues such as internal war.[16]

The principles underpinning this regime have also become divided. "Traditional" humanitarian actors—including the ICRC as well as other organizations such as MSF—continue to focus on the duty of humanitarian organizations to provide aid in accordance with the principles of neutrality, impartiality, and independence.[17] Other humanitarian organizations—including Oxfam, World Vision, and CARE—today favor a rights-based approach that sees them acting both in a more overtly political manner and linking humanitarian assistance directly to human rights. This, Urvashi Aneja argues, not only expands the range of goods and services that fall under humanitarian assistance but also "shifts attention from the needs of civilians to the duties and responsibilities of external actors."[18]

The international refugee regime is based in international law (particularly the 1951 Convention Relating to the Status of Refugees and its 1967 protocol), in the role played by formal institutions, particularly the UNHCR,[19] and in state policy and practice. Hence, this regime is based on a foundation of social norms that define that refugees need legal protection and multilateral assistance. This was not true at the beginning of the regime: When the UNHCR was originally created, it had exclusively a legal mandate toward refugees. This shifted in the 1950s as the UNHCR responded to a series of international crises, which led to an expansion of the organization's duties to include assistance.[20]

The refugee convention established a range of basic minimum standards for the treatment of refugees, stipulated that refugees cannot be prosecuted for illegal entry, and, most important, introduced a legal norm of nonrefoulement. It defines refugees as

> any person who owing to well-founded fear of being persecuted for reasons of race, religion, nationality, membership of a particular social group or political opinion, is outside the country of his nationality and is unable, or owing to such fear, unwilling to avail himself of the protection of that country; or who, not having a nationality and being outside the country of his former habitual residence as a result of such events, is unable or, owing to such fear, unwilling to return to it.[21]

The convention is seen as so important that it has been referred to as the "Magna Carta of international refugee law."[22] Yet, the convention's definition is limited in a number of ways. These include a focus on state-based persecution, rather than other persecution such as that caused by nonstate actors or from situations of generalized violence, and that refugees are defined in an "essentially individualistic" way in the convention.[23] This means that a range of forced migrants do not actually fall within the convention's definition of refugee status. In its own practices, the UNHCR has undertaken prima facie recognition, whereby individuals can acquire refugee status without having to justify their fear of persecution based on the objective circumstances of mass displacement and the obvious refugee character of the individuals so affected, but signatories are not required to do so.[24] Similarly, many states also offer complementary protection to refugees who do not fall within the convention's definition but nevertheless face threats of persecution in their own countries. Such practices include leaves to stay on humanitarian grounds and temporary stays against removal.[25]

The IDP protection regime is relatively recent, dating back to the end of the Cold War.[26] Critical to this regime are the guiding principles on internal displacement. While nonbinding, the guiding principles use as their foundation existing international human rights law, humanitarian law, and refugee law.[27] There has also been a move to adopt the principles into binding legal instruments, particularly in Africa. In particular, the 2009 African Union Convention for the Protection and Assistance of Internally Displaced Persons in Africa (the Kampala Convention), ratified in 2012, deliberately replicates the normative structure introduced by the guiding principles.[28] The principles describe IDPs as "persons or groups of persons who have been forced or obliged to flee or to leave their homes or places of habitual residence, in particular as a result of or in order to avoid the effects of armed conflict, situations of generalized violence, violations of human rights or natural or human-made disasters, and who have not crossed an internationally recognized State border."[29]

The principles restate the international legal rights that IDPs are entitled to; hence, they establish a norm that IDPs are entitled to the same legal protections as other citizens. And they establish that "the primary duty and responsibility for providing humanitarian assistance to internally displaced persons lies with national authorities" but that "appropriate actors have the right to offer their services. . . . Consent thereto shall not be arbitrarily withheld."[30]

While there is no central actor assigned a duty of assistance or protection to IDPs, the UN-based cluster approach was introduced in 2005 in order "to provide much-needed predictability and accountability for the collaborative response to IDPs."[31] Each of the eleven clusters has a designated lead agency. These include a range of transnational actors, including UN agencies such as the UNHCR and key NGOs such as the IFRC.[32] While the cluster approach has increased leadership, predictability, and the effectiveness of aid delivery, the system has also worked most effectively when "host government agencies have taken the lead (such as in Ethiopia and the Philippines); the least successful are those with a multitude of international participants, weak cluster leadership, and confusion about roles."[33] Unfortunately, it is when state authorities are unable, or unwilling, to act that the internally displaced most need an alternative form of protection.

Creating a Regime Complex

The growing complexity of global governance means that linkages frequently develop across regimes. Kal Raustiala and David G. Victor were the first to suggest that overlaps between regimes could lead to a regime complex, "an array of partially overlapping and nonhierarchical institutions governing a particular issue-area."[34] More recently, Karen J. Alter and Sophie Meunier have focused on an allied but broader notion of "regime complexity" as referring to the "presence of nested, partially over-lapping, and parallel international regimes that are not hierarchically ordered."[35] With a third view, Amandine Orsini, Jean-Frédéric Morin, and Oran Young suggest a regime complex is a "network of three or more international regimes that relate to a common subject matter; exhibit overlapping membership; and generate substantive, normative, or operative interactions recognized as potentially problematic whether or not they are managed effectively."[36] We can see across these three definitions a clear idea of what constitutes a regime complex—multiple overlapping and nonhierarchical regimes within a common subject.

The focus of this work has been primarily on how actors, principally states, can use regime complexity in a strategic manner, such as by undermining obligations through forum-shopping and by shifting regimes.[37] And yet regime complexes are, by their nature, messy in several ways. First, new international problems tend to be accommodated within existing regimes and formal international organizations, rather than having new, separate structures created. Further, the regime complexity literature has also primarily focused on state agency, particularly through the creation of new rules and legal arrangements,[38] rather than on the agency—and basic practices—of actors within these regime complexes. Examining actor-based practices within a regime complex provides an alternative way of seeing directly the unanticipated effects that regime complexes may generate. For "divided actors"—those whose formal mandates and roles encompass multiple regimes within the complex—interactions between regimes define the space in which these organizations operate and their capacities to do so. This suggests that, at a deeper level, regime complexes constitute basic organizational practices.

By incorporating a number of distinct regimes (see figure 8.1 below), the development of the IHR complex has created three significant contradictions for the actors involved in its individual component regimes. The first contradiction reflects the status of the subject. Each regime (with foundations in international law) focuses on people with particular statuses: civilian, refugee, internally displaced person. Hence, while the person is the subject of the regime complex, people can simultaneously have multiple statuses and fall within different regimes.

Individual actors are aware of these potential contradictions. When the guiding principles on internal displacement were first proposed, the ICRC objected on two points. The first was that humanitarian law did "afford protection to the internally displaced" but that "its scope extends a great deal further," though this neglects the fact that many IDP situations occur in situations where

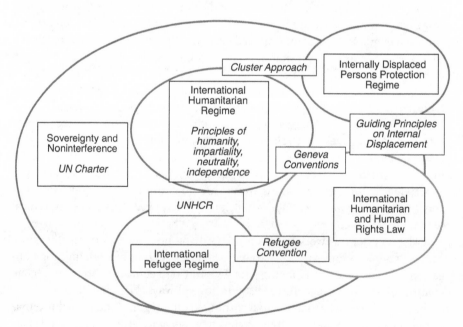

Figure 8.1: The International Humanitarian Regime Complex

international humanitarian law is not applicable.[39] The second point was that the ICRC felt no need to single out IDPs when other categories could have just as pressing needs, and hence there was no need for an alternative set of practices: "A global view of the different needs and an impartial response to them will prevent unjustified distinction between the various categories of victims. The ICRC has never attempted to define the term 'internally displaced person,' simply because all displaced persons fall within the category 'civilian population.'"[40]

The second contradiction is that some humanitarian actors may *cross several regimes* within the complex and therefore find their own roles divided. Thus, as noted above, the UNHCR has both a legal protection and assistance mandate for refugees. More recently, the UNHCR has actively recognized and sought out complementary overlaps, such as by expanding its role beyond refugees to incorporate IDPs.[41] With this shift, the UNHCR effectively became a key institutional actor in both the refugee and IDP regimes.

The third contradiction reflects that each of these regimes is based in a specific understanding of state sovereignty, yet each provides a different view of the role of the state in the humanitarian process. The international refugee regime accords status to those individuals who are outside of their own state and cannot count on its protection. Yet not all host countries are signatories to the convention, nor do all provide the full rights embodied in the convention to refugees in their territory. The UNHCR can only operate in a country if it is invited to do so, and "governments have a range of mechanism[s] for frustrating the work of UNHCR, including preventing access to regions of the country, isolating UNHCR Representatives and denying entry for visiting missions from headquarters."[42]

For both the IHR and the IDP protection regime, state consent can be critical for access. Yet the nature of sovereignty has been questioned through the development of the R2P doctrine. In first proposing the R2P concept in 2001, the International Commission on Intervention and State Sovereignty sought to recast existing debates around rights of humanitarian intervention to instead introduce a responsibility or duty for the international community to take action to respond or avert mass atrocities.[43] Five years later in its document "Resolution 60/1: World Summit Outcome," the UN recognized the R2P doctrine, establishing that "each individual State has the responsibility to protect its populations from genocide, war crimes, ethnic cleansing and crimes against humanity," that the international community should "help States to exercise this responsibility," and that the international community has a responsibility to act through the Security Council on a case-by-case basis "should peaceful means be inadequate and national authorities are manifestly failing to protect their populations from genocide, war crimes, ethnic cleansing and crimes against humanity."[44]

In the ten years since, the R2P doctrine has provided an important focus for how the international community should respond. Alex Bellamy argues that it has created "a collection of shared expectations."[45] Jennifer Welsh suggests it has created a "duty of conduct" for members of the international community "to identify when atrocity crimes are being committed (or when there is threat of commission) and to deliberate on how the three-pillar framework might apply."[46] Critically, as I will argue below, the R2P doctrine has triggered a shift in how sovereignty is understood, which has had direct effects on the IHR complex.

The IHR Complex and the Response to Syria

The scale of the humanitarian crisis created by the Syrian Civil War well illustrates how these contradictions can play out in practice for transnational humanitarian actors. In seeking to provide the civilian population with assistance, these actors have faced two significant issues. The first issue is that the victims of the conflict had a range of different and overlapping statuses defined by geography. The second issue is that the Syrian government has used the pretext of its sovereign consent to limit the ability of these transnational actors to operate within its territory and to significantly impede aid delivery within the country, particularly to rebel-held areas.

More so than in most conflicts, geography has been a significant factor in affecting the humanitarian assistance and protection that Syrians can receive. Obviously, there is a key distinction based on whether affected civilians can leave the country as refugees or remain within the country as IDPs. But, in this case, even being outside the country has not guaranteed full protections under international law. Resettlement to third countries has not been widespread. While the UNHCR has worked to create resettlement places for Syrian refugees in third countries, that had only created some 227,497 places across thirty-two countries by April 2016.[47]

Instead, 95 percent of the five million refugees produced by the Syrian conflict have remained within the region in Lebanon, Jordan, Turkey, and Iraq. The UNHCR and other humanitarian actors have operations in each country. But their legal status is precarious. Turkey is the only one to have signed the 1951 refugee convention. Yet that government has "expressly maintained its declaration of geographical limitation upon acceding" and is not legally bound to apply the convention to Syrian refugees.[48] The right of nonrefoulement, or nonreturn to a country where a refugee will face persecution, is customary law and therefore applicable to all countries.[49] But other core rights for refugees, including nonpersecution for illegal entry, freedom of movement, and access to basic services, are not.

These governments have committed significant support to their refugee populations, but evidence suggests all four governments are under significant strain. Lebanon, for example, has received 1.1 million refugees, almost 20 percent of its population.[50] There the government has supported the refugees residing with host families or other informal settlements, rather than in camps. As of January 2016, Turkey was hosting 3.1 million registered refugees from Syria and Iraq, and its government estimated that it has spent over $7 billion since the start of the crisis.[51]

The legal situation for IDPs within Syria is worse. The Syrian government does not admit it has IDPs. As Dr. Chaloka Beyani, the UN's special rapporteur on the human rights of IDPs, has noted, "The Government stated its position that the Syrian Arab Republic was not suffering from a phenomenon called 'internally displaced persons' but rather had been subject to a series of terrorist attacks undertaken by armed outlaws. As such, persons being assisted were referred to as 'people who left their homes as a result of the current events.'"[52] The unwillingness of the Syrian government to provide IDPs with legal rights is in spite of the guiding principles' clear applicability in this situation. It reflects a rejection of the principles providing protections for IDPs against arbitrary displacement and against attacks on those not participating in hostilities, as well as IDPs' right to receive unimpeded access to humanitarian assistance.[53] This has had direct consequences for the internally displaced population, with most IDPs continuing to "face significant protection concerns in relation to the ongoing conflict . . . [g]iven the near absence of areas providing safety."[54]

The second issue has been one of consent to operate within Syria. All international NGOs need to first register with the government to legally operate within Syria, but by October 2015 only fifteen NGOs had received approval.[55] Further, while the government's official position is that humanitarian agencies can go anywhere, as Ben Parker, the former head of OCHA in Syria, has noted, "every action requires time-consuming permissions, which effectively provide multiple veto opportunities."[56] In particular the government has sought to limit where humanitarian organizations operated. Until October 2013, it was willing to support "cross-line" aid deliveries—aid that originated in Damascus but may then cross into opposition-held areas—but was unwilling to support cross-border aid, as the border regions are generally held by the rebels.[57]

Lack of government consent always leaves transnational humanitarian actors with a set of unpalatable choices: "When humanitarians cross into opposition-controlled areas without State consent, for example, humanitarian space in State-controlled areas can be compromised."[58] In Syria, UN agencies were unable to operate without the Syrian government's consent. Other humanitarian organizations, such as MSF, made the decision to operate illegally to provide aid to rebel-held areas: "We feel that by crossing the border even illegally we are legitimate since the needs are huge and almost no one is present to assist the population."[59]

Beginning in 2013, these issues triggered a remarkable campaign on the part of the transnational humanitarian community to push for action by the UN Security Council. Human Rights Watch and Oxfam began the action but were then joined by the ICRC and Interaction, the alliance of US-based international relief organizations.[60] The Security Council has the primary role at the international level to maintain international peace and security. Since the end of the Cold War, it has interpreted large-scale refugee and IDP flows as falling within this responsibility.[61] However, the Security Council has rarely taken action on the issue of government consent to humanitarian assistance, and the few cases where it was addressed were all within wider contexts of peacekeeping operations.[62]

It is perhaps surprising, therefore, that when faced with this pressure, the Security Council moved to take a series of actions. These began in October 2013 with a presidential statement drafted by Australia and Luxembourg.[63] As a statement it was nonbinding and did not have the same legal force a resolution would have, but it did reflect the unanimous will of the council. The statement noted the council's "grave concern" that several million Syrians need "immediate humanitarian assistance, and without urgent increased humanitarian action, their lives will be at risk." The statement explicitly noted that the Security Council was "appalled" at the level of violence and condemned the widespread violation of human rights and international humanitarian law by the Syrian government. It also urged the Syrian government to remove bureaucratic obstacles and to facilitate the expansion of international assistance and access, including across borders. Draft language, however, had been much more forceful, suggesting that the Security Council might bypass the Syrian government and introduce humanitarian corridors into the country.[64]

Following the statement, the Syrian government did increase the number of cross-line convoys approved and allowed cross-border assistance from Jordan, Lebanon, and Iraq but continued to block any assistance from Turkey.[65] In December 2013, this led MSF to argue that "if the Syrian government remains the main channel for the overwhelming majority of international humanitarian aid, millions of people will continue to be deprived of adequate assistance."[66]

With the failure of the Syrian government to ameliorate its actions, the Security Council subsequently passed a unanimous resolution demanding that "all parties, in particular the Syrian authorities, promptly allow rapid, safe and unhindered humanitarian access for UN humanitarian agencies and their implementing partners including across conflict lines and across borders."[67] Stronger language including the possibility of sanctions was once again removed during the negotiating process.[68]

And yet Syria similarly ignored this resolution. The UN Emergency Relief Coordinator publicly argued that the "continued withholding of consent to cross-border and cross-line relief operations . . . is arbitrary and unjustified."[69] A coalition of international lawyers similarly argued that in denying such access, the Syrian government has engaged in "blatant disregard for the most basic rules of international humanitarian law."[70]

This triggered a second resolution in which the Security Council decided that "the United Nations humanitarian agencies and their implementing partners are authorized to use routes across conflict lines . . . with notification to the Syrian authorities."[71] The resolution also established a monitoring mechanism to ensure only humanitarian relief was provided. This change did improve aid delivery, with the UN noting that "a record number of people were reached with food assistance in August [2014]. . . . There have also been openings in access across conflict lines, with some cross-line deliveries of food, health and water and sanitation supplies in Aleppo . . . , Idlib and Rif Dimashq."[72] The Security Council renewed this mechanism in December 2015, noting that it was "gravely distressed by the continued deterioration of the devastating humanitarian situation" and "gravely concerned at the lack of effective implementation of its resolutions."[73]

Beyond the immediate aid delivered, it is important to note that by explicitly removing the requirement for Syrian authorities to consent to aid flows, the Security Council both created a new precedent and further redefined sovereignty, providing a significant boost to the transnational humanitarian community. This reinforced both the norms of humanitarian action and access but also established that it is within the scope of the council to investigate and take action in situations where such access is denied in violation of international law. How this affects sovereignty is subtle. Both Resolutions 2139 and 2165 reaffirmed the sovereignty and territorial integrity of the Syrian state. While Resolution 2139 referenced the R2P, it is an oblique reference, stressing that "the primary responsibility to protect its population lies with the Syrian authorities."[74] And yet, clearly underpinning this shift was a view that the Syrian authorities were not fulfilling their responsibilities toward their own population and that, at least with respect to humanitarian action, the council could take action.

Conclusions: Interactions and Regime Complexity

The transnational humanitarian community operates within an IHR complex. This complex introduces a number of potential contradictions with respect to the status of individuals, with respect to actions by organizations within the complex, and with respect to state sovereignty. First, with respect to status, people can have multiple simultaneous statuses as civilians, as victims of displacement, and so on. However, these statuses may not be accepted by all critical actors—the Syrian government does not accept that its own population is internally displaced, while refugee-receiving countries in the region have generally not signed the 1951 refugee convention.

Second, individual transnational actors wrestle with different responsibilities across these regimes. Here, sovereignty plays a key role in limiting the assistance that UN actors can provide within Syria, for example, while other non-UN-aligned NGOs can intercede and ignore the government. Individual actors do not have the authority within the regime complex to overcome these dilemmas, though some, like MSF, can avoid them by acting illegally. The Security Council's role with respect to humanitarian assistance in Syria, however, suggests one way in which some of the contradictions within the regime complex can be bridged. Only it has the authority and capacity to direct action by the Syrian government.

Unfortunately, humanitarian assistance alone cannot end a crisis like Syria's. Sadako Ogata, the UNHCR high commissioner from 1991 until 2000, famously argued that "there are no humanitarian solutions to humanitarian problems."[75] Asylum represents one form of protection for the Syrian population. But, as the numbers of refugees reach past five million, this is becoming limited. By expanding humanitarian assistance within Syria, the international community can provide lifesaving help even while waiting for a political solution.

Notes

1. John Hudson, "UN Envoy Revises Syria Death Toll to 400,000," *Foreign Policy*, April 22, 2016; European Commission Humanitarian Aid Office, "Syria: IDPs and Refugees in Neighboring Countries," March 9, 2016, http://reliefweb.int/map/syrian-arab-republic/syria-idps-and-refugees-neighbouring-countries-echo-daily-map-09032016; United Nations Office for the Coordination of Humanitarian Affairs, *Syrian Arab Republic: 2016 Humanitarian Needs Overview*, October 2015, https://www.humanitarianresponse.info/en/system/files/documents/files/2016_hno_syrian_arab_republic.pdf.

2. Michael Barnett, "Humanitarianism as a Scholarly Vocation," in *Humanitarianism in Question: Politics, Power, Ethics*, ed. M. Barnett and T. G. Weiss (Ithaca, NY: Cornell University Press, 2008), 239.

3. Office for the Coordination of Humanitarian Affairs [OCHA], *Humanitarian Bulletin: Syrian Arab Republic 13–26 March 2014* (New York: OCHA, 2014); US Agency for International Development [USAID], *Syria: Complex Emergency Fact Sheet #18: Fiscal Year 2014* (Washington, DC: USAID, 2014).

4. Fiona Terry, *Condemned to Repeat? The Paradox of Humanitarian Action* (Ithaca, NY: Cornell University Press, 2002), 19.

5. Barnett, "Humanitarianism as a Scholarly Vocation," 253.

6. Active Learning Network for Accountability and Performance in Humanitarian Action (ALNAP), *The State of the Humanitarian System: 2012 Edition* (London: Overseas Development Institute, 2012), 9, 29.

7. Global Humanitarian Assistance, *Global Humanitarian Assistance Report 2013* (Bristol, UK: Development Intiatives, 2013), 4.

8. UN General Assembly, "Resolution A/RES/46/182: Strengthening of the Coordination of Humanitarian Emergency Assistance of the United Nations," December 19, 1991, annex I.

9. Stephen D. Krasner, "Structural Causes and Regime Consequences: Regimes as Intervening Variables," *International Organization* 36, no. 2 (1982): 186.

10. See Marc A. Levy, Oran R. Young, and Michael Zurn, "The Study of International Regimes," *European Journal of International Relations* 1, no. 3 (1995): 270; Oran R. Young, "International Regimes: Toward a New Theory of Institutions," *World Politics* 39, no. 1 (1986): 106.

11. Robert O. Keohane and Joseph S. Nye, *Power and Interdependence*, 2nd ed. (Glenview, IL: Scott, Foresman, 1989), 259, 266.

12. Jennifer Sterling-Folker, "Competing Paradigms or Birds of a Feather? Constructivism and Neoliberal Institutionalism Compared," *International Studies Quarterly* 44 (2000): 112.

13. Phil Orchard, *A Right to Flee: Refugees, States, and the Construction of International Society* (Cambridge, UK: Cambridge University Press, 2014), 29; Gary Goertz, *International Norms and Decisionmaking: A Punctuated Equilibrium Model* (Lanham, MD: Rowman & Littlefield, 2003), 15.

14. Mark Neufeld, "Interpretation and the 'Science' of International Relations," *Review of International Studies* 19, no. 1 (1993): 43; Andreas Hasenclever, Peter Mayer, and Volker Rittberger, *Theories of International Regimes* (Cambridge, UK: Cambridge University Press, 1997), 165.

15. Barnett and Weiss, "Humanitarianism: A Brief History of the Present."

16. David P. Forsythe, "The ICRC: A Unique Humanitarian Protagonist," *International Review of the Red Cross* 89, no. 865 (2007): 66.

17. Terry, *Condemned to Repeat?*, 19.

18. Urvashi Aneja, "International NGOs and the Implementation of the Norm for Need-Based Humanitarian Assistance in Sri lanka," in *Implementation and World Politics: How International Norms Change Practice*, ed. Alexander Betts and Phil Orchard (Oxford, UK: Oxford University Press, 2014), 89.

19. Nicholas Van Hear, "Editorial Introduction," *Journal of Refugee Studies* 11, no. 4 (1998): 342. See also G. Loescher, "The International Refugee Regime: Stretched to the Limit?," *Journal of International Affairs* 47, no. 2 (1994): 352.

20. Orchard, *Right to Flee*.

21. Convention Relating to the Status of Refugees, 1951, Article 1 A. (2).

22. The Editor's Desk, "The Refugee Convention at 50 . . . ," *Refugees* 2, no. 123 (2001): 2.

23. Jerzy Sztucki, "Who Is a Refugee? The Convention Definition: Universal or Obsolete?," in *Refugee Rights and Realities: Evolving International Concepts and Regimes*, ed. Frances Nicholson and Patrick M. Twomey (Cambridge, UK: Cambridge University Press, 1999), 58; Guy S. Goodwin-Gill and Jane McAdam, *The Refugee in International Law*, 3rd ed. (Oxford, UK: Oxford University Press, 2007), 23.

24. Jean-François Durieux and Jane McAdam, "Non-Refoulement through Time: The Case for a Derogation Clause to the Refugee Convention in Mass Influx Emergencies," *International Journal of Refugee Law* 16, no. 1 (2004): 11.

25. Matthew J. Gibney, *The Ethics and Politics of Asylum: Liberal Democracy and the Response to Refugees* (Cambridge, UK: Cambridge University Press, 2004), 8.

26. Phil Orchard, "Protection of Internally Displaced Persons: Soft Law as a Norm-Generating Mechanism," *Review of International Studies* 36, no. 2 (2010).

27. Walter Kälin, "The Guiding Principles on Internal Displacement as International Minimum Standard and Protection Tool," *Refugee Survey Quarterly* 24, no. 3 (2005): 29–30.

28. Allehone Mulugeta Abebe, "The African Union Convention on Internally Displaced Persons: Its Codification Background, Scope, and Enforcement Challenges," *Refugee Survey Quarterly* 29, no. 3 (2010): 42; Phil Orchard, "Implementing a Global Internally Displaced Persons Protection Regime," in Betts and Orchard, *Implementation and World Politics*.

29. OCHA, *Guiding Principles on Internal Displacement* (New York: OCHA, 1999), 1.

30. Ibid., 13.

31. Tim Morris, "UNHCR, IDPs and Clusters," *Forced Migration Review* 25 (2006).

32. OCHA, *Consolidated Appeals Process: Appeal for Improving Humanitarian Response Capacity; Cluster 2006* (New York: OCHA, 2006). The eleven clusters and cluster leads are protection in conflict situations (UNHCR) and disaster situations (UNHCR / Office of the High Commissioner for Human Rights / United Nations Children's Fund [UNICEF]); camp coordination and management (UNHCR and International Organization for Migration); early recovery (UN Development Programme); emergency shelter in conflict situations (UNHCR) and in disaster situations (IFRC); health (World Health Organization); water, sanitation, and hygiene (UNICEF); nutrition (UNICEF); education (UNICEF and Save the Children); food security (Food and Agriculture Organization and World Food Programme [WFP]); logistics (WFP); and telecommunications (OCHA). United Nations, *Handbook for the Protection of Internally Displaced Persons* (New York: UN Global Protection Cluster Working Group, 2010), 45; UN Humanitarian Response "Clusters," http://www.humanitarian response.info/clusters.

33. Elizabeth Ferris and Sara Ferro-Ribeiro, "Protecting People in Cities: The Disturbing Case of Haiti," *Disasters* 36, no. s1 (2012): S53; Julia Steets et al., *Cluster Approach Evaluation 2 Synthesis Report* (Paris and Berlin: Groupe URD and the Global Public Policy Institute, April 2010), 9.

34. Kal Raustiala and David G. Victor, "The Regime Complex for Plant Genetic Resources," *International Organization* 58, no. 2 (2004): 279.

35. Karen J. Alter and Sophie Meunier, "The Politics of International Regime Complexity," *Perspectives on Politics* 7, no. 1 (2009): 13.

36. Amandine Orsini, Jean-Frédéric Morin, and Oran Young, "Regime Complexes: A Buzz, a Boom, or a Boost for Global Governance?," *Global Governance: A Review of Multilateralism and International Organizations* 19, no. 1 (2013): 29–30.

37. Alter and Meunier, "Politics of International Regime Complexity"; Alexander Betts, "Institutional Proliferation and the Global Refugee Regime," *Perspectives on Politics* 7, no. 1 (2009).

38. Raustiala and Victor, " Regime Complex," 279.

39. Jean-Philippe Lavoyer, "Commments on the Guiding Principles on Internal Displacement," *International Review of the Red Cross*, no. 324 (1998).

40. Ibid. The ICRC has since shifted to recognizing the guiding principles as a "valuable benchmark." International Committee of the Red Cross, *ICRC Position on Internally Displaced Persons (IDPs)* (Geneva: ICRC, 2006): 3.

41. Alexander Betts, "Regime Complexity and International Organizations: UNHCR as a Challenged Institution," *Global Governance: A Review of Multilateralism and International Organizations* 19, no. 1 (2013): 75.

42. Gil Loescher, Alexander Betts, and James Milner, *The United Nations High Commissioner for Refugees (UNHCR): The Politics and Practice of Refugee Protection into the Twenty-First Century* (Milton Park, UK: Routledge, 2008): 82.

43. International Commission on Intervention and State Sovereignty, *The Responsibility to Protect* (Ottawa: International Development Research Centre, 2001).

44. UN General Assembly, "Resolution 60/1: World Summit Outcome," 2005, 30.

45. Alex J. Bellamy, *Global Politics and the Responsibility to Protect: From Words to Deeds* (Milton Park, UK: Routledge, 2011), 84.

46. Jennifer Welsh, "Implementing the 'Responsibility to Protect': Catalyzing Debate and Building Capacity," in Betts and Orchard, *Implementation and World Politics*, 136.

47. Mona Chalabi, "Where Are the Syrian Refugees Going?," *Guardian*, January 29, 2014, http://www.theguardian.com/news/datablog/2014/jan/29/where-are-the-syrian-refugees

-going; UNHCR, "Resettlement and Other Admission Pathways for Syrian Refugees," August 31, 2016, http://www.unhcr.org/protection/resettlement/573dc82d4/resettlement -other-admission-pathways-syrian-refugees-updated-31-august.html.

48. UNHCR, "States Parties to the 1951 Convention Relating to the Status of Refugees and the 1967 Protocol," 2011, http://www.unhcr.org/3b73b0d63.html.

49. UNHCR, "Note on the Principle of Non-Refoulement," 1997, http://www.refworld .org/docid/438c6d972.html.

50. Amnesty International, "Syria's Refugee Crisis in Numbers," February 3, 2016, https://www.amnesty.org/en/latest/news/2016/02/syrias-refugee-crisis-in-numbers/.

51. European Commission, "Turkey: Refugee Crisis," April 2016, http://ec.europa.eu/ echo/files/aid/countries/factsheets/turkey_syrian_crisis_en.pdf.

52. UN General Assembly, *Protection of and Assistance to Internally Displaced Persons: Situation of Internally Displaced Persons in the Syrian Arab Republic* (New York: United Nations, 2013), 17.

53. OCHA, *Guiding Principles on Internal Displacement*.

54. UN General Assembly, *Protection of and Assistance to*, 7, 10.

55. OCHA, "Syrian Arab Republic: Humanitarian Presence: Registered International NGOs (as of 28 October 2013)," 2013.

56. Ben Parker, "Humanitarianism Besieged," *Humanitarian Exchange*, no. 59 (2013): 3.

57. Human Rights Watch, "Syria: Authorize Cross-Border Humanitarian Aid," February 11, 2013, https://www.hrw.org/news/2013/02/11/syria-authorize-cross-border-humanitarian-aid.

58. Global Protection Cluster, *Global Protection Cluster Roundtable: Cross-Border Humanitarian Relief Operations* (Geneva: United Nations, 2014): 4.

59. RN Breakfast, "Delivering Aid in Warzones," ABC Radio (2013), http://www.abc .net.au/radionational/programs/breakfast/delivering-aid-in-warzones/5082648.

60. Human Rights Watch, "Syria"; Peter Maurer, "IHL and Humanitarian Principles Are Non-Negotiable: Syria Is No Exception," February 15, 2014, https://www.icrc.org/eng/ resources/documents/article/editorial/2014-02-15-syria-maurer-humanitarian-principles .htm; Oxfam International, "Aid Agency Calls for Improved Humanitarian Access to Syria as Needs Escalate," April 30, 2013, http://www.oxfam.ca/news/oxfam-calls-for-improved -humanitarian-access-to-syria; Interaction, "Statement by Interaction Member CEOs on the Third Anniversary of the Syrian Civil War," March 6, 2014, https://www.worldvision.org/ press-release/statement-interaction-member-ceos-third-anniversary-syrian-civil-war.

61. Bruce Cronin, "International Consensus and the Changing Legal Authority of the UN Security Council," in *The UN Security Council and the Politics of International Authority*, ed. Bruce Cronin and Ian Hurd (London: Routledge, 2008); T. G. Weiss and D. A. Korn, *Internal Displacement: Conceptualization and Its Consequences* (Oxford, UK: Routledge, 2006).

62. Alex J. Bellamy, "Opening the Door to Humanitarian Aid in Syria: Significance, Challenges, and Prospects," *IPI Global Observatory*, July 17, 2014, https://theglobalobservatory .org/2014/07/opening-door-humanitarian-aid-in-syria-significance-challenges-prospects/.

63. UN Department of Public Information, "Security Council, Appalled at Deteriorating Humanitarian Situation in Syria, Urges Eased Access for Relief Workers, Including across Conflict Lines," October 2, 2013, https://www.un.org/News/Press/docs/2013/sc11138.doc.htm.

64. "Syria Crisis: UN Security Council Demands Aid Access after Chemical Weapons Deal," Associated Press, October 1, 2013.

65. Antonio Galli, "Humanitarian Negotiations: Syria, Sudan, Cross-Border Operations, and Armed Non-State Actors," *PHAP: Professionals in Humanitarian Assistance and Protection* (2013).

66. Médecins Sans Frontières, "Syria: Urgent Need for Cross-Border Aid," (2013).

67. UN Security Council Resolution 2139, "Syria- Humanitarian Assistance," February 22, 2014, http://www.un.org/en/ga/search/view_doc.asp?symbol=S/RES/2139(2014).

68. Michelle Nichols, "U.N. Security Council Unanimously Approves Syria Aid Access Resolution," Reuters, February 22, 2014, http://mobile.reuters.com/article/idUSBREA1L0 OV20140222?irpc=932.

69. "There Is No Legal Barrier to UN Cross-Border Operations in Syria," *Guardian*, April 29, 2014.

70. Ibid.

71. UN Security Council Resolution 2165, "Middle East," July 14, 2014.

72. UN Security Council, "Implementation of Security Council Resolutions 2139 (2014) and 2165 (2014): Report of the Secretary-General," 2014.

73. UN Security Council Resolution 2258, "Middle East (Syria)," December 22, 2015.

74. UN Security Council Resolution 2139, 4.

75. Cited in David Rieff, *A Bed for the Night: Humanitarianism in Crisis* (New York: Simon & Schuster, 2002), 22.

9

Women's Advocacy Groups in Peace Negotiations

MIRIAM J. ANDERSON

It is now a globally accepted norm for women to participate in peace negotiations. This has been the result of women's transnational activism in individual states experiencing conflict and their efforts at the international level, which has resulted in strengthened global norms on women, peace, and security. Although there are now multiple United Nations (UN) Security Council resolutions that address women, peace, and security, women face continued resistance to participating in peace talks. Despite these barriers, women are often successful in gaining a place at peace negotiations and in securing women's rights in peace agreements. Transnationally networked women's civil-society groups are now playing important roles in peace negotiations and in shaping the terms of the resulting peace settlements.

The prevalence and influence of women in individual peace negotiations marks a notable departure from earlier periods. During World War I, for example, more than twelve hundred women from over thirty countries, some of whom would shortly thereafter form the Women's International League for Peace and Freedom—the organization discussed by Catia Cecilia Confortini in chapter 2—held a women's peace conference called the International Congress of Women in The Hague in 1915.[1]

The women there made a number of demands similar to those called for by women today seeking to participate in peace negotiations: an all-women's peace conference, women's presence at any official negotiations, and universal suffrage.[2] Perhaps needless to say, they were unsuccessful in achieving these demands.

Several aspects of the 1915 International Congress of Women share commonalities with the way that transnational civil society women's organizations seek to influence their states mired in conflict today. First, like the International Congress of Women, they create gender-based organizations. This is likely because they face barriers to participate in the leadership of mainstream mobilizing structures such as political parties, governments, and militaries or rebel groups. In 1915, very few women in the world had the right to vote, let alone serve in parliaments or governments. Today, despite holding the right to vote and to stand for elected office in the vast majority of states worldwide, women are still underrepresented in formal politics.[3] A women-only organization, then, provides space for women to participate as well as to advance feminist ideals not found in the other mobilizing structures dominated by men. Second, and closely related to the previous point, the women's meeting in 1915 emphasized the transnational gender-based identity of the women at the congress, which served to trump the attendees' national identities. Women's groups that mobilize and demand access to peace negotiations today often use an explicitly gender-based identity and actively recruit women from multiple sides of the conflict, which emphasizes their nonpartisanship. Third, the women at the international congress tied the issue of universal suffrage to peace. Likewise, the women participants in peace negotiations today often pursue longer-term feminist objectives through the peace negotiations that go beyond seeking an end to the cessation of hostilities. In both the 1915 case and the contemporary cases, women seeking to participate in peace negotiations conceptualize peace as going beyond a cease-fire. Specifically, they seek to create a framework articulated in the peace agreement for a postconflict society that includes a more equitable role for women in the state.

This chapter provides some background on women's peace advocacy groups, women's rights provisions in peace agreements, and on the global women's, peace, and security agenda. It then focuses on the role that women activists can play in influencing the outcome of peace negotiations. In offering a portrait of women peace advocates who seek participation in peace processes, it considers how this group of actors is organized, how it interact with other actors, how it communicates both internally and externally, how it influences conflict and peace, and finally how it reflects developments in transnationalism.

Peace negotiations and the peace agreements that emanate from them mark key historical events in the lives of states. Peace agreements may be seen as "'roadmap[s]' for a country's subsequent peacebuilding efforts."[4] As constitutional moments, many peace agreements set out the frameworks for the creation of postconflict institutions, power-sharing agreements, and changes to legislation.[5] Women's rights clauses are now found in many peace agreements, and such provisions include women's electoral quotas, the creation of offices devoted to women's rights, and changes to inheritance legislation.[6]

Between 1975 and 2011, about 40 percent of conflicts that generated peace settlements produced at least one that included references to women.[7] The bulk of these gender-inclusive peace agreements were signed after 1989.[8] It should be noted that the strength and content of these provisions are diverse, but what they hold in common is that the vast majority are framed in human rights language.[9] What is striking about the women's rights language found in peace agreements is that it overwhelmingly reflects international norms on women rather than the diverse set of local norms as might be expected. For example, a number of peace agreements refer to international women's rights instruments such as the Convention on the Elimination of All Forms of Discrimination against Women, the Convention on the Nationality of Married Women, and the Declaration of the Southern African Development Community.[10] The references to international documents found throughout a diverse set of agreements point to a transnational homogenizing mechanism at play.

Furthermore, the references in peace agreements also reflect the two themes in international women's rights instruments—women as equal to men, as well as women as vulnerable and in need of special initiatives and protections. For example, the Agreement on the Basis for the Legal Integration of the Unidad Revolucionaria Nacional Guatemalteca, a Guatemalan peace agreement from 1996, refers to women under "sectors requiring specific priority attention." Likewise, the 1991 Rwandan N'Sele Ceasefire Agreement and the 1993 Rwandan Arusha Accords identify vulnerable groups as "women, children, the aged and the handicapped," who will be "specifically taken care of" within the repatriation program.

In addition, language on women's rights within the agreements reflects the three principles underpinning human rights: inherent dignity, equality, and inalienability.[11] In other words, the implied or explicit justification for claims of women's rights is premised on the inherent dignity of human beings. The principle of equality is that human rights apply to each individual equally, and inalienability means that human rights endure despite particular circumstances and behavior. Again, the reproduction of human rights principles across agreements begs explanation.

It is women's advocacy groups that are largely responsible for the form and presence of women's rights in contemporary peace agreements. There are numerous examples worldwide of women who lobby for inclusion in peace negotiations and are often successful.[12] I wish to draw a distinction here between women's advocates, in particular, and the other capacities in which women can participate. In addition to participating in a peace process as women's advocates from civil society, they can often serve as the representatives of the warring parties, of mainstream political parties, or as mediators.

However, women are underrepresented in all of those roles in peace negotiations. Over the eighteen-year period from 1992 to 2010 "only 2.5% of negotiators, 4% of signatories, and 9% of delegations were women."[13] Among these examples of women's participation in cases where women were members of male-dominated delegations, women were unable or unwilling to advance substantive prowomen demands. For example, women participated in the Sudanese peace process concerning Darfur, as members of the Sudan People's Liberation Movement/Army's negotiating team from 2006 to 2009. These women proposed a women's electoral quota of 25 percent, which was initially taken up by the male leaders on the negotiating team, who then reduced it to 5 percent and subsequently dropped the demand altogether.[14] As well, women were members of the Farabundo Martí National Liberation Front's rebel group in El Salvador but did not advocate for women's rights specifically during the negotiations.[15] In other words, the aforementioned cases are those that demonstrate descriptive but not substantive representation of women.[16] Although all peace processes have not yet been coded for whether there were self-identified women's civil-society groups present, we do know that in a number of cases such groups have participated with the explicit objective of advancing women's interests.[17] In this chapter then, I discuss women's substantive representation in the form of all-women's peace advocacy groups. These are groups that self-identify as women's advocates and seek to participate in peace negotiations.

The chapter illustrates how women peace advocates exemplify complex transnationalism, defined in this volume as "the increasing number, scope, interactions, and influence of transnational actors on diplomatic and governance processes where states have invited as participants, been forced to respond to, or have become reliant upon the expertise of transnational actors and where transnational actors increasingly interact directly with each other." Through women's activism worldwide, states and nonstate armed groups have been pressured to accept women's presence and demands at peace negotiations. As already noted, this has occurred at both the level of individual states and at the global level as embodied in the multiple UN Security Council resolutions on women, peace, and security. Although women still face hurdles to participating in formal processes, they have successfully put the issue of women, peace, and security on the global agenda and have presented themselves as legitimate actors in peace negotiations. With so much at stake in peace talks, representatives from wide swaths of society deserve representation at these negotiations. As 52 percent of the world's population and often constituting a higher percentage of a society following an armed conflict, women are the majority of the population and deserve representation at processes determining fundamental aspects of their future state.

More broadly, literature on women and politics suggests that social rupture, including conflict, promotes gender disruption, which may be conducive to women entering formal politics.[18] Women and men often play different roles during conflict that are less possible during peacetime. Women, for example, might serve in armed forces, join peace or political movements, run businesses, or become refugees or displaced persons.[19] These experiences may be transformative—in particular, women may for the first time begin to conceive of themselves as political actors or as individuals who have a role to play in the public sphere. Those who observe women in these new roles may also have their perceptions altered regarding women's ability to perform roles in the public sphere during peacetime.[20] Those are the mechanisms that are theorized to lead to transformed gender roles as a result of conflict.

Recent scholarship indicates that local women's participation in peace negotiations leads to peace of a longer duration in the short term.[21] As well, it suggests that gender-inclusive agreements lead more quickly to the adoption of women's electoral quotas than in cases where there is no peace agreement or a peace agreement without women's rights provisions.[22]

Organization: A Gender-Based Identity

Common to the organization of a number of women's groups seeking entry into their country's peace negotiations is a gender-based identity. Throughout the Burundian peace process from 1998 to 2000, both Burundian women peace activists and their international allies emphasized their shared identity as women as of primary importance and a rationale for pursuing a shared agenda. In appealing for unity among women from across the ethnic divides of the conflict, they used such statements as "In Burundi it is said that women have no clan, no ethnic group, no regional identity. This forces us to be sensitive to the miseries of all Burundians, whether Hutu, Tutsi or Twa."[23] Similarly, at the All-Women's Peace Conference held as a component of the official negotiations, the United Nations Development Fund for Women (UNIFEM), which was hosting the event, stated explicitly that the women present should focus on "women's issues"—particularly their marginalization in society only—and not address the issues over which the conflict had been waged.[24]

Likewise, in Northern Ireland, women created a political party, the Northern Ireland Women's Coalition, that won the right to participate in the peace talks held between 1996 and 1998. The strategic employment of a gender-based identity helps women's advocacy groups to avoid the contentious issues of the conflict. In this case, the party stated explicitly that it held no position on the "Constitutional Question"—whether Northern Ireland would remain part of the United Kingdom—other than that should it be decided peacefully. The strategy of sticking to "women's issues" only serves three possible purposes. First, it offers women who have not previously identified themselves as political to become involved in advocacy. Second, it ensures that the fissures of the conflict are not opened among the women advocates. Third, it is a subversive strategy that allows women to appear less threatening. Instead of them claiming already occupied ideological territory claimed by politicians who are predominantly men, women create a claim to new terrain over which men are not contesting.

The leadership of these women's advocacy groups demanding access to peace negotiations springs out of existing mobilizing structures. Many of the women who become active in peace negotiations, or at least call for women's participation, are already involved in women's advocacy. In the cases of Burundi, Northern Ireland, and Macedonia, for example, at least one of the women who held a leadership position among the women's advocates who were leading the charge to be included in the peace talks had attended the UN's Fourth World Conference for Women held in Beijing in 1995.[25] As a result of their being linked to transnational feminist networks, they were aware of other women's efforts to shape peace negotiations and were familiar with international women's rights documents.

It is due to the participation of local women in transnational feminist networks that peace agreements consist of women's rights clauses predominantly framed in human rights language and in accordance with international norms on women's rights.[26]

Communication: Internal and External

To achieve their objectives of influencing the peace process, women's peace advocacy groups must effectively communicate their message to recruits, to peace negotiation decision makers, and, when necessary, to out-of-country allies. A key component of communication is framing demands in an effective way. As noted in the previous section, a gender-based identity serves to appeal to women who have not previously identified as political, bridge the divides of the conflict, and appear less political and therefore less threatening to decision makers. To communicate their message and demands, they use a variety of practices reflecting their transnational linkages.

More concretely, communication among members of the peace advocacy group and their allies occurs in person. For example, in 1997, the Geneva-based nongovernmental organization (NGO) Femmes Africa Solidarité organized the African Women's Mission to Burundi, which included a high-level delegation of prominent African women. While in Burundi, the group held a three-day workshop for about a hundred Burundian women to promote women's participation in the peace process.[27] The following year, the African Women's Committee on Peace of the Organization of African Unity (OAU) sponsored a peace conference for Burundian women in Kampala, Uganda, attended by sixty-five Burundian women, the results of which were set to be presented at the upcoming official peace talks.[28] These meetings suggest that women's peace advocacy groups use face-to-face meetings to build awareness of the peace process and women's involvement in it, as well as rely on the sponsorship of international organizations and international NGOs.

To communicate to the general public and decision makers, women peace advocates have organized a number of public events. In Macedonia in 2001, for example, women held daily demonstrations in public squares holding up signs calling for peace in both Macedonian and Albanian.[29] The form of the silent public demonstrations imitated those used by the transnational feminist group Women in Black.[30] In Burundi, women held a march for peace.[31] By holding demonstrations, women communicate their message for peace and assert their presence in the public sphere.

Interaction with Others

The nature of transnational embeddedness becomes obvious when examining the interactions of the various groups of women involved in achieving gender-inclusive peace negotiations. Various cases illustrate the role that transnational feminist networks play in helping local women get to the peace table. The Burundi case involved local women activists from civil society, as well as women who were appointed by their political parties to participate in an all-women's peace conference. It took considerable effort on the part of numerous women to ensure that the conference proceeded. First, seven women observers traveled in July 1998 to Arusha, Tanzania, where the peace talks were being held, to insist on observer status.[32] With support from allies, including the OAU and the facilitator of the peace talks, Nelson Mandela, they were able to achieve their objective,[33] and then they worked with allies in the regional UNIFEM office in Nairobi, Kenya. UNIFEM's New York office lobbied Nelson Mandela and the negotiation team to agree to the all-women's peace conference, which was held as part of the official talks.[34]

Calling upon more powerful actors is an example of the "boomerang model"[35] where local activists seek support from their international counterparts when they are unable to influence decision makers in their own state. These external actors then pressure the decision makers who were previously resistant to the local activists' demands. In this case, the decision makers were resistant to local Burundian women's efforts to be included in the peace talks, and consequently the Burundian women aligned themselves with external actors who were able to persuade previously recalcitrant actors.

The boomerang model features several times throughout this volume to describe the interactions of a diverse set of actors. In chapter 4, Jennifer M. Brinkerhoff describes how "diasporans become important actors in a 'boomerang effect,' whereby internal actors use diasporans to voice, promote, and engage what cannot be done within the borders of the homeland." In chapter 5, Ariel I. Ahram and John Gledhill illustrate how the promotion of ideas by political exiles can be understood through the boomerang model, where individuals such as Osama bin Laden and Ayatollah Ruhollah Khomeini used transnational networks to further their own agendas because they were blocked from doing so directly by their home states. And in chapter 6, David Malet notes that foreign fighters "aim to create a boomerang effect upon their home societies by virtue of their enhanced capacities." Complex transnationalism within which war and peace are conducted, then, features the boomerang effect employed by both peace-promoting and violence-wielding actors.

The particularly dense transnational interactions among local, regional, and global actors are illustrative in the Burundian case. As discussed, Burundian women seeking access to the peace talks worked with regional allies to help them achieve their objectives. Simultaneously, UNIFEM's New York office was lobbying the UN Security Council to create a resolution on women, peace, and security. One of the proponents of that policy sought to create a positive example of women's participation in the peace process and selected the Burundian case.[36] UN Security Council Resolution 1325—the first of multiple resolutions on women, peace, and security—was passed several months after the Burundian peace agreement that included numerous references to women, which the women who attended the All Women's Peace Conference had recommended. This example illustrates complex transnationalism, where the efforts of local, regional, and global actors, all part of a transnational advocacy network, were influential both in enabling Burundian women to participate in their country's peace process, as well as in the passage of a Security Council resolution.

During the current crisis in Syria, an array of actors has joined together to carve out a role for women in any future negotiations. In 2015, UN special envoy for Syria, Staffan de Mistura, reached an agreement with Scottish legislators for "training Syrian peacemakers in negotiation and communication skills to best prepare them to maximise their role in [any peace] talks held."[37] De Mistura created a Syrian Women's Advisory Board, which traveled to Edinburgh, Scotland, for four days of talks and a conference at the Scottish Parliament in 2016.[38] The organization Beyond Borders Scotland has been instrumental in promoting the work of the Syrian Women's Advisory Board and the Scottish Parliament.[39] This case is exemplary of the various actor types interfacing to promote a particular component of an anticipated peace process.

Women's Peace Advocacy Groups and War and Peace

Women's peace advocacy groups now impact peace negotiations because of strong transnational feminist networks and global norms promoting women's rights.

Due to their successful efforts in gaining access to negotiations and compelling the Security Council to pass a series of resolutions on women, peace, and security, women now play and are likely to continue to play an influential role in the governance of peace promotion. Unlike the international environment of 1915 where women could only hope to make demands outside of the corridors of power, women now have the backing of the Security Council to shape the terms of peace and the aftermath of conflict.

Despite the global norm, however, women still have to struggle to be included in negotiations.[40] This reflects the fact that high-level decision making in formal politics is still predominantly the province of men. The impact of resolutions such as 1325 remains to be fully realized.

More research is needed to determine how and under what conditions women's participation in peace negotiations translates into gains for women. To date, we know that gender-inclusive peace agreements accelerate the average time needed for the adoption of a women's electoral quota,[41] as well as that a gender-inclusive process influences positively the duration of peace in the short-term.[42] We still do not know the processes by which women's rights in peace agreements are most likely translated into postconflict gains for women, how women's participation in peace negotiations might best be sustained to ensure women's postconflict participation in the public sphere, and whether there are marked differences in success rates if women participate in different capacities during peace negotiations.

Complex Transnationalism in War and Peace

Complex transnationalism is evident in examining women's advocacy groups and peace talks. The various case studies referenced here illustrate the dense and many interactions among the women participants in any given case and their allies in neighboring countries, other women participants in states worldwide, prominent politicians in other states, and various representatives in international organizations. These connections are possible due to communications technology and also due to an increasingly globalized feminist activist program. Due to the UN's women's world conferences and other regional meetings, women advocates have many opportunities to form networks and coordinate with others working in war-torn states. Through association with such networks, women become familiar with international standards, practices, and documents, such as the Beijing Declaration and Platform for Action and the Convention on the Elimination of All Forms of Discrimination against Women. Such contacts ensure that activists are socialized into the language and expressions of human rights that create similar language in peace agreements worldwide.

The frequency of including women's rights in peace accords has increased markedly since 1989,[43] and since 2000 a series of Security Council resolutions have called for gender-inclusive peace talks and agreements. Women's advocacy groups at peace negotiations are becoming a normal feature of peace processes. Accordingly, women's groups now regularly impact the terms of the peace settlements and are regular players in these extralegislative processes. Women participants in peace negotiations have gone from having to fight individual case battles to having Security Council resolutions that call for their participation in every case. This progression from isolated cases to the creation of a global policy on their participation in peace negotiations marks a process similar to that identified in David Malet's chapter on foreign fighters. Foreign fighters have featured in numerous conflicts, but it has been only recently that the Security Council has issued resolutions, attempting to regulate them and create uniform global policies. The responsivity of the Security Council to transnational actors demonstrates a departure from the UN Charter's focus on interstate conflict. The body's multiple resolutions on transnational actors influencing war and peace indicates a demonstrable shift from an interstate to a transnational world politics.

Notes

1. Gertrude Bussey and Margaret Tims, *Women's International League for Peace and Freedom* (London: George Allen & Unwin, 1965), 17; Catia Cecilia Confortini, *Intelligent Compassion: Feminist Critical Methodology in the Women's International League for Peace and Freedom* (New York: Oxford University Press, 2012), 9.

2. "Report of the International Congress of Women," paper presented at the International Congress of Women, The Hague, Netherlands, April 28–May 1, 1915.

3. Inter-Parliamentary Union IPU, "Women in Parliaments: World and Regional Averages (Statistical Archive)," http://www.ipu.org/wmn-e/world-arc.htm.

4. Kara Ellerby, "(En)Gendered Security? The Complexities of Women's Inclusions in Peace Processes," *International Interactions* 39 (2013): 439–60.

5. Miriam J. Anderson, "Transnational Feminism and Norms in Peace Processes: The Cases of Burundi and Northern Ireland," *Journal of Intervention and Statebuilding* 4, no. 1 (2010): 1–21.

6. Miriam J. Anderson, "Gender and Peacemaking: Women's Rights in Contemporary Peace Agreements," in *Peacemaking: From Practice to Theory*, ed. Andrea Bartoli, Susan Allen Nan, and Zachariah Mampilly (Santa Barbara, CA: Praeger Security International, 2011), 344–77; Miriam J. Anderson, *Windows of Opportunity: How Women Seize Peace Negotiations for Political Change* (New York: Oxford University Press, 2016).

7. Miriam J. Anderson and Liam Swiss, "Peace Accords and the Adoption of Electoral Quotas for Women in the Developing World, 1990–2006," *Politics and Gender* 10, no. 1 (2014): 33–61.

8. Ibid.

9. Anderson, *Windows of Opportunity*; Anderson, "Gender and Peacemaking."

10. Anderson, *Windows of Opportunity*, 29.

11. For a discussion of the three principles underpinning the concept of human rights, see Christian Tomuschat, *Human Rights: Between Idealism and Realism* (Oxford, UK: Oxford University Press, 2008).

12. Kate Fearon, *Women's Work: The Story of the Northern Ireland Women's Coalition* (Belfast, UK: Blackstaff Press, 1999); Kate Fearon and Monica McWilliams, "The Good Friday Agreement: A Triumph of Substance over Style," *Fordham International Law Journal* 22, no. 4 (1999): 1250–72; Sanam Naraghi Anderlini, "Women at the Peace Table: Making a Difference," in *Peace Book*, ed. Comfort Lamptey and Gretchen Sidhu (New York: UNIFEM, 2000); Sanam Naraghi Anderlini, *Women Building Peace: What They Do, Why It Matters* (Boulder, CO: Lynne Rienner, 2007).

13. Kara Ellerby, "A Seat at the Table Is Not Enough: Understanding Women's Substantive Representation in Peace Agreements," *Peacebuilding* (2016).

14. Ellerby, "(En)Gendered Security?"

15. Ellerby, "Seat at the Table."

16. Ibid.

17. For women's inclusion to meet the test for inclusion as envisaged by Security Council Resolution 1325, (1) the topic of women needs to be an explicit agenda, (2) women must have access to the peace process, and (3) there must be female advocacy within the process. Ibid. This can be contrasted with my finding that conflict length, a gender-based identity, access to the peace process, and avoidance of the key conflict-generating issues of the conflict are instrumental to success. See Anderson, *Windows of Opportunity*.

18. Kathleen M. Fallon, Liam Swiss, and Jocelyn Viterna, "Resolving the Democracy Paradox: Democratization and Women's Legislative Representation in Developing Nations, 1975–2009," *American Sociological Review* 77, no. 3 (2012): 380–408; Jocelyn Viterna and Kathleen M. Fallon, "Democratization, Women's Movements, and Gender-Equitable States: A Framework for Comparison," *American Sociological Review* 73, no. 4 (2008): 668–89; Melanie M. Hughes, "Armed Conflict, International Linkages, and Women's Parliamentary Representation," *Social Problems* 56, no. 1 (2009): 174–204; Melanie M. Hughes, "Windows of Political Opportunity: Institutional Instability and Gender Inequality in the World's National Legislatures," *International Journal of Sociology* 37, no. 4 (2007): 26–51.

19. Veronika Fuest, "'This Is the Time to Get in Front': Changing Roles and Opportunities for Women in Liberia," *African Affairs* 107, no. 427 (2008): 201–24; Aili Mari Tripp et al., *African Women's Movements: Changing Political Landscapes* (New York: Cambridge University Press, 2009); Georgina Waylen, *Engendering Transitions: Women's Mobilization, Institutions, and Gender Outcomes* (Oxford, UK: Oxford University Press, 2007); Jane Jaquette, ed. *The Women's Movement in Latin America: Feminism and the Transition to Democracy* (Boston: Unwin Hyman, 1989); Donna Pankhurst, "Women and Politics in Africa: The Case of Uganda," *Parliamentary Affairs* 55, no. 1 (2002): 119–28; Gretchen Bauer and Hannah E. Britton, eds., *Women in African Parliaments* (Boulder, CO: Lynne Rienner, 2006).

20. Holly J. McCammon et al., "How Movements Win: Gendered Opportunity Structures and U.S. Women's Suffrage Movements, 1866 to 1919," *American Sociological Review* 66, no. 1 (2001): 49–70; Holly J. McCammon, Harmony D. Newman, Courtney Sanders Muse, and Teresa M. Terrell, "Movement Framing and Discursive Opportunity Structures: The Political Successes of the U.S. Women's Jury Movements," *American Sociological Review* 72, no. 5 (2007): 725–49.

21. Laurel Stone, "Women Transforming Conflict: A Quantitative Analysis of Female Peacemaking," (2014).

22. Anderson and Swiss, "Peace Accords and Adoption of Electoral Quotas."

23. Enid D. Burke, Jennifer Klot, and Ikaweba Bunting, *Engendering Peace: Reflections on the Burundi Peace Process* (Nairobi: UNIFEM, 2001), in Anderson, *Windows of Opportunity*, 67.

24. Burke, Klot, and Bunting, *Engendering Peace*, 66.

25. Anderson, *Windows of Opportunity*.

26. Ibid.

27. Ibid., 63.

28. Ibid.

29. Ibid., 101.

30. Ibid., 109–10.

31. Ibid., 64.

32. Burke, Klot, and Bunting, *Engendering Peace*, 7.

33. Ibid., 8–11.

34. Ibid., 14.

35. Margaret Keck and Kathryn Sikkink, *Activists beyond Borders: Advocacy Networks in International Politics* (Ithaca, NY: Cornell University Press, 1998), 13.

36. Anderson, *Windows of Opportunity*, 65–66. For a detailed discussion of how the Security Council resolution was passed, see Jennifer F. Klot, "UN Security Council Resolution 1325: A Feminist Transformative Agenda?," in *The Oxford Handbook of Transnational Feminist Movements*, ed. Rawwida Baksh and Wendy Harcourt (New York: Oxford University Press, 2015), 723–45.

37. Libby Brooks, "Scotland to Train Female Syrian Peacemakers in Conflict Resolution," *Guardian*, November 29, 2015.

38. "Sturgeon Holds Talks on Role of Women in Syrian Peace Process," *Herald Scotland*, May 7, 2016.

39. Ibid.

40. Ellerby, "Seat at the Table."

41. Anderson and Swiss, "Peace Accords and Adoption of Electoral Quotas."

42. Stone, "Women Transforming Conflict."

43. Miriam J. Anderson and Liam Swiss, "A High Price to Pay: Social Rupture and Gender Inclusive Peace Agreements, 1975–2011," paper presented at the International Studies Association's annual conference, 2016, Atlanta, GA.

10

Containing Conflict

Authoritative Transnational Actors and the Management of Company-Community Conflict

KATE MACDONALD

Amid intensified competition for land available to private investors in sectors such as mining, agribusiness, and forestry, disputes over land between transnational investors and local communities are emerging in many parts of the world as an increasingly visible form of transnational conflict. Whereas land conflicts were once seen as a quintessentially "local" problem to be managed by national or subnational political authorities, they are now becoming transnationally politicized. Such conflicts may be expressed in episodes of violent confrontation between members of local communities and police, military, or private security officials.[1] At other times, they take the form of nonviolent resistance or protest, or are channeled through formal political, administrative, or legal channels for managing social and political contestation.

Governance of such community-company land conflicts aims in part to channel these conflicts into nonviolent forms and to ensure their management by systems of legal and political rule. In many cases, such governance processes are dominated by national and subnational agencies responsible for law and order and for the administration of land allocation and use. Increasingly the governance of conflicts of these kinds has also been performed by *transnational authoritative actors*—reflecting more recognition of the responsibilities of transnational companies or international agencies for such conflicts, as a result of their links to contested land acquisitions through supply chain, financing, or broader political relationships.

A number of institutional initiatives enable both state and nonstate actors to take on transnational-conflict management responsibilities. Some major international financial institutions have created independent accountability or grievance-handling bodies, such as the World Bank Group's Compliance Advisor Ombudsman for the International Finance Corporation and Multilateral Investment Guarantee Agency (IFC-CAO, or simply CAO). It has also become increasingly common for multistakeholder governance schemes that set standards for business activity in relation to particular commodities to adopt dispute-handling entities of a similar kind. Establishment and ongoing development of a formal complaints system by the Roundtable on Sustainable Palm Oil (RSPO) is a clear example of this trend.

In accordance with the core questions addressed by this volume, this chapter begins by analyzing how such transnational authoritative actors are organized and how they interact with both governments and other kinds of transnational actors in the course of their efforts to influence processes and outcomes of company-community land disputes. Analysis focuses on the role of the CAO and the RSPO dispute-resolution mechanisms in managing a series of interconnected conflicts in the Indonesian palm oil sector, involving the Singapore-based company Wilmar and local communities in the Indonesian province of West Kalimantan and on Sumatra.[2] Discussion draws on research conducted during 2012 and 2013 in Indonesia,[3] where land conflicts involving companies and communities have posed a major governance challenge and prompted extensive efforts to contain and manage conflict involving transnational as well as national and subnational authorities. Indonesia's recent pathway to development has been characterized by significant changes to patterns of land ownership. Land that had previously been controlled by small-scale farmers has been appropriated for a range of commercial agricultural uses, notably palm oil, while there has also been extensive clearing of forests for new plantations. Conflicts over land have proliferated, with estimates putting the number related to palm oil in the hundreds or even thousands. These conflicts are often driven by disputes over land boundaries, the legality of land-purchasing or licensing processes, or the terms on which land-sharing arrangements between plantation owners and smallholders are established.

The chapter then focuses on the sources of influence that transnational authoritative actors such as the CAO and the RSPO are able to draw on in shaping the dynamics and outcomes of company-community conflicts. Existing literature on transnational governance has generated significant insights into distinctive sources and limits of influence available to transnational authoritative actors, with a particular focus on private transnational authorities. By examining together two transnational authoritative actors that have sought influence over localized land conflicts—one a private, multistakeholder scheme and one an intergovernmental entity—the chapter's analysis reveals that private and public transnational actors can experience very similar challenges in establishing effective influence. Such challenges include reliance on incomplete and fragile "soft" forms of authority and on governance strategies that require cooperation among multiple authoritative actors. These difficulties are compounded by tensions between the expectations of audiences at different governance levels, whose deference and sometimes active cooperation is required for these strategies to succeed.

Finally, the chapter reflects on implications for wider analysis of transnationalism, focusing on the role of transnational actors in authoritative governance processes. Transnational authority is shown to be fragile and often transient, requiring transnational actors to rely heavily on collaborative and interactive strategies of influence as they struggle to balance the competing demands of multiple constituencies. These findings have specific implications for our understanding of the sources and limits of influence that transnational authoritative actors can exercise in containing and managing conflict. They also have broader implications for our understanding of the interactive character of governance processes within an environment of complex transnationalism, understood as "the increasing number, scope, interactions, and influence of transnational actors on diplomatic and governance processes where states have invited as participants, been forced to respond to, or have become reliant upon the expertise of transnational actors and where transnational actors increasingly interact directly with each other" (as defined by David Malet and Miriam J. Anderson in the introduction to this volume).

Transnational Actors in the Governance of Corporate-Community Land Conflict

Before exploring the dynamics and dilemmas of transnational influence in greater depth, it is useful to introduce the transnational character of the land conflicts, together with key attributes of the transnational actors that seek to assert authority in the governance of these conflicts.

It is important to recognize at the outset that political analysis at national and subnational levels remains very important in understanding both the drivers of company-community land conflict and institutional efforts to prevent or contain that conflict. Conflict dynamics are closely linked to both historical patterns of land dispossession and capitalist development and to more recent political and economic shifts in the post-Suharto era (since 1998). Land conflicts are often compounded by weaknesses and contradictions in government regulation at subnational, national, and sometimes international levels in relation to land and forest regulations, customary land rights, environmental protection, and climate policy. Despite the weaknesses of national and subnational governance processes for managing land conflicts linked to palm oil production, there exists a range of mechanisms at these levels for managing such disputes, which analysis of transnational interventions must take into account. These include administrative grievance channels linked to the National Land Agency, the Plantation Department, the Ministry of Environment, courts and court-sanctioned mediation processes, the national human rights institution Komnas HAM, and customary dispute-resolution processes, as well as a range of more ad hoc and locally distinct mechanisms involving district regents called *bupatis*, provincial governors, district or provincial representative councils, police, and security agencies.

These land conflicts are also underpinned by overlapping transnational structures of different kinds. The first kind encompasses the transnational organization of finance, investment, and supply chains in the sector. Many foreign and Indonesian companies operate in Indonesia's palm oil sector, and it draws on significant levels of foreign finance.[4] The sale of palm oil is also highly international, with Asian markets figuring strongly, alongside those in Europe and elsewhere. Large transnational companies such as Nestlé and Unilever play an important role in shaping palm oil supply chains, as well as the megaprocessing and trading companies that dominate global palm oil trade, alongside large numbers of smaller growers, processors, retailers, and other players. Sophisticated transnational coordination and governance is required to sustain broader transnational financing and supply chain relationships within the sector, illustrating the high levels of complex, transnational interdependence within a globalizing political economy emphasized by early writing on transnationalism.[5]

The transnationalization of these conflicts also involves mobilization by nongovernmental organizations (NGOs) and associated social actors. NGO mobilization seeking to contest corporate land appropriation has often been connected to wider campaigning and policy work on issues of human rights, support for smallholder livelihoods, deforestation, and related concerns regarding biodiversity and climate change. Such issues have been taken up by a number of prominent international NGOs, including the World Wildlife Fund (WWF), Greenpeace, Friends of the Earth, some national affiliates of Oxfam, and more issue-specific NGOs such as the United Kingdom's Forest Peoples Programme.[6] International NGOs have worked together with a number of NGOs at national and subnational levels within Indonesia. Among many others, the Indonesian NGO Sawit Watch is devoted to scrutiny of the palm oil sector, while others such as the environmental forum WALHI have been active in tackling interconnected social, environmental, and indigenous issues. Connections among international, national, and local NGOs working on these issues have tended to be held together through a small core of intensively coordinated organizations, such as the close and sustained coordination between

Sawit Watch and the Forest Peoples Programme, linked to broader but much looser networks organized around particular issues, events, or campaigns.

Transnational actors have played important roles in placing conflicts of these kinds on the international agenda, thus shaping the wider political environment in which transnational governance emerges. Moreover, as we will see, networks of national and international NGOs have played important roles in brokering links between transnational mediators and local communities, enabling intervention of transnational authorities where this would otherwise not be possible. Nonetheless, these actors are distinct from the *authoritative* transnational actors that are the subject of this chapter. Who then are these actors, and over whom and what do they exercise or assert authority? How are these transnational actors organized, and how do they interact and communicate with other actors?

The first transnational authoritative actor examined here is the CAO, an independent accountability and grievance-handling body designed primarily to manage conflicts associated with business activity funded by the World Bank's private-sector lending arms, the International Finance Corporation (IFC) and the Multilateral Investment Guarantee Agency (MIGA). As its name suggests, the CAO comprises three elements: a compliance auditor, which assesses the IFC's adherence to its own social and environmental policies; an advisory arm, which advises the World Bank Group on how the IFC's and MIGA's social and environmental performances can be improved; and an ombudsman arm, which provides recourse for people affected by IFC or MIGA projects and facilitates mediation between companies, communities, and other affected parties.[7]

The ombudsman arm of the CAO—the most directly involved in managing individual land disputes—does not adjudicate the merits of any individual complaint or impose solutions. Rather, it provides dispute-resolution specialists, who work with disputing parties to "identify and implement their own solutions."[8] In performing its mediation function, it requests parties to recognize its authority as an expert and independent mediator and to respect the ground rules of mediation worked out on a case-by-case basis through the mediation process. The most direct addressees of such authority claims are companies financed through IFC loans, which are expected as a condition of their loans to comply with the IFC's performance standards, which lay out detailed social and environmental expectations regarding business activity. Addressees also include other parties to land disputes, such as members of local communities, other companies within palm oil supply chains, and government agencies involved in managing land disputes at the local level.

The second significant transnational authoritative actor engaged in governing these company-community conflicts is the RSPO, a multistakeholder organization that sets social and environmental standards for business activity in the palm oil sector. The RSPO has established a formal complaints system that incorporates a dispute-resolution facility designed to facilitate the mediation of individual conflicts and a complaints panel, which is empowered to adjudicate disputes arising from complaints and provide recommendations to the RSPO board on appropriate remedies.[9] Corporate members of the RSPO are central targets of the RSPO's authority; it also directs more limited claims of authority at external parties to specific disputes, such as landowners, workers, or smallholders affected by the business activity of RSPO members. Member companies are expected to adhere to the RSPO's social and environmental standards and to submit to its complaint-handling procedures when disputes arise.[10] Other parties are expected to follow RSPO procedures in documenting and submitting complaints and to follow relevant procedures designated by RSPO-appointed mediators.

Both the CAO and the RSPO also assert authority over a range of state and nonstate actors with whom they interact and from whom they seek "deferential conduct" in the form of political support, as well as the provision of resources to support their ongoing operation. The CAO seeks such support from the member governments that authorize and resource its activities. The RSPO seeks similar forms of support: All RSPO members pay financial membership fees, staff from some member organizations contribute considerable time to support RSPO governance and policy activities, and the RSPO receives significant sources of funding from other state and private donors.[11] More broadly, both authorities seek political support for their activities from NGOs and other actors involved in public advocacy on relevant issues.

Being constituted as part of an intergovernmental entity, the CAO is not strictly a transnational actor, according to a definition that stresses nonstate constitutive character as a critical feature. Nonetheless, it can be understood as a transnational actor in a number of salient dimensions. The public purposes it promotes are cross-border in nature and focused on governance of the private entities that the IFC and MIGA finance. The key constituencies with which the CAO engages in carrying out these purposes are likewise nonstate and cross-border, and, as we will see, access to the resources and authorization that enable them to act in accordance with their mandates depend on their ability to mobilize support from a range of nonstate and governmental actors. The RSPO conforms more straightforwardly to the definition of a transnational actor used in this volume, insofar as it not only pursues transnationally oriented governance objectives but is constituted as a wholly nonstate entity, and its sites of operation and modes of communication, coordination, and governance operate across national borders.

Transnational Influence over the Management of Company-Community Conflict

This chapter's analysis of the role of such transnational actors in governing conflict focuses on the management of disputes between the Singapore-based palm oil company Wilmar and local communities in Indonesia. The CAO has played a particularly important role in these disputes. Three complaints about Wilmar were made to the CAO by a coalition of community organizations and NGOs from 2007 to 2011. These complaints relate to alleged specific instances and wider patterns of social and environmental abuses, including illegal use of fire to clear lands, clearance of primary forests and areas of high conservation value, and the takeover of indigenous peoples' customary lands without due process or their free, prior, and informed consent. The RSPO has had a more minor role in brokering dialogue between conflicting parties at certain stages of the dispute, as well as providing reference standards around which dialogue between parties has sometimes been framed. Intervention by these dispute-resolution bodies has contributed to the partial resolution of conflict in two of the Indonesian locations (Sambas and Riau) but has failed to achieve much influence over outcomes in the complex and protracted disputes in Jambi Province. Influence on wider policy and practice in the sector has likewise been discernable but small. The central analytical focus here is on trying to make sense of both the sources and limits of the influence that transnational actors bring to bear on local conflicts and the distinctive dilemmas and challenges they face in attempting to do so.

We first examine the sources and dynamics of authority that transnational actors have drawn on as a basis for influencing the management of localized company-community conflicts. Their influence has depended, first, on soft forms of authority, grounded with reference to moral standards or claims to expertise.[12] Second, they have made use of interactive strategies involving collaboration or coordination with other actors at national and subnational levels.

Soft forms of authority have underpinned the ability of transnational dispute-handling institutions to induce deference from addressees through a number of interconnected channels. First, moral authority linked to codified standards propagated by these institutions can play an important role in framing broader processes of dialogue. For example, the authority that comes from the public affirmation of RSPO standards, together with the multistakeholder processes within the RSPO, creates a space within which brokerage of dialogue and dissemination of ideas can take place. In a dispute between Wilmar and communities in West Kalimantan that was brought to the RSPO, RSPO standards set the normative backdrop for dialogue among the company, the complainants, and the RSPO, as reflected in the letters sent back and forth through the RSPO at key points of the dispute.[13] Although moral authority of this kind does not provide sufficient leverage to induce companies to engage with negotiations if they are otherwise reluctant to do so, such moral standards can influence negotiations by shaping the terms within which reason-giving occurs, "requiring justification and persuasion in terms of applicable rules and relevant facts."[14]

Both RSPO standards and the IFC's own social and environmental performance standards loosely framed the subsequent mediation process that was carried out by the CAO—though this framing process was often subtle and indirect.[15] According to one CAO mediator, "In my observation, in negotiations it was rarely discussed about the standards. So, maybe, this is like the standard, something that is already in your head. And when there is an issue that is difficult to settle, sometimes one of the parties or one of us will remind everybody, 'Hey, don't forget that. . . . This standard asks you to do this or that.'"[16]

Relatedly, *expertise* can play an important role in underpinning transnational authority and leverage over local conflict dynamics. For example, the CAO's authority in its role as mediator has depended importantly on recognition by the addressees of its expertise and experience in this role and its claim to independence and neutrality in the management of disputes. In this case, addressees have deferred to the CAO's authority at least in part because of the latter's capacity to influence the former's beliefs about the right way to go about mediating conflicts. According to one local government official, "Many parties had tried, but not resolved [the conflict]. . . . Maybe we missed something we don't understand. So, if there is another party that is more professional in mediation, we really welcome that . . . [and] the biggest role is from the CAO, because they have more experience. They understand how this mediation process works."[17] Of relevance here is not only expertise in the sense of knowledge but also functional capacity derived from accessible resources. According to one government official involved in management of the conflict, "We don't have certain people that work on [conflicts] full time. We can't, so the manpower is lacking. We know that the government has so many things to do . . . and there are also other conflicts. . . . So, when this one came along, we said, 'Wow, thank God, there is a party that would like to help!'"[18]

Such soft forms of authority are mainly useful in enabling the CAO to encourage the parties to the conflict to participate in a CAO-facilitated mediation process; they give the CAO little direct influence over the outcomes of negotiations between parties. Nonetheless, the CAO's ability to establish an authoritative role in brokering communication between conflicting parties can help facilitate processes of dialogue and negotiation through which broader dynamics of persuasion or the reshaping of interests may be set in train.

Significant limits to the direct influence over conflict dynamics and outcomes able to be derived from soft authority demand that transnational actors rely extensively on *interactive strategies of influence*, in which transnational actors enlist the resources of broader networks of actors in support of their goals. Such collaborative strategies are illustrated by the CAO's approach to managing mediation between a subsidiary of Wilmar and communities in Jambi Province. After a prolonged mediation between companies and communities facilitated by the local NGO Setara ran aground, the CAO established what it referred to as a joint mediation team, involving direct collaboration between the CAO and selected participants from local government. The team included members of the provincial government drawn from several relevant ministries, as well as from the Batang Hari District government.

Building relationships with government actors is an important means through which transnational actors can try to influence conflict outcomes, since governments typically retain key sources of authority and influence. For instance, they physically control distributions of land and decisions about who can access it on what terms (both through the licensing process and through broader frameworks for allocating land rights), and they can impose such decisions coercively through the use of police and security forces, both of which have been actively deployed on behalf of the company at several points in the conflict between Wilmar's subsidiary and local communities in Jambi. Collaboration with the government can also help to confer legitimacy on the CAO process itself, enabling the final agreement to "gain recognition from the government, and also to gain legitimation and legalization from the government."[19]

This collaboration was explicitly founded on voluntary terms of engagement: The CAO mediators were clear that they lacked authority to compel government actors to participate, indicating that they therefore relied on the involvement of individual government officials who were "moved by their personal and institutional visions" to share responsibility for participating in the mediation process. In this sense, the CAO's moral authority and expertise underpinned its capacity to motivate voluntary engagement by government officials with CAO mediation procedures. By enlisting government participation in mediation processes, the CAO mediation team was able to benefit from the specialized knowledge of government actors regarding the intricacies of local land management practices, thereby strengthening the efficacy of mediation processes. Conversely, CAO mediators also hoped to contribute to effective conflict management by strengthening the capacity of local government, through supporting the development of networks, relationships, and information sharing between departments and between government and communities, promoting visits of government bureaucrats to local communities, and by developing individual and institutional capacity specifically with regard to complaint handling.

The Limits of Transnational Influence

Sources of authority of the kinds described above can be important in enabling transnational actors to exert influence over the dynamics and outcomes of local company-community conflicts, despite these conflicts remaining deeply embedded in national and subnational politics. However, reliance on moral authority, expertise, and collaborative strategies—often characteristic of transnational authority—also entails distinctive constraints on such influence. As the discussion below illustrates, such challenges are experienced in very similar ways by the CAO—an intergovernmental entity—and the nongovernmental RSPO. This analysis has important implications for understanding both mechanisms and effects of transnational efforts to influence conflict management at the local level.

First, reliance on soft authority entails familiar constraints associated with its nonlegal character and consequent challenges of securing compliance.[20] Although accepting an IFC loan entails binding obligations on companies to comply with the IFC performance standards, participation in mediations under the CAO's ombudsman arm is voluntary, and the conflicting parties need to appoint CAO mediators by mutual agreement. Companies are incentivized to engage with such mediation processes either to avoid compromising their ongoing access to IFC finance or to guard against broader adverse reputational effects. The RSPO likewise lacks the capacity to command compliance, relying instead on the mobilization of other incentives or pressures. If a member company fails to engage constructively with attempts to mediate conflicts to which it is a party, the RSPO has the option of decertifying them. The extent to which companies are encouraged to comply with RSPO directives then depends on the degree of market pressure to achieve RSPO certification from palm oil purchasers such as Unilever or financial institutions involved in financing the palm oil sector.

Such soft authority is particularly constrained because of the ability of companies targeted by CAO and RSPO authority to voluntarily exit the market relationships in which the authority of these institutions is grounded. Companies can repay their IFC loans early as a means of concluding formal contractual obligations to adhere to the IFC's performance standards, as Wilmar did following a prolonged CAO mediation in Jambi Province. Companies also have the option of selling subsidiaries that become embroiled in particularly difficult conflicts—a strategy also employed by Wilmar in this case. Wilmar sold the relevant subsidiary in April 2013 to a company that was not an RSPO member, leading to the loss of RSPO as well as CAO authority over the dispute.[21] Moreover, many companies have shown themselves to be willing to leave the RSPO if they feel that the obligations of membership are becoming too demanding, as illustrated in the Indonesian context by the palm oil producer association GAPKI leaving the RSPO in 2011 in response to disagreement with certain standards.[22]

Such examples highlight the contingency and transience of the authority wielded by transnational dispute-resolution institutions in land conflicts. In this sense, the leverage of these transnational bodies over companies remains highly contingent on the concerned company's choices about the patterns of business relationships it enters into and on what terms it chooses to exit. In effect, then, patterns of wider pressures and incentives arising from the broader social, political, and market environment in which the companies act place structural limits on the potential scope of CAO and RSPO authority.

These limits to the authority and influence of transnational actors not only have adverse implications for the effectiveness of these actors in helping to contain and appropriately manage company-community conflicts but can also be detrimental to their legitimacy. Particularly from the perspective of NGO constituents of the RSPO (including both members and observers or critics), a major source of criticism of the RSPO's grievance-handling processes has focused on the RSPO's failure to decertify companies that neglect to deal properly with ongoing disputes. Even those NGOs that are more sympathetic and supportive of the RSPO are themselves under pressure from their own constituents to take a strong stance on this issue.[23]

Endorsement by these NGO constituencies contributes significantly to legitimizing RSPO processes among consumer, investor, and government audiences, thereby influencing the market incentives of the companies to stay involved. As a result, where such authorization is undermined, a destabilizing vicious cycle may be created, whereby a withdrawal of NGO legitimation weakens the market value of remaining in the RSPO, thus weakening the incentives for companies to bear the costs of complying with RSPO standards and in turn further weakening the capacity of the RSPO to exercise leverage in support of its mandate.

Vicious cycles of weakening authority can also be observed with regard to the resources and operational autonomy available to the RSPO. Limited material resources and organizational capacity are major challenges for operation of the RSPO's complaint-handling process, and its credibility and capacity also suffer as a result of the low independence of the complaints panel from the RSPO board and sometimes also from parties to particular disputes.[24] More broadly, the weak institutionalization and autonomy of RSPO complaint processes has tended to push dialogue between parties outside formal RSPO procedures, further undermining the credibility and authority of the process. Yet mobilizing external resources, and convincing members to entrust the procedures with greater delegated authority and autonomy, is difficult to achieve when levels of credibility and trust in the process are low. Moreover, there are some immediate practical imperatives for the grievance panel to maintain little autonomy from its members, not only because the willingness of members to delegate to the RSPO is weak but also because the direct engagement of companies and NGOs in the grievance process can help ensure that negotiated outcomes are sufficiently in accordance with these parties' interests to be sustainable. To the extent that weak autonomy compromises the independence and associated authority of the mechanism itself, these dynamics confront transnational actors with significant dilemmas.

Also in the case of the CAO, failures to satisfy the expectations of NGO constituencies as a result of constrained authority can undermine both legitimacy and effectiveness. For example, national and international NGOs involved

in bringing complaints to the CAO sometimes view its mandate as encompassing attempts to influence corporate practices and government policy frameworks
in the palm oil sector as a whole, to the extent that these are actively facilitated
or tacitly endorsed by IFC lending. Although the CAO has undertaken some ad
hoc attempts to engage with the RSPO, government agencies, and other intergovernmental bodies on such policy issues, the CAO has generally interpreted
its mandate as being limited to a narrower focus on managing specific disputes.[25]
Resulting disappointment with CAO processes among some NGOs and others
can mean that such groups are less willing to invest in supporting these processes
or to encourage others to do so. This can further undermine the CAO's effectiveness because of the CAO's reliance on collaborative networks or other
interactive governance strategies that often include NGOs alongside government. For example, the CAO sometimes relies on local, national, and international NGOs to help communities to access the CAO mechanism or build
sufficient capacity to engage meaningfully in mediation processes. The CAO is
therefore able to carry out its role more effectively if it can secure ongoing support from these groups.

Reliance on interactive strategies of influence can also generate significant
challenges for transnational efforts to influence conflict-management processes
to the extent that strategies of stakeholder management are seen to undermine
actors' impartiality or neutrality. For example, the CAO has sometimes undertaken capacity-building activities targeting communities involved in the disputes, in the form of support for community knowledge of land-registration and
boundary-mapping processes, local organizational capacity building, or negotiation strategies. The CAO may also perform an implicit brokerage role: By con-
ferring legitimacy on NGOs that work closely with local communities, the CAO
can help these organizations gain enhanced credibility or visibility in the local
political environment, in turn enabling them to build new channels of dialogue
with companies or government actors. The new roles and relationships that the
local NGO Setara was able to build with company and local government actors
through participation in the CAO mediation in Jambi illustrates this potential.
Yet intervening in ways that redistribute capacities or resources among parties to
the conflict has the potential to undermine a key ground of the CAO's claim to
authority, namely its claim to neutrality. This is a dilemma that CAO mediators
were keenly aware of: "The mediator . . . is facing a dilemma . . . between his role
as mediator with the need to improve competency, capacity, capability. . . . If we
do not hold ourselves back from the desire to help one party in increasing their
capacity, this may be considered as being on one side. . . . Increasing their capacity means increasing their power, and this might be considered as a threat to the
other party. It's a dilemma, isn't it?"[26]

The RSPO has also faced tensions between attempts to influence conflict
dynamics and outcomes through persuasion, brokerage, or network building and

its ability to secure authority based on claims of neutrality and independence. For the RSPO, these tensions have centered on the challenges of managing the perceived appropriateness of its relationship with government. Many of the conflicts that the RSPO and member companies are mandated to manage are pervasive throughout the palm oil sector, and their underlying causes are deeply connected to gaps and contradictions within government policy and regulatory frameworks. If the RSPO were to fulfill the expectations of some NGO constituencies regarding strengthened standards and conflict prevention in the sector as a whole, it would need to build strong collaborative relationships with producing-country governments.

Yet in the cases examined here, establishing authorization from the Indonesian government for its operations demands that the RSPO refrain from activities that might encourage perceptions that it threatens the government's authority or national sovereignty. According to an RSPO staff member, "You might not see this written anywhere, but the RSPO has strict understandings that we don't get involved in national legislation because we are not elected—we are strictly voluntary. So, we don't interfere in government legislation or rules and that sort of thing. That is for members to do. We don't have anything to do with government." Refraining from any perceived challenge to state authority is also important for maintaining authorization from producer organizations that often have a preference for policy agendas to remain under the control of their own governments, rather than what they see as a foreign-controlled entity.[27]

Although manifested in differing ways, these challenges can all create tensions between the desire of transnational authoritative actors to adopt governance strategies that would enable them to pursue their mandates effectively and the need to satisfy stringent and often contradictory conditions of authorization from government, business, and civil society audiences.

These tensions can give rise to significant structural constraints on the capacity of transnational authoritative actors to influence conflict dynamics and outcomes. The capacity of transnational actors to establish and exercise authority over those they seek to influence depends on the degree of alignment between stakeholder understandings of mandates to be pursued and the roles, powers, and resources that are authorized for such purposes. Constraints on the influence of transnational authoritative actors can thus be understood in one important sense as linked to misalignment in these structures of authorization and legitimation.

One significant challenge results from conflicts among the terms of authorization conferred by different constituents. Dispute-resolution bodies need to construct authority relations with multiple constituencies, each of which may recognize authority on different terms (on different grounds, with different understandings of mandates, and with different ideas about the limits to justified power associated with these mandates and grounds). In other words, there is a disjuncture or incongruence between grounds of authority required to satisfy different addressees of the authority relationship, with no established means of seeking resolution across these through a unified process of public discourse, negotiation, or aggregative decision rules. The lack of institutional means of resolving these tensions contributes to a persistent disconnect between the expectations placed on these actors and the outcomes they are able to deliver.

The disappointment of stakeholder expectations that results can take a number of forms, depending on which aspects of the expectations are unmet and which stakeholders are concerned. First, expected mandates might not be achieved, as in the case of NGOs being disappointed that the CAO has failed to tackle broader conflict in the sector or that the RSPO has neglected to enforce designated requirements of certification. Second, the limits of authorized power might be overstretched, as in the case of companies resisting the imposition of what they see as excessively demanding obligations concerning conflicts in which they are involved. Third, the conditions or grounds on which authority has been granted may be violated, as can occur when attempts by transnational actors to engage and influence wider governance networks are called into question for lacking appropriate forms of neutrality or independence. These potential sources of stakeholder dissatisfaction sit in tension with one another, as transnational actors often lack the capacity to deliver on what some stakeholders consider to be appropriate mandates without deploying strategies and powers that other stakeholders consider outside the scope of their authority.

The consequences of these tensions can vary, depending in turn on the responses of different stakeholders to such scenarios. When the direct parties to the conflict (palm oil companies and communities) are dissatisfied, on the grounds that public purposes are not being adequately advanced and/or that appropriate limits on powers are being overreached, they can simply exit the relationship—either by withdrawing from the mediation or by withdrawing altogether from the economic relationships to which the mediation bodies are attached. Both the RSPO and the CAO suffer from this problem in similar ways—the RSPO through the ability of companies to exit the RSPO and the CAO through the ability of companies to prepay loans and seek alternative sources of finance. Communities in both cases can simply decline to use transnational mechanisms to seek redress for their grievances.

Authority can be further undermined if such forms of dissatisfaction lead support to be withdrawn by wider stakeholder audiences such as corporate or financial entities, NGOs, and governments, all of which confer authority and resources on transnational dispute-resolution bodies in important ways.[28] This is also a concern for both the RSPO and the CAO, though it presents more intense dilemmas for the RSPO. The character of its multistakeholder governance gives it less operational autonomy from these wider external stakeholders, meaning that the resources and leverage underpinning its operations depend in very immediate ways on the ongoing authorization of market and NGO audiences. Legitimation from these wider audiences is still important for the CAO, but such wider forms of influence are filtered through a state-based governance structure, creating higher immediate levels of operational autonomy. Despite this difference of degree, however, the basic structure of the dilemmas of transnational action is the same for both actors.

These dynamics and dilemmas have distinctive consequences for the strategies that transnational actors need to undertake if they want to enhance their influence over local conflict dynamics and outcomes. Attempts to enhance their own authority and resources are important but are usually insufficient to enable them to fulfill their mandates. Rather, the limits to the influence and authority that transnational dispute-resolution bodies wield autonomously mean that they also need to undertake interactive governance strategies, which involve enlisting and weaving together external sources of authority to promote their objectives.

Many collaborative governance strategies can easily be interpreted as overstretching the boundaries of what some stakeholders recognize as the legitimate scope of authoritative actors' powers or roles. Their influencing strategies thus seek to weave together sources of authority that are not only limited in scope in problematic ways but also fragile and liable to dissolve when they attempt to use them. They are forced to build strategies based on interaction with actors that sometimes work to support them but can easily be switched to divert, neutralize, or undermine their sources of authority. Navigating this contested and complex political environment requires that these actors build nested strategic games, in which leverage must be exercised not only directly over regulatory subjects but also over the wider social and political environments that in turn condition the preferences, incentives, and available choices of such actors.

Analysis of these dynamics and dilemmas of transnational action helps us to understand why transnational interventions in local land conflicts are often so difficult, frustrating, and rife with controversy. Conflicting expectations and hopes are built into the negotiations around mandates, and to some extent the existence of contradictory expectations seems to be a precondition for the establishment of the authority—an organized hypocrisy of sorts. Such tensions among different constituencies appear hardwired in some senses into the structure of transnational governance arrangements of these kinds—reflecting the contradictory configurations of power and interest that are present within the divergent market and political environments in which transnational bodies intervene.

Conclusion

This chapter has focused on two specific transnational actors—the RSPO and CAO—both of which have played an important role in attempting to manage company-community land conflicts in the Indonesian palm oil sector. Analysis of their internal organization and external interactions has focused on their operation as *authoritative* transnational actors, seeking to govern conflicts associated with transnational business activity. This focus resonates strongly with the examination of transnational governance presented by Virginia Haufler in this volume, in which transnational civil society and business actors were shown to have adopted common, interactive approaches to governing conflict linked to transnational business activity. This is also similar to the common cause and efforts that Miriam J. Anderson (chapter 9) identifies between transnational civil society and international organizations in promoting women's participation in peace negotiations.

While the transnational authoritative actors examined in this chapter were shown to exercise some significant forms of influence over the course and outcomes of company-community conflicts, such influence was also revealed to be structurally constrained. Transnational authority remains contested and fragile, as transnational actors struggle to balance the conflicting demands and expectations of their multiple constituencies. Effective influence by transnational actors has thus often depended on their ability to deploy collaborative or interactive governance strategies—enlisting resources and political support from other state and nonstate actors in support of their goals.

The importance of interactive strategies in a multilevel, transnational governance context has often been recognized by scholars of transnational network governance and from within an emergent literature that examines "steering mechanisms" within complex, multilayered governance systems. Such interactive strategies are acknowledged to be complex and difficult to execute effectively. The analysis presented in this case has highlighted an additional challenge based on the need for transnational actors to juggle contradictory expectations regarding the proper boundaries of their mandates, the range of resources and powers that constituencies are willing to authorize, and the exigency of authority claims that subjects of authority are willing to accept.

Under these circumstances, disappointment by some constituents of transnational authoritative actors seems inevitable, creating forms of authority that are fragile, underdeveloped, and beset with persistent legitimacy dilemmas. Yet demands for transnational actors to take responsibility for the social conflicts created in part as a result of their own transnational activities mean that efforts to construct and sustain transnational authority oriented toward the management of such conflict is likely to persist. Understanding these dilemmas, and how these difficult balancing acts can be managed, is not only of importance to practitioners concerned with the effective and legitimate management of transnational social and economic conflicts. It is also of broader theoretical interest for scholars of transnationalism.

Notes

1. For example in the Indonesian context, see Colchester Marcus, Patrick Anderson, Asep Yunan Firdaus, Fatilda Hasibuan, and Sophie Chao, "Human Rights Abuses and Land Conflicts in the PT Asiatic Persada Concession in Jambi: Report of an Independent Investigation into Land Disputes and Forced Evictions in a Palm Oil Estate," Forest Peoples Programme, 2011, http://www.forestpeoples.org/sites/fpp/files/publication/2011/11/final-report-pt-ap-nov-2011-low-res-1.pdf; Institute for Policy Analysis of Conflict, *Indigenous Rights vs. Agrarian Reform in Indonesia: A Case Study from Jambi* (Jakarta: Institute for Policy Analysis of Conflict, 2014).

2. Wilmar is a large company with palm oil plantations in many countries around the world, including in multiple locations in Indonesia, and there is documentation of many such conflicts throughout its operations. See, for example, Lembaga Gemawan Milieudefensie and KONTAK Rakyat Borneo, *Policy, Practice, Pride and Prejudice: Review of Legal, Environmental and Social Practices of Oil Palm Plantation Companies of the Wilmar Group in Sambas District, West Kalimantan (Indonesia)* (Amsterdam: Friends of the Earth, Netherlands, 2007).

3. Analysis draws on sixty-two interviews and focus groups involving over 150 individuals, including staff of companies and NGOs working on land-management issues in the palm oil sector, Indonesian government officials, staff and board members of the RSPO and CAO, and members of communities affected by palm oil production.

4. Precise figures are unreliable, due to complex patterns of indirect financing through the intermediation of multiple regional banks.

5. Joseph S. Nye and Robert O. Keohane, "Transnational Relations and World Politics: An Introduction," *International Organization* 25, no. 3 (1971).

6. Oliver Pye details configurations of local and transnational activists in the palm oil sector in greater depth in "The Biofuel Connection: Transnational Activism and the Palm Oil Boom," *Journal of Peasant Studies* 37, no. 4 (2010).

7. Rukaiyah Rofiq and Rian Hidayat, *Mediation: A Strategy or a Final Objective? Some Notes Based on the Experience of Mediating Conflicts between PT Asiatic Persada and the Suku Anak Dalam (Batin Sembilan) in Jambi Province*, Forest Peoples Programme, 2013, http://www.forestpeoples.org/sites/fpp/files/publication/2013/11/setara-report-pdf.pdf.

8. "How We Work: Ombudsman," CAO, http://www.cao-ombudsman.org/howwework/ombudsman/.

9. "About the CAO: Who We Are," CAO, http://www.cao-ombudsman.org/about/whoweare/index.html.

10. The standards against which complaints can be brought are defined as "any alleged breaches of specified RSPO Statutes, By-laws, motions approved by the General Assembly, or any other approved articles, including the Principles & Criteria for Sustainable Palm Oil Production, Certification System and RSPO Code of Conduct." See Herakles Farms, "Letter to RSPO," http://www.rspo.org/file/PDF/Complaints/NPP_APPLICATION_LETTER.pdf.

11. CAO mediator, interview with author, Jambi, February 2013.

12. Kenneth W. Abbott et al., "The Concept of Legalization," *International Organization* 54, no. 3 (2000); Nico Krisch, "The Structure of Postnational Authority," 2015, available at SSRN 2564579.

13. Endorsement of RSPO standards played a particularly important role in framing a series of letters sent from Wilmar to the RSPO general-secretary between October 2007 and January 2008, as well as in earlier written responses by the company to a Friends of the Earth report that had documented some of the complaints against the company.

14. Kenneth W. Abbott and Duncan Snidal, "Hard and Soft Law in International Governance," *International Organization* 54, no. 3 (2000), 421–56.

15. The IFC's performance standards are of greater relevance to the CAO's compliance function, where interpretation of specific rules and identification of violations is the central function being performed.

16. CAO mediator, author interview, Jambi, February 2013.

17. Provincial Plantation Department official, author interview, Jambi, February 2013.

18. Ibid.

19. "Complaints System Components & Terms of Reference," Roundtable on Sustainable Palm Oil, www.rspo.org/publications/download/33dc47007811e3d.

20. Abbott and Snidal, "Hard and Soft Law."

21. Rofiq and Hidayat, *Mediation*.

22. In Cameroon also, the company Herakles Farms withdrew from RSPO membership after a complaint was brought against it under the RSPO's New Planting Provisions by a coalition of NGOs. Roundtable on Sustainable Palm Oil, "Financial Institutions," http://www.rspo.org/members/complaints/status-of-complaints/view/45.

23. There are a number of examples in which NGOs such as Oxfam Novib and WWF that have been supportive of the RSPO have been criticized by media and other NGOs for failing to push the RSPO hard enough on such issues. See Grassroots, *Beyond Certification: Reforming RSPO's Complaints System to Meet Stakeholder Expectation* (Kuala Lumpur: Grassroots, 2013).

24. Throughout the duration of the Wilmar-community conflicts discussed here, the RSPO complaints panel comprised largely or exclusively RSPO executive board members, sometimes (as in the Wilmar case) including direct parties to the complaints. This has been a major source of public criticism of the grievance procedure.

25. For example, one CAO staff member interviewed cited the issue of health impacts on agricultural workers in Nicaragua, where they tried to get other international organizations to pick up the issue, despite it being outside of their mandate.

26. Author Interview, February 2013.

27. Elements of the producer associations in both countries have expressed hostility to NGOs, and in both countries there have been prominent attempts to establish government-controlled rivals to the RSPO.

28. This distinction resonates with Benjamin Cashore's distinction between tier 1 and tier 2 audiences, though the distinction is between those who are and are not direct parties to the conflict, not those who are members of a particular governing entity. See "Legitimacy and the Privatization of Environmental Governance: How Non-State Market-Driven (NSMD) Governance Systems Gain Rule-Making Authority," *Governance* 15, no. 4 (2002).

Conclusion

Complex Transnationalism

MIRIAM J. ANDERSON and DAVID MALET

This book has provided a comparative examination of a range of transnational actors and how they interact with states and each other in the conduct of war and peace promotion. One hundred years after the term "transnational" was introduced to the study of international conflict, it has come to characterize several different bodies of literature that are not typically read collectively by scholars in the subfields into which the discipline of international relations has been divided. This stovepiping has meant that the similarities and differences between these actors, as well as their collective impact on war and peace, have been obscured. Examining these actors together produces important insights into the contemporary conduct of war and peace in global politics and to the nature and behavior of transnational actors.

Researchers studying transnational civil society (TCS) can learn more about transnational organizations by studying how transnational corporations and transnational violent actors operate. Despite profound differences in some respects, there are a number of points of comparison that become evident when examining these actors alongside each other. All use framing to legitimize participation in conflicts in disregard of state sovereignty. All mobilize various constituencies to pressure states and nonstate actors to change their policies and behavior. All of these actor types promote the legitimacy of nonstate stakeholders in the governance of peace, the regulation of markets, and the conduct and management of conflict.

The cases presented in this book demonstrate that these actors are increasingly engaging with each other directly and are also afforded roles in governance by states. Because there are nonstate actors centrally involved in the governance of war and peacemaking, it is vital to adopt a unified approach that captures the scope of influences on global conflict and its management. The concept of complex transnationalism—defined as *the increasing number, scope, interactions, and influence of transnational actors on diplomatic and governance processes where states have invited as participants, been forced to respond to, or have become reliant upon the expertise of transnational actors and where transnational actors increasingly interact directly with each other*—more accurately reflects the mechanisms of world politics in the realm of war and peacemaking than does a state-centric model of international relations.

Transnational actors play a variety of linked roles in war and peacemaking. They conduct violence both at the behest of the state, as well as against it. In chapter 7, Matthew LeRiche demonstrated the importance that private security professionals and private military security companies now play in offering armed protection for foreign humanitarian and civilian personnel, such as those who serve as TCS humanitarian aid workers, as Phil Orchard illustrated in chapter 8. Such companies also provide training for national militaries in a number of African states paid for by UN agencies, joining the historical ranks of TCS entities such as the Knights of Columbus in providing supplemental services to state militaries, as portrayed by Luke Flanagan in chapter 1. David Malet in chapter 6 illustrated how foreign fighters play key roles in insurgencies, drawn by their transnationally based identities to wage war against states. These actors finance their activities through transnational criminal networks and the extraction of natural resources similarly to how other rebel groups use conflict minerals, as described by Virginia Haufler in chapter 3. In chapter 5, Ariel I. Ahram and John Gledhill illustrated the role of exiles in promoting terrorism in the name of a transnationally based religious identity in a manner similar to that of the Zairean diaspora's activities in support of armed groups, described by Jennifer M. Brinkerhoff in chapter 4. Kate Macdonald in chapter 10 detailed governance of resource conflicts through international forums, including both international organizations and transnational actors. Miriam J. Anderson described in chapter 9 similar interactions concerning women's participation in peace negotiations, as did Catia Cecilia Confortini in chapter 2 regarding the participation of the Women's International League for Peace and Freedom (WILPF) in international organization forums. As the respective chapters detailed, the exercise of violence by nonstate groups has become a major preoccupation of national governments and international organizations and shows no sign of abating in the foreseeable future.

States are responding to nonstate sources of violence in new ways. In response to foreign fighters (chapter 6), for example, states now regularly use drone strikes because traditional military actions are not effective against transnational networks that do not have fixed assets or that operate across a variety of states, including allies and nonallies. Ahram and Gledhill illustrated how states' responses to exiles are dependent upon their ability, which is increasingly limited, to control cross-border networks and media communications. In the case of private military companies (chapter 7), which are often employed by the state, their prominence may be linked, in part, to neoliberal trends of outsourcing. The responses by states to transnational groups advocating and/or carrying out violence has required the use of new military and communication technologies to counter those used by the groups.

A key feature of transnational actors in war and peace is that these actors *interact with other transnational actors and not solely states*. National WILPF chapters formed coalitions with "peace and social justice organizations on locally based initiatives," as Confortini detailed. Such an arrangement meant the strengthening of combined causes with the use of shared expertise and resources. As described by Haufler, corporations, international and subnational NGOs, and states work together in the Kimberley Process to curtail the sale of diamonds that fund conflicts. As noted by Ahram and Gledhill, the perpetrators and immediate targets of terrorism are often nonstate actors. Contemporary war and peace promotion includes many interactions between transnational actors that may or may not include states, suggesting that a state-based approach to understanding contemporary war and peace would miss central dynamics of these events and processes. States, of course, remain major global actors in the conduct of war and in peace promotion. Transnational actors still rely upon states, international organizations, and the global infrastructure that they have created to advance their goals.

The collection of actors in this volume speaks to the centrality of transnational actors to war and peacemaking. They impel state and nonstate actors to take particular paths in governance, in diplomacy, and in the waging of war and peace. They introduce flows of political influence and policymaking opportunities and constraints. They are significant players in international relations who can be both nefarious and self-interested, as well as altruistic and inclusive—regardless of whether they employ strategies of coercion or conscience.

Examining transnational actors collectively yields observations about the key features of globalized war and peace. The first of these is deterritorialization. Because of developments in communication technology, individuals and groups face lowered opportunity costs to engage in transnational causes. For recruiters in the case of foreign fighters, for example, this means access to thousands of potential recruits via social media. In the cases of diasporans and women peace activists, this means being able to solicit allies (the "boomerang model") in service of their respective causes.

Deterritorialization produces fluidity, by which we mean the ability of individuals and groups to play roles in changing capacities over time. Diasporans, for example, are more easily able to return to their countries of origin and take up governmental posts. Private security professionals have often served as members of national armies and then serve in private military security companies in multiple countries worldwide. Fluidity produces a blurring of identities and allows for the enhancement of expertise that can be transferred from one arena or identity to another.

Individuality is another key feature highlighted in this volume. To date the role of individuals as transnational actors has received little attention, but as the chapters on diasporans, exiles, and private security professionals indicate, individuals can now be key players in various transnational groups and dynamics.

A key question raised by the increased salience of transnational actors in the conduct of war and peace promotion is that of legitimacy. Does the ability for more actors to participate in these key processes signal a democratization of global governance? Or, since many of these actors use violence to achieve their objectives, does it signal a silencing of democratic processes by those who can compel compliance with force? The question of legitimacy will likely persist as these transnational dynamics intensify.

It is tempting to conclude an examination of transnational actors made one hundred years after the introduction of the term by asking what lies ahead in the second transnational century. In fact, the cases presented in this book demonstrate that international relations have not shifted fundamentally between the First World War and the war on terrorism; all of the types of transnational actors surveyed were already in existence and impacting war and peacemaking before 1916. It would be inaccurate to call the hundred years leading to 2116 as only the second transnational century if the label is applied based on the mere existence of transnational actors.

Instead, a century after Randolph S. Bourne's establishment of the paradigm of transnationalism, and nearly a half-century after Joseph S. Nye and Robert O. Keohane's development of a framework for analyzing the impact of transnationalism on world politics, we can identify two trends evident in the changing influence of the transnational on war and peace. One is the evolving landscape of world politics and how it has permitted transnational actors to adapt to new opportunity structures. The second is how the scholarship of world politics is changing to permit a richer understanding of complex transnational dynamics.

Throughout the era of the world wars and the first half of the Cold War, transnational actors remained either entities based in a single state that operated transnationally or as loose confederations of nationally based units. By the latter half of the Cold War and the unipolar two decades that followed, developments in communication and transportation technologies made it practical for transnationally dispersed networks to coordinate operations and engage resources worldwide. This process of globalization has promoted the growth of a self-reinforcing feedback loop in which the growing familiarity of transnationalism has fostered increasing cosmopolitanism and bestowed a legitimacy on the international political activities of nonstate actors, leading to expanded roles in global governance and further integration of emerging transnational dynamics.

Meanwhile, the occurrence of a large number of civil wars and often postcolonial fragile states during the past century has created opportunity structures in zones of "thin sovereignty" for the emergence of governance by private authority, sometimes by antistate entities and sometimes at the behest of the international community. The high cost to civilians in so-called low-intensity conflicts and shifting norms accompanying growing cosmopolitanism have brought human security issues to the forefront of international security concerns, creating opportunities for expert nonstate entities that provide forms of governance during interventions and peacebuilding. The increasingly networked dynamic of both global governance and the infrastructure of globalization have also created critical nodes that can be disrupted by actors wishing to make their presence felt but lack the state's capacity to make war or enforce sovereignty.

But despite the growing influence of transnational actors, nationalism remains a potent force countervailing transnational ties. In 2016, the centenary of "Transnational America," nationalists in the United Kingdom prevailed in a referendum on leaving the European Union. In other Western countries that year, nationalist candidates enjoyed unexpected success with anti-immigrant, antitrade campaigns that gave voice to publics who felt threatened by the globalization that Bourne saw as a source of strength. Following the referendum, the *New York Times* published an op-ed titled "Britain's Flight Signals End of an Era of Transnational Optimism." The "Brexit" referendum, President Donald Trump's pledge to tighten borders and erect an interstate wall, and the anti-immigrant sentiment within vocal segments of Western populations signal that nationalism remains potent.

In the course of coming decades, it will be worth watching to see whether the anxieties regarding the increasing power of transnational forces will lead to counteractions by states seeking to reclaim authority. States retain the power to change many of the structures that have enabled transnational actors to flourish, from the openness of global communications and trade to the absence of major wars mobilizing nations. Authoritarian regimes that have effectively shut down the Internet within their countries in response to civil-society protests during the 2010s illustrate one such response. The international community may also make renewed efforts to expand global governance through international organizations rather than outsourcing to surrogates.

Advances in technology have facilitated the rise of transnational actors, and it seems reasonable to expect that they will continue to do so, in the form of enhanced communications in commercial development. But technological or industrial change may bring disruptive developments as well. Scarcity of resources, whether energy, minerals, or water, could magnify the importance of private suppliers.

Often patterns are only fully appreciated with a wide perspective. Currently students of international relations are trained to examine particular categories of actors and the literatures related directly to that subfield. Scholars are socialized to read journals and attend conference panels with familiar topics and names. With a narrow focus, it can be difficult to observe broad trends.

But transnationalism increasingly factors in security studies and in collaboration across national and disciplinary boundaries. The trend toward pluralism in methodology, and in the legitimation of a wider array of actors and phenomena to be studied, affords the opportunity to appreciate the growing complexity of interactions impacting conflict and negotiated settlement. In the second century of our conception of transnationalism, transnational actors will play still greater roles in war and peace, and scholars of international relations must be prepared to see the forest for the trees.

CONTRIBUTORS

Ariel I. Ahram is associate professor of government and international affairs at Virginia Polytechnic Institute and State University. His substantive research focuses on issues of security and development, particularly in the Middle East. His book, *Proxy Warriors: The Rise and Fall of State-Sponsored Militias* (Stanford University Press, 2011), examines the emergence and evolution of armed non-state actors that collaborate with governments. Dissenting from current policy orthodoxy, he argues that efforts to fix weak and frail states are unlikely to reduce the power of militias and that human and international security can often be improved by empowering, not repressing, armed nonstate forces.

Miriam J. Anderson is assistant professor in the Department of Politics and Public Administration at Ryerson University in Toronto. She holds a PhD from the University of Cambridge, and has served as a visiting scholar at Columbia University. Her publications include *Windows of Opportunity: How Women Seize Peace Negotiations for Political Change* (Oxford University Press, 2016); articles in *Politics and Gender, Refugee Studies,* and *Intervention and Statebuilding*; as well as chapters in edited volumes. From 1999 to 2002, Dr. Anderson served as a human rights monitor for the Organization for Security and Co- operation in Europe in Croatia. During this period she also monitored elections in Bosnia- Herzegovina and in Croatia for the Office for Democratic Institutions and Human Rights.

Jennifer M. Brinkerhoff is professor of public administration and international affairs at George Washington University. She holds a PhD in public administration from the University of Southern California in Los Angeles. Her publications include seven books, as well as five coedited journal issues and over sixty articles and book chapters. Her most recent book is *Institutional Reform and Diaspora Entrepreneurs: The In-Between Advantage* (Oxford University Press, 2016). She is the 2016 winner of the Fred Riggs Award for Lifetime Achievement in International and Comparative Public Administration, for "significant and widely recognized contributions to the conceptual, theoretical or operational development of international and comparative or development administration." Dr. Brinkerhoff has consulted for multilateral development banks, bilateral assistance agencies, nongovernmental organizations, and foundations. Regarding diasporas and development, she has advised and provided training to the US State Department and the US Agency for International Development (USAID) and to diaspora organizations and government officials in the Netherlands and Sweden. She wrote *Technical Guidance on Engaging Diasporas in Conflict Settings* for USAID's Center for Conflict Mitigation and Management.

Catia Cecilia Confortini is associate professor and codirector of the Peace and Justice Studies Program at Wellesley College. She holds a PhD from the University of Southern California's School of International Relations, as well as a master's degree in international peace studies from the Joan B. Kroc Institute for International Peace Studies at the University of Notre Dame. She is the author of *Intelligent Compassion: Feminist Critical Methodology in the Women's International League for Peace and Freedom* (Oxford University Press, 2012). She has published extensively on the contributions of women's peace activism to peace studies. Her new project, "Bio-Pink: Gender, Power and the Transnational Diffusion of Breast Cancer Governance in Nigeria," is situated at the intersection of feminist global health and peace research. It examines the diffusion of biomedical and pink-ribbon cultures of breast cancer in the global South, specifically Nigeria. She is international vice president of the Women's International League for Peace and Freedom (2015–18).

Luke Flanagan is a teacher of politics at Bexhill Sixth Form College, East Sussex, United Kingdom. To date his research has focused on regionalism in Canada's Maritime provinces and questions of identity among Canadian soldiers in Britain during the First World War. He has published in the *British Journal of Canadian Studies* and has recently contributed to an edited collection titled *Big Worlds: Politics and Elections in the Canadian Provinces and Territories* (University of Toronto Press, 2016). He is under contract with McGill-Queen's University Press to publish a manuscript based on his PhD thesis, which analyzes the Maritime Union debate from 1960 to 1980. Dr. Flanagan has worked for the Scottish Parliament and the British Association for Canadian Studies, in addition to teaching at the University of Edinburgh, where he received his PhD, and at Memorial University of Newfoundland.

John Gledhill is associate professor of global governance in the Department of International Development, University of Oxford. He was previously an LSE Fellow in Global Politics at the London School of Economics and Political Science.

In his research, writing, and teaching, Gledhill investigated conflict processes, nonviolent protest movements, state formation and dissolution, peacekeeping, and transnational social mobilization. His recent publications have appeared in PS: *Political Science and Politics*, *Security Studies*, *Nationalities Papers*, and *Asian Security*.

Virginia Haufler is associate professor in the Department of Government and Politics at the University of Maryland. She directs the Global Communities program, and is affiliated with the Center for International Development and Conflict Management. She is affiliated with the Harrison Program on the Future Global Agenda and the Center for International Development and Conflict Management at the University of Maryland. Her research examines the role of the private sector in global governance, the global regulation of industry, and the rise of industry self-regulation and corporate social responsibility. She is currently writing a book on corporations and conflict prevention. She serves on the Advisory Board of the Center for the Study of Business Ethics, Regulation and Crime (C-BERC) and of the OEF Foundation, and has been advisor or board member of the Peace Research Institute Frankfurt, the UN Global Compact, the Principles for Responsible Investment, and Women in International Security. She has consulted for both international organizations and the nonprofit sector.

Matthew LeRiche is asisstant professor of global studies and director of the Global Leadership Center at Ohio University. He focuses on political and conflict risk analysis, initially specializing in the political and security dynamics and the role of international actors and norms in South Sudan where he lived and worked for several years. LeRiche holds a PhD in war studies from King's College London, was a postdoctoral fellow at the London School of Economics and Political Science, and has been a lecturer and instructor at Memorial University of Newfoundland and the Royal Military College of Canada. His book *South Sudan: From Revolution to Independence* (Oxford University Press, 2012) is considered an authoritative account of how South Sudan became the world's newest state. He has worked widely in security-sector reform, with a focus on defense education and political risk.

Kate Macdonald is senior lecturer at the University of Melbourne, having held previous positions at the London School of Economics and Political Science, the Australian National University, and Oxford University. Her research focuses on the politics of transnational production and business, with a particular focus on social, labor, and human rights regulation of global business. Recent publications include *The Politics of Global Supply Chains: Power and Governance beyond the State* (Polity Press, 2013) and articles in *Ethics and International Affairs*, the

Review of International Studies, *Governance*, the *Journal of Business Ethics*, the *European Journal of International Law*, and *Third World Quarterly*.

David Malet is director of the Security Policy Studies program of the Elliott School of International Affairs at George Washington University. Previously he taught at the University of Melbourne, where he was associate director of the Melbourne School of Government, and at Colorado State University–Pueblo, where he was director of the Homeland Security Studies Program and the University Honors Program. He is the author of *Foreign Fighters: Transnational Identity in Civil Conflicts* (Oxford University Press, 2013) and of *Biotechnology and International Security* (Rowman & Littlefield, 2016). He provides media analysis regularly on international security issues and American politics.

Phil Orchard is senior lecturer in international relations and peace and conflict studies at the University of Queensland and the research director of the Asia-Pacific Centre for the Responsibility to Protect. His research focuses on international efforts to provide legal and institutional protections to forced migrants and war-affected civilians. He is the author of *A Right to Flee: Refugees, States, and the Construction of International Cooperation* (Cambridge University Press, 2014), which won the 2016 International Studies Association Ethnicity, Nationalism, and Migration Studies Section Distinguished Book Award, and the forthcoming book *Protecting the Internally Displaced: Rhetoric and Reality* (Routledge, 2017). He is also the coeditor, with Alexander Betts, of *Implementation in World Politics: How Norms Change Practice* (Oxford University Press, 2014).

INDEX

Arabic names beginning with the prefix 'al-' are alphabetized by the name itself.